Follow Me, Friend

A Memoir of Undiagnosed PTSD,
and the Healing Power of the
Horse-Human Relationship

Cheryl L. Eriksen

PRAISE FOR CHERYL L. ERIKSEN

Cheryl's life has been an incredible journey—a journey that should happen to no one, especially a little girl. Yet through her writings and work with horses, she becomes an incredible inspiration for so many who have sadly suffered a similar fate. *Follow Me, Friend* is a must for anyone who has been abused or know someone who has, no matter what form—but especially the abuse that comes from that dim voice inside that says the act was somehow your fault and you'll never amount to anything. Know that you are not alone. I commend Cheryl for her bravery and her amazing spirit.

— ROBIN HUTTON, *NEW YORK TIMES* BEST-SELLING AUTHOR OF *SGT. RECKLESS, AMERICA'S WAR HORSE*

Cheryl's memoir, *Follow Me, Friend*, is a powerful and engaging story. I felt transported into her life, both as an observer and as if living her life with her. It provides a potent and heartbreaking description of living with intense depression, anxiety, and PTSD, while at the same time providing hope through her resilience and the strength and healing that came through her relationship with her horse. This book has had a profound impact on me, both personally and as a mental health professional, leading to a deeper understanding of these mental health issues and the beautiful power of horses, dogs, and friendships in our healing journeys.

— LYNN THOMAS, LCSW, EAGALA FOUNDER AND PRESIDENT OF HORSES FOR MENTAL HEALTH

Follow Me, Friend brings a unique depth to the story of a girl and her horse, layering adeptly descriptive prose of stable and farm life, with distressing experiences on the road to emerging as a survivor. This is an emotionally compelling page-turner on the repercussions of abuse, the importance of friends, and the healing power of close relationships with horses and dogs. Eriksen's intimate and insightful telling is interwoven with engaging horse and dog stories, while taking the reader along on her path to hope and peace. *Follow Me, Friend* is also relevant in truly comprehending the impact and need for today's youth protection preventative and educational measures.

— CARYN SAPPELLI, YOUTH PROTECTION COORDINATOR FOR A NATIONAL YOUTH EQUESTRIAN ORGANIZATION

First Edition 2021 - 9798494744517

Copyright © 2021 by Cheryl L. Eriksen

All rights reserved.

No part of this book may be reproduced in any form or by any electronic or mechanical means, including information storage and retrieval systems, without written permission from the author, except for the use of brief quotations in a book review.

Cover illustration © Ruth Sanderson

Cover design by Mallory Rock of Rock Solid Book Design (www.RockSolidBookDesign.com)

Edited by Dori Harrell, Breakout Editing

Formatting and internal illustrations - Kai Viola, Phoenix Formatting (https://phoenixformatting.com)

CONTENTS

Preface	ix
Prologue	1
Part I **A HORSE CALLED DISSOCIATION**	
Chapter 1	5
Chapter 2	13
Chapter 3	23
Chapter 4	29
Chapter 5	35
Part II **DIVIDED MIND, STOIC SMILE**	
Chapter 6	43
Chapter 7	47
Chapter 8	55
Chapter 9	63
Chapter 10	69
Chapter 11	75
Chapter 12	81
Chapter 13	87
Chapter 14	99
Part III **FOLLOW ME, FRIEND**	
Chapter 15	107
Chapter 16	113
Chapter 17	121
Chapter 18	129
Chapter 19	133
Chapter 20	141
Chapter 21	145

Part IV
PATH OF THE PEACE HORSE

Chapter 22	157
Chapter 23	161
Chapter 24	163
Chapter 25	167
Chapter 26	171
Chapter 27	177
Chapter 28	181
Chapter 29	187
Chapter 30	193
Chapter 31	201
Chapter 32	211
Chapter 33	219
Chapter 34	225
Chapter 35	231
Chapter 36	237
Chapter 37	243
Chapter 38	255
Chapter 39	265
Chapter 40	273
Chapter 41	287
Epilogue	293
Acknowledgments	299
A Note About the Cover Art	303
Additional Resources for Survivors and their Families/Friends	305
About the Author	307
Also by Cheryl L. Eriksen	309

To Little Cheryl

You are brave
You are beautiful
And through this book, you are finally free.

PREFACE

When I first started thinking about writing this memoir, my desire was to write the book I wish I could have read when I was twenty—something that would give that younger version of me some clue that I was not crazy, there was an explanation for what I was going through, and that I didn't have to go it alone. *Follow Me, Friend* is the end result. As I researched, learned, and healed, I came to understand that there were many others having the same experiences, suffering in silence, afraid to seek help. These same people had family, friends, and loved ones who perhaps saw the signs but did not know what they were observing or how to help. I realized this book could help them too. Finally, I realized this book could reach beyond childhood trauma and help shed light on the effects of PTSD on relationships, behavior, social engagement, decision-making, finances, ability to maintain employment, etc. We, as a society, are increasingly aware of PTSD in veterans, but there are many more people from different walks of life experiencing and inhibited by the effects of trauma and PTSD on their daily lives. I hope this memoir reaches and helps many people better understand what is happening to them and that healing is possible.

AUTHOR'S NOTE

This is a work of creative nonfiction. The events, conversations, and locations have been recreated to the best of my memory and from the personal journals I kept. Some of this happened long ago and in situations of extreme stress. I've done my best to represent people, events, and conversations accurately. Dialogue is written from the author's memory and are not intended to represent word-for-word transcripts—however, the author has made every effort to accurately convey the essence, meaning, and emotion of each conversation. In many cases, names, identifying features, occupations, and specific details or locations have been altered or omitted to protect the innocent, myself included.

A special note for survivors—while I've tried to keep it from being too graphic, this work does include mention and some description of depression, anxiety, disassociation, self-harm, and childhood sexual abuse. It's not the whole book, but it is there, and as a fellow survivor, I wanted you to know.

PROLOGUE

As I lay back on the soft carpeting, listening to the gentle tones of the guided meditation, I closed my eyes. She came to me then, standing just ahead, at the start of a long, narrow path. Yellow light glowed all around us. Trees dripping with Spanish moss enclosed us within this secret, safe place. She turned away from me, and I followed her.

The path twisted into murky darkness. Sharp, black thorns encroached upon us, threatening to tear at my clothes and skin. I hesitated. She paused, turning her neck to look at me. The peace emanating from her gentle eyes touched my soul. A breeze lifted her mane. She blinked once, then again, and her soft brown eyes spoke within me. "Follow me, friend," she seemed to say. "Follow me. I'll help you through this."

I drifted back from the vision, the floor reaching up to cradle my body. My eyes fluttered open. The horse, my horse, had spoken. But it would be years before I would truly listen.

A BITING winter wind raked its icy teeth across my bare arms. Inwardly I felt numb, my insides like that of a tattered rag doll, cold and dead, with just enough stuffing to hold me upright. Swaying in the doorway, I looked down at my bare feet and then stepped into the fresh snow. The pain was not immediate. With my T-shirt flapping wildly in the bitter wind, I walked several steps into the snow-drenched yard before the icy, stabbing cold penetrated my naked feet. *I look like a lunatic,* I thought.

"You are a lunatic," the angry voice in my head hissed.

My eyes darted around the yard and landed on my neighbor's house. *Can they see me? Normal people don't act like this.*

"You're not normal," the inner voice jeered.

Moving faster, I disappeared into the tree line. Shivering hard now, wearing only a T-shirt and pajama pants, I sat in the snow, my body sinking into the fluffy white powder. For a moment, a warm memory flowed over me. I recalled hours playing in the snow as a little girl, wrapped in the warmth of my snow suit and the safety of intact innocence. The image shattered and fell away.

Shaking uncontrollably, I lay back in the snow, teeth chattering hard. I looked up at the gray winter sky, willing the cold to destroy me. Barren trees bent away from the wind, their dry branches clicking and popping as they struggled against the harsh cold. My muscles clenched. My shivers deepened. The subfreezing wind tore at my flesh, seeking my bones.

How much time had passed? Twenty minutes? Thirty? *This will take too long.* Hopelessness, cold and heavy, clung to me like thick, sucking mud, pulling me ever downward. Someone would come home and find me before I froze to death. Find me and stop me. But worse than that, they would know for certain what I'd worked so hard to hide for decades. I am absolutely *crazy*.

I rose and headed back toward the house, trying to look nonchalant and normal as my bare feet carried my pajama-clad body through the shin-deep snow. As always, I would tell no one, adding this episode to my ever-deepening pool of secrets.

Nothing important happened today. Nothing at all.

PART I
A HORSE CALLED DISSOCIATION

CHAPTER ONE

A magnificent black horse careened across an open field at a full gallop, his long dark tail streaming out behind him like that of an inky-black comet. His lustrous coat glistened like obsidian in the warm summer sun. He wore no saddle or bridle, but astride his sturdy back—a young girl. Strong muscles slid easily under his sleek coat.

His mane looked like a glorious sail catching the wind. It flowed from his neck, wrapping around my hands and gently caressing my arms as I held him tightly. The wind whipped at my face, bringing tiny tears to my eyes. I urged him along even faster. The stallion's hooves thundered beneath me, clods of dark earth flying up on either side of us. Ahead, an imposing stone fence loomed in our path.

I lowered my body and pressed my left ear near to the right side of his sleek neck. "Let's go," I whispered against the wind.

The black horse burst forward, each powerful stride consuming the ground beneath us. Together we effortlessly sailed over the fence. Landing on the far side, we galloped on. The horse tossed his head triumphantly. I let go of his mane and placed a hand on either side of his robust neck, feeling the fire within him …

"Cheryl? Hey, Cheryl?"

My black horse dissolved at the sound of the intrusive voice.

"What?" I responded, irritated.

"What are you looking at?"

"Nothing." I looked away, returning my gaze outside the van window. "I was just thinking."

I didn't want to talk. I never wanted to talk, fearful I'd say something stupid, something that proved what a worthless idiot I was. Or worse, accidently give away some clue that confirmed what I feared was true—my utter and complete insanity. The other dozen or so kids excitedly pointed out the window at the magnificent horse farms while the van carried our 4-H club through the horse-dotted landscape of Kentucky's beautiful Bluegrass Region. I gazed at the rolling landscape, hoping I would not be disturbed again. Wishing I could disappear into the seat cushions, I strained my eyes and my imagination until my black horse reappeared.

It was July 1989, and I was twelve.

I suppose many children have similar daydreams fueled by books and movies about seemingly magical relationships between a child and the horse only he or she could tame. However, my imaginings were more than daydreams—they were a place I went to be safe, to feel normal. A place I could hide from a reality I was not equipped to handle. If I were old enough then to put my complex feelings it into words, I'd say I felt disconnected from my body, hanging on by a thin thread, being jerked along by a demented puppet master, with no control over what would happen to me, or when.

By the time I turned ten, I'd become fairly certain something was seriously wrong with me, that indeed, I was crazy. I felt as if I possessed some innate defect, perhaps a flaw in my genetic makeup that made me offensive to others. My feelings of being abnormal compounded as I grew older.

Looking around at my classmates, I could see I wasn't like them. They were happy, laughing, at ease with themselves and their peers. I felt weird, out of place, and filled with shame, like I'd done something terrible, something unforgiveable. I desperately grasped at bits and pieces of characters from favorite TV shows and movies, imitating them, trying to understand and mimic what a normal person acted like—hoping somehow I could become one.

At one time, when I was still very small, I felt normal. After carrying the self-hatred for so long, those early years seem more like a memory from someone else's life rather than something I'd experienced.

Those early years were spent as part of "just us girls"—my mom, my older sister, Andrea, and me. I don't have a memory of living with my dad, my parents having divorced when I was two years old. Both grandfathers passed away before I was born, relegating their role in my life to one of a handful of pictures and stories. Often my maternal grandmother would care for my sister and me when Mom was working or needed a night off. We were latchkey kids, at times attending summer camps, day care, and after-school programs—all of which kept us entertained while Mom worked full time as an occupational therapist in a school for children with severe mental and physical disabilities.

In my mind, my dad was something of an enigma, a mystery to unravel, a treasure to seek and hold on to. He worked for General Motors, traveling around the world for the automaker. One such trip occurred before my parents divorced, and the entire family lived in Singapore for a few months in the late 1970s. I celebrated my second birthday there. I remember almost nothing from that time, aside from my mother's laughter when I grabbed and ate the heads off the little ducks on my birthday cake.

When they separated, Mom took us girls and moved back to Kalamazoo, Michigan, her hometown and the place her mother and sister still lived. Dad stayed in their home in a Detroit suburb and continued to travel for his work, which took him to Africa and then to Spain, where he stayed for a couple years. Spain sounded exotic to me, although at that age I didn't really grasp where he was or what he was doing. Just that he was far away and doing something important, something that other kids' fathers were not doing. Dad returned to the states every six months to visit family and see his daughters. I eagerly anticipated a visit from Dad, cleaning my room, carefully picking my clothes—I wanted to impress him.

Dad would bring his sister, my aunt Charlotte (also my godmother), and his mother, my grandma Eriksen, from the east side of the state to Kalamazoo. When he returned from Spain, he came more frequently and sometimes attended a Little League game, horse show, or other important event.

When we were older, Andrea and I would visit Dad and stay with him for a week over the summer. This was a special time, a chance to step into Dad's world, which seemed so different from my own. His home was filled with antiques and exotic items from his travels. It didn't look like any home I'd ever seen before. I felt special being there.

I had a close connection with my maternal aunt and uncle, my uncle sometimes taking the role of father figure in those early years, showing me how to oil my baseball glove, helping me use a tool, putting together a bicycle, or setting up the camper so us girls could camp at Yogi Bear's Jellystone Park—something I loved and looked forward to every year.

Mom, Andrea, Grandma, and my aunt, uncle, and cousins all spent birthdays and holidays together, attended Detroit Tigers baseball games, and played or watched Little League games at the same ball park. Baseball. That was something I loved and could share with the whole family.

"Are we winning?" I would ask, crawling onto my mother's bed. Back then, few baseball games were televised, so Mom would listen to them on the radio in her bedroom—the only place we had a radio out of earshot of the TV.

"And at the bottom of the seventh, Tigers are up, four to three …" Ernie Harwell's familiar voice crackled through the radio, answering my question before Mom could.

"Yay! We're winning!" I lay down next to Mom and snuggled up close beside her, feeling warm and safe. I loved to be close to Mom—

she would hug me and tell me how much she loved me. She often read to me and Andrea at night before bed. I loved the Value Tales series, which told stories of famous people like Louis Pasteur and Benjamin Franklin and were illustrated and written for kids. My favorite story was of Jackie Robinson, the first African American baseball player to break the modern-era Major League Baseball color line.

My mom's side of the family loved baseball. Her father took his daughters to watch the Detroit Tigers play when they were young girls. My mom made sure my sister and I had the same experience. I loved going to Tiger Stadium and watching the games. In 1984 we all went to the World Series and watched the Tigers win game four, before clinching the title the next night by winning game five. I was seven that fall, just a couple months shy of my eighth birthday.

Mom, Andrea, and I attended the Methodist church just down the street, close enough we could walk when the weather was nice. There I enjoyed a supportive church family, becoming fond of my favorite Sunday school teachers in first and third grade. Mr. and Mrs. Butler, and Mrs. Friedman and Mrs. Dartmoore, respectively. Mrs. Friedman was my then best friend's grandmother.

When I was about eight, Mom remarried, and Rick joined our family. We moved to a larger home and changed schools, but we stayed with the same church. Summers now included a family road trip, during which I saw much of the United States. Desert landscapes, palm trees, mountains, historical monuments, national parks, the Grand Canyon—every summer brought a new adventure.

Adding Rick to the household was challenging for my sister and me. I worried that Dad might think he was being replaced, that he would think we loved Rick more than him. I didn't know how to express this to Mom, Dad, or Rick, so I withdrew into myself, trying not to get too close to Rick while elevating Dad to a celebrity status in my mind. Confused, I didn't know how to make everyone happy.

Not an outgoing kid, I could at least hold my own in a group, play with kids on the playground at school, and make friends with the neighborhood kids. I spent hours outside, running barefoot in the summer, the hot asphalt burning my feet and causing me to jump onto the crisp, sunburned grass for relief. I loved being outside, the fresh air on my face, the smell of the earth, the feeling of climbing high into the pine trees behind our house.

In the fall, the cool evening air chilled my bare arms and nipped at my face, but worry that Mom would call me in, bringing an abrupt end to my playing, kept me from going home in search of a jacket. When darkness finally fell over our neighborhood, and I could no longer deny the streetlights had come on long ago. I'd wander home to the soft, yellow glow emanating from the windows, inviting me in for dinner.

Wintertime, I spent hours playing in the deep Michigan snow. Sledding, building snow forts and snow horses—it seemed I never felt the cold. When I think back on those times, I am filled with serenity at the memories of playing with friends and running all over the neighborhood without fear, guided only by a deep sense of adventure and a desire to explore the world around me.

I was normal, until I wasn't.

LIKE THE FIRST sharp stabs of winter penetrating the gentle warmth of fall, something shifted. My world tilted, and I slowly disappeared. To the casual observer, or even my own family, it was not an abrupt change one might take note of, but over time, a very complete one. Still tugged along by that invisible puppet master, controlled by something I couldn't, *or wouldn't*, remember, I gradually turned inward and closed myself off from others, withdrawing into my imagination, where the black horse lived. My relationships changed, I played less frequently with kids in the neighborhood, and I spent more time alone, burying myself in the stories of Walter Farley's Black Stallion series.

"No one really likes you. No one wants to be with you. You're a terrible person, worthless garbage, a pathetic waste of a human life." The internal monologue was harsh and endless—also true. When had it started? I could no longer remember a time when the inner voice wasn't there. I

became the weird kid at school, socially awkward and full of self-hate. Crushing guilt blackened my heart. Anxiety roiled within me. I had done something horrible, something unforgiveable. I just couldn't remember what. Afraid to put myself in a situation where my secret might be discovered, I avoided my peers, preferring to sit alone in a darkened corner, wishing I were invisible, trying to disappear into my imagination.

The times I felt confused and angry, I wanted to lash out, to yell or scream, to do something to stop that hateful inner monologue. I remember one summer, feeling that angst, the noise of anger filling my head, resentment covering my world like it'd been dipped in sticky black mud. I accidently spilled boiling-hot water on my hand. The pain was intense and brought tears to my eyes. But it also brought something else—a clarity to my mind and a lifting of the blackness. The physical pain made me feel normal, even if only for a moment. Because I had caused the pain myself, it also gave me a sense of control.

When I think back on those times, I view them from far away, as if floating near the ceiling. I can see the young version of myself, horse book clutched in both hands, in the soft yellow glow of the Raggedy Ann night light, but she is far below me, like a piece of someone else's memory.

"OH, CHERYL!" Mom gasped when I removed my shirt.

It was our annual pre-summer ritual, probably the summer before fourth grade, Andrea and I were trying on clothes to see what still fit from the previous summer.

"What?" I yelped, terrified I had done something wrong.

"You're *fat!*" my sister said loudly, more as an observation than a condemnation.

I had apparently gained an alarming amount of weight in a relatively short time.

"You're going to have to go on a diet!" Andrea added.

"NO!" I screamed. "NO!" Panic rose in my voice. "I'll work it off playing outside! Please! No diet!"

I felt terrified at the prospect. Fat was ugly, fat was wrong, but somehow fat was also *safe*.

CHAPTER TWO

Living in the city, I never had exposure to real horses. In fact, the first horse I remember meeting stood larger than life—a Clydesdale statue at the entrance to Busch Gardens in Tampa Bay, Florida, where my mom, grandma, sister, and I were vacationing. I was seven. This magnificent statue enamored me with horses. Inexplicably compelled to stay with the statue, I sat under one enormous raised hoof, gazing up at the marvelous creature. I had never felt this way before. A fierce desire to be in the presence of that magnificent animal overtook me. Somehow, I felt safe in the protective shadow of that horse.

A mechanical horse by the name of Sandy became my first horseback ride. Sandy held her place at the local grocery store in Kalamazoo, awaiting excited children to sit on top of her cold, steel body. She wore a real leather saddle and bridle, which, in my world, created an accurate representation of an authentic horseback-riding experience. When I placed a penny in the box near her shoulder, she moved slowly in a back-and-forth rocking motion. I imagined Sandy and I were galloping together across magnificent open fields. The low rum, rum, rum of her motor became the rumble of her thundering hooves as we rode far beyond the busy store to a secret place only we knew about.

My interest in horses grew exponentially with each exposure. One horse book soon turned into an entire collection. Notebooks and later sketchbooks became filled with horse drawings. Horse posters covered my bedroom walls. When I was eleven, I got my first Breyer horse model—I still have it, along with a couple hundred or so of its friends. It was a blossoming friendship that had begun the previous year, which would soon launch my horse zeal from strong interest to life-altering obsession.

I met Sarah at a mutual friend's beach party the summer I was ten. By that time I wasn't good at making friends. I struggled to trust others—not a conscious decision, just another string frequently pulled by the invisible puppet master. I felt certain I had no redeeming qualities, and that incessant internal monologue had assured me this was true. I probably wouldn't have said anything if Sarah hadn't spoken first. I'd never met someone interested in everything I was. From favorite reading material to hobbies and everything in between, it seemed like we were cut from the same cloth. Perhaps the most exciting part—Sarah was also a horse lover. I'd never had a friend who loved horses so much she wanted to constantly talk about them, read about them, and draw them—just like me.

Sarah and I connected thoroughly. So unusual for me to feel immediately comfortable with a new friend. Barely able to comprehend what had happened, I floated through the afternoon on a cloud of disbelief. Sarah actually seemed to genuinely like me. *Me.*

Inevitably, the party ended and we went our separate ways. I sat in the backseat of our family car and waved goodbye to my new best friend while the warm summer breeze blew the familiar smells of fresh water, sand, and seaweed in from the lake. I could hardly wait to see her again.

Sarah and I didn't live on the same side of town, and we went to different schools and churches. However, at every opportunity one of us would sleep over at the other's house, where we'd stay up long into the night talking of horses and playing with our Breyer horse models. Neither of us owned a real horse, but we dreamed of the day when we would each have a farm of our own and would fill it with horses and other animals. Sarah had recently started riding lessons, and I went to see her ride one evening. I stood in awe of her as she sat astride a big, beautiful gray horse. I wanted to be just like her.

For my eleventh birthday Sarah gifted me with a riding lesson with her instructor, on a horse named Robbie. A bold and magical step. Now my horse experience was no longer fully intertwined with my imagination. For the first time I had the opportunity to gain actual experience with a *real* horse. Magical.

"How was the lesson?" Mom asked as I climbed into the car.

"It was great! Robbie is so cool. He's an Arabian, like the Black Stallion, but he's gray."

"What did you learn?"

"I learned how to brush him and put on his saddle and bridle. Carrie told me I should know how to do everything myself. That would make me a *real* horseman. I learned how to get on him and hold the reins and ask him to go …" I clicked my seat belt into place, and Mom started the car as I chattered on. I was excited but also anxious because I wanted to ask for something. If the answer was no, I would be devastated. But I had to try. I took a deep breath, pushing my anxiety down within me.

"I asked Carrie if I could take more riding lessons on Robbie. She said yes." I looked at Mom intently, trying to read her face. "So can I? Please?"

Mom sighed, but not with irritation. I suspect now she saw this question coming long before I'd worked up my nerve to ask. Mom agreed, and I soon began taking weekly riding lessons on Robbie. The next year I joined Sarah's 4-H club, an atmosphere that gave my horse passion a significant boost from strong interest to undying obsession.

Our 4-H club was called the Kalamazoo Kontenders, and we were made up of city kids without horse access. However, the leader, Kathy, had many connections with people willing to provide a free lease, so each of us had a horse to work with and show. A half-Arabian, half-Appaloosa gelding was one such horse. When I met Splatters in March 1990, the entirety of my horse experience consisted of one year of formal riding lessons. Splatters had four years of experience being a horse, which was to his advantage. But between the two of us, I had considerably more riding experience, making me just knowledgeable enough to get myself into more than a few bad situations.

Splatters was not what you'd describe as a show horse, nor did he seem to be the product of a very-well-thought-out breeding. He was a small, rather scrawny horse with crooked legs, a skinny ewe neck, and a variety of other minor conformational deficiencies. Of course, I saw none of his physical shortcomings—to me he was the most beautiful horse in the world. Splatters had a lovely deep-chestnut-colored Appaloosa pattern. His face, neck, shoulders, and upper legs were flecked chestnut and white with a bright-white blanket covering his back and hind quarters. He had dozens of dark chestnut spots of various shapes and sizes over his whole body, with solid chestnut coloring on his knees and hocks. Splatters had four white socks and a white mane and tail. His beautiful baby face was crowned with long but shapely chestnut-colored ears.

When I first began riding him, Splatters challenged me repeatedly. He'd spook; I'd fall. He'd bolt; I'd fall. He'd trip; I'd fall. It didn't take long for Splatters to teach me how little I knew about riding horses and, more importantly, how to stay topside and out of the dirt. Periodically, I took riding lessons on Splatters, which was when I began to understand how to communicate with a horse and shape his behavior.

Near the end of our second year together, Splatters and I were able to walk, trot, and canter under saddle, executing circles, serpentines, and other figures. I now felt ready to enter our first dressage class, a sport with a rich tradition of classical horsemanship techniques designed to build strength and balance in the horse and rider so they can perform great athletic maneuvers with nearly imperceptible cues from the rider. At least that is what it's supposed to look like.

Riding lessons, 4-H, and horse showing took up most of my time outside of school. Summers were filled with family vacation and horse shows, leaving me little time for anything else. As a result, I gave up Little League, although I maintained my love of baseball. I had no time for extra school activities, which was fine with me. I didn't fit in there. I was still active in my church, mostly in youth group. Friends I'd known from early childhood were comfortable for me to be with, but making new friends—that I couldn't seem to do very easily. But like the other changes in myself, I didn't think on it. In truth, it made perfect sense. After all, there was something wrong with me—surely others could sense it. Everything bad was my fault. Everything.

ON THE HOT, humid July morning of our first dressage class, an event where an individual horse and rider pair perform a specific series of movements, or "test," in front of a judge. I saddled Splatters as he stood tied to the horse trailer, munching hay from my new, red hay bag. After bridling the horse and donning my helmet, I climbed aboard. Giving Splatters a gentle squeeze with my legs, I pointed him in the direction of the dressage ring.

The outer perimeter of the ring was made up of several PVC posts about two feet high, with plastic chain strung between each post. Each section of chain ran through an opening near the top of the post so that the chain started high, then drooped down to about six inches from the ground level before rising up to the next post. The pattern repeated all the way around the ring. At one end there was an opening with no chain—the entrance.

There were several horses and riders milling around the grounds that morning, preparing for the day's events, but Splatters and I found the dressage ring empty. I was a much better rider than when I'd first met Splatters a year and a half before, but in the grand scheme of things, still inexperienced. I rode the gelding into the dressage ring at a walk and took him around the perimeter a couple times. This seemed to go OK, so I squeezed him into a trot.

Splatters trotted off willingly enough, and for the first several strides things went well—until he spied his hay a short distance away. Giving his head a defiant toss, the horse attempted to hop out of the arena—landing with his front feet outside the enclosure, his body straddling the chain. I sat a moment, contemplating my rebuttal, and then proceeded to tug at his mouth, asking him to walk backward into the dressage ring. Big mistake. Splatters shuffled his feet backward obediently but hooked a front hoof on the plastic chain. The gelding panicked, running backward pulling the chain with him. One by one, the slack loops in the chain snapped up taut as Splatters continued backward. With the chain tight and the horse still moving, the PVC pipes ripped out of the ground one after another—indeed an alarming sight.

Terrified, Splatters leapt into the air, spinning away from the horse-eating barrier. At this particular airborne moment, I lost my seat and tumbled off, landing with a painful thud in the grass. The rearing, twisting motion that unseated me also succeeded in releasing the chain from Splatters's feet. He trotted a couple steps away, lowered his head, and grazed, as if nothing had happened. My face burned with embarrassment while one-thousand angry butterflies tore through my stomach. I quickly looked around, hoping no one had seen. *What an idiot! Who let you believe you're capable of training a horse?*

I gathered myself, rose to my feet, and dusted off my pride as I went to retrieve the now calm and collected Splatters. Realizing no one had witnessed the debacle, my shame faded slightly, but I was still furious with myself. *You are so worthless.* The words in my mind stoked the embers of self-hatred burning within me. I dreamed of becoming a professional horse trainer someday, although deep down that voice within reminded me I would never be successful. *Too fat. Too stupid. You'll never be good enough.* I looked around me and saw only thin, beautiful girls with well-trained horses. It seemed they effortlessly won class after class. I longed to be like them, but I never would be. Something was wrong with me. *Damaged, broken, useless.*

Despite, or perhaps in defiance of that negative self-talk, by the end of our fourth year together, Splatters and I were competitive with our peers. We had become a strong team and developed a close friendship. We started winning some of our classes against tough competition. I'd become a stronger, more confident rider. Through trial and error, I'd learned how to communicate with Splatters, to shape his behavior, and to help him understand what I asked of him. I still had a significant amount to learn before I could think of myself as a competent trainer, but perhaps I was on my way.

Sarah and I grew closer as friends in those first years in 4-H. We hung out together whenever we could and of course talked about nothing but horses. Sarah took Robbie, the horse we'd each taken our first lessons on, to the same horse shows as I took Splatters to, and the horses soon became best friends, just like us.

"It's so cute how much they love each other." Sarah reached down and stroked Robbie's neck, then turned in the saddle and did the same for Splatters. Sitting astride our mounts, Sarah and I waited in the staging area outside the show ring. Splatters nuzzled Robbie's neck.

"Awww!" we sang in unison, then laughed.

The loud speaker crackled to life, announcing the first call for our Hunt Seat Equitation class.

"I guess I'd better go warm up a little." I picked up the reins hanging loosely on Splatters's neck.

"Me too." Sarah took up the slack in her own reins. I took a deep breath, the show-ring jitters rising within me. "Good luck BFF. You be good, Robbie."

"You too. You'll do great!" Sarah turned Robbie away and headed toward the warm-up area. That was how it was with us, competitors but always best friends first. Just like Robbie and Splatters.

In summer of 1993, the owners who had been kind enough to loan Splatters to me were ready to have him back. Although devastated and inconsolable, I understood how lucky I'd been to have this horse all to myself for those years. That knowledge did not dull the sensation of having my heart ripped from my chest and stomped into the ground. In Splatters I'd found a friend to confide in, one I felt safe with and who would never pass judgment on me, despite my flaws and shortcomings. Someone I could talk to in a way I never felt comfortable when interacting with people. My time with Splatters taught me there was one place I could be myself, one place where I could believe I was a good person, even if only for a while. I felt safe with him and took great comfort just being in his presence, not unlike I'd felt several years ago under the huge raised hoof of the horse statue in Florida.

Connecting with Splatters also helped me open up and let in new friends, something I'd struggled with as I grew older. Somewhere along the road between childhood and adolescence, I'd learned to distrust my ability to recognize good people from bad. People were not always what they seemed. Some were dangerous, like a razor blade hidden inside your Halloween candy—not always evident, but harmful just the same. But with Splatters it was different. I made friends because he was friendly. He helped me reach out, and I blossomed a little.

While still close to my mom, I could never tell her any of these things I felt. When younger, I had felt safe telling her my secrets, but as I grew older, I knew I couldn't allow her to know my true thoughts. My feelings of worthlessness, my self-hatred—if Mom knew what I was really like, how could she possibly still love me? Surely she would be ashamed of me. I couldn't risk losing her love. Not that she'd ever said or done anything to make me believe she would withdraw her love. Still, without knowing why, my fear was very real.

SALTY TEARS SOAKED Splatters's soft neck and shoulder. I pressed my face into his hair and hugged him while I cried my goodbyes. He wrapped his head and neck around me like a warm hug. Nuzzling my hands and pockets, he looked at me expectantly. *Does he know what is happening?* I looked into his soft brown eyes and whispered goodbye as I slipped off his halter for the last time. With one final search of my hands, Splatters trotted off to graze with his buddies in the back pasture.

No longer tracing slow, jagged lines down my cheeks, the tears flowed freely as my body shook with the pain of the loss of my friend. I looked down at the black-and-gray halter with the attached silver nameplate I'd bought for it. The halter, pictures, and memories were all I had left. I looked at Splatters grazing in the distance and waved goodbye. Slinging his old halter over my shoulder, walking away, I wondered if I'd ever see him again. *Would I ever feel that safe again?*

Late one night, shortly after saying goodbye to Splatters, I seriously contemplated suicide for the first time. Lying in a heap on the cold linoleum of our front hallway, a kitchen knife clutched tightly in my right hand, I listened as my inner voice taunted me. *"You're worthless garbage!"* The voice hissed. *"You deserve to die!"* I nodded warily in agreement, the kitchen knife tracing a thin, shallow line along my upturned wrist.

CHAPTER THREE

Dry brown leaves crunched under our shuffling feet as Mom and I walked up the driveway of the nineteenth-century brick farmhouse. Determined to never lose another horse as I'd lost Splatters, and with my mother's blessing, sixteen-year-old me pooled my meager savings with my pitiful earnings from a part-time job at Wendy's, and I set out to find a horse of my own. I'd started the job just after my final county fair with Splatters, pinching every penny in the few months since then, while searching for a horse I could afford. Today we'd see the results of my efforts. I'd come to see the only horse I'd found that was a close match to my dream horse (I'd been looking for a black Arabian, of course) and also somewhat close to falling within the parameters of my derisory budget. Expecting our arrival, the owner emerged from the barn leading a stunning gray gelding, shod front feet clip-clopping loudly on the asphalt drive.

When little girls dream of wandering through enchanted forests on the back of a magnificent horse, I suspect they imagine a horse like Corky. A stunning Arabian gelding with a steel-gray coat, winter-white tail dragging the ground, brilliant white stockings reaching up and over his knees and hocks, and a silvery flowing mane. He only needed the horn of the mystical unicorn or the wings of the mythical Pegasus to complete the fantasy.

"Well, this is Corky!" the owner, Nancy, said with a smile. "I wanted to bring him out here so you could get a good look at him in the light." She stopped and posed the young gelding. "We'll take him back to the barn and saddle him up to ride."

"How did he get his name?" I asked. Corky sounded more like the name of a tubby round pony, not a gallant Arabian whose predecessors were bred to carry Bedouin warriors into battle.

"Well," Nancy began, "when he was a foal, he was always getting into trouble, sticking his nose where it didn't belong. He was really a corker—you know, a little stinker!" She chuckled. "So I called him Corky."

After riding the lanky gray gelding, I felt convinced he was the one for me. Although still inexperienced under saddle, Corky was willing and brave. His smooth gaits were a pleasure to ride and magnificent to see. I felt an instant connection between us, like two old souls reuniting in a new life.

Despite his lack of a coal-black coat, Corky was everything I could ask for in a horse. I told Nancy I had $1,000 to put down on the horse and asked (without much hope) if I could make payments of $100 a month on the remainder, knowing I'd need the bulk of my earnings to cover board and expenses for my new horse. Be it the hand of God or simply a fellow horse lover wanting to help a young girl get her first horse, I can't say (though I suspect it was a bit of both), Nancy never mentioned the original $3,000 price tag, which was well out of my range. Had Mom known we were going to see a $3,000 horse, she never would have allowed the trip. To my surprise, Nancy said she was asking only $1,500 for the gray gelding. She agreed to term payments, and that was it. Corky was mine!

Corky came into my life just before my seventeenth birthday. I had been riding and showing horses for about five years, and, as is so common with people who are still new to horses, I assumed I knew much more than I truly did. I'd learned a great deal from Splatters and figured that made me ready to handle another green-broke four-year-old. Luckily, Corky was a level-headed and patient teacher. That first year was a magical 365 days of discovery—I discovered how much I still didn't know about horses, while Corky discovered creative ways to teach me to not take myself too seriously.

Our first day together fell on a warm autumn day at the end of October. Orange and yellow leaves caught the golden light of the sun and danced on the breeze trickling over the treetops. I walked Corky from the main barn at the boarding stable down to the large indoor arena, thinking it would be fun to turn him loose in the enclosure to let him explore. The indoor arena had two large doors. The one on the far end was open a few feet, allowing the warm breezes to chase out the damp, cold air trapped inside from the previous night's subfreezing temperatures. I noticed a semisolid gate constructed of two-by-fours and lattice leaning across the opening, as if to create a barrier to prevent a horse from exiting the arena through the open door. At only about two and a half feet tall, the gate looked too short to keep a horse confined. I dismissed that thought, figuring the gate wouldn't be there if it wasn't intended to contain the horses. Yeah, I know, but it made sense at the time.

I walked Corky into the arena, slipped off his halter, and stood back a step, expecting him to toss up his head and gallop around the space, kicking up his heels at the sheer joy of being "free" in the sixty-by-one-hundred-foot enclosure. However, Corky didn't run or jump or even move. He simply stood just as I'd left him. He swung his head around and looked at me, as if to say, "OK, genius, now what?" I flung my arms in the air and made clicking noises with my tongue. Seemingly amused, Corky flicked an ear in my direction, then sauntered off toward the open door with the jump-gate barrier.

Aha! Success! The horse was moving.

Corky stopped at the jump-gate barrier, peering out the open doorway. His nostrils flared, drinking in the smells of his new home. *That's nice. He's content here.* I sighed with satisfaction. Corky sighed too (*Ah yes, we're connecting!*) then slowly rocked back on his hindquarters and elegantly hopped over the gate.

"Hey!" I ran to the door. "Corky!" *You idiot. You've been a horse owner for less than twenty-four hours, and he's already escaped!* Lacking the grace Corky possessed in exiting the arena, I stumbled over the gate into the partially enclosed field next to the arena. Corky grazed happily near the trailhead leading to the large cross-country jumping field located near the back of the property. With a flick of his ear in my direction, he acknowledged my expert horse-handling techniques as far superior to anything he'd encountered before.

In my haste to reach my truant horse, I had forgotten to grab his halter and lead rope. Now, afraid to let the gelding out of my sight, I did not want to return to the arena in order to retrieve them. I flapped my arms and made clicking noises—universal horse-person code for "move away from me, horse"—thinking perhaps I could herd him back into the arena. Corky did not even lift his head but simply continued to graze, an entertained look etched upon his face. Inching closer to Corky, I continued my arm flapping and clicking noises, looking like an awkward, half-crazed chicken. The horse jogged toward the trailhead, sending an amused toss of his head in my direction. I ran back in the same direction to attempt to block the opening. Corky stopped, lowered his head, and started grazing again.

I am such an idiot. Frustration and fear rose within me.

I needed a new plan. What could I use as a rope? I had just one idea, but it wasn't something I wanted to try if there was a chance anyone would see me. I crept up to Corky. Taking one last look around, I quickly reached under my sweatshirt and unhooked my bra. I pulled my arms inside my shirt and slid the bra strap off each shoulder, then returned my arms to the sleeve holes, pulling the bra out of my sleeve with my right hand. What a sight I'd be if anyone had discovered me leading my horse around with my bra wrapped around his neck! Lucky for me, it seemed Corky felt my lesson was well learned and willingly followed me back to the arena with the aid of my bra rope. Safely within the confines of the arena, I released Corky and quickly ducked behind some jumps to replace my bra. The gelding stood nearby with an amused look on his face. Well played, Corky. Well played.

Corky possessed a gentle, kind spirit and extraordinary intelligence. He taught me to be a "thinking horseman," one who relied on horse-human connection, communication, and mutual respect. The training methods using force and dominance I'd learned up to this point simply didn't work with Corky. He demanded more from me than the common assumption a horse was simply a reactionary animal and not a sentient being. I spent hours observing Corky and other horses, seeking to understand how to communicate in a way that made sense to him.

Because of Corky, I became a better rider and a gentler trainer. In the saddle and from the ground, Corky hardly required a touch—he simply followed my every move, like we were the same being occupying two different bodies. I grew a lot as a horsewoman in those last years of 4-H with Corky. Much of that growth I owed to my new 4-H leader and riding instructor, Lana.

Lana showed me how to teach Corky to use his body correctly. She taught me how to ride him using my legs primarily and my hands secondary. I learned a lot from Lana, but one thing really stuck with me, and I carried it forward with every horse I've worked with since—eliminating the use of training gadgets (equipment that uses force to produce desired results). These gadgets are illegal in the show ring for a reason. Draw reins, martingales, and other leverage devices are shortcuts that produce artificial and unsustainable results. "If you can't show with it, don't train with it." Her words became my training mantra.

Just like Splatters, Corky made it easy for me to connect with my peers.

Like a beckoning lighthouse on a fog-shrouded pier, Corky's beauty and personality drew people to him, and consequently to me. Just by being himself, he acted like a buffer, a safe way for me to connect with others. Some of my peers and even professional horse trainers and show judges were impressed by him, his training, and his accomplishments. These were things I had taught him. A small but withering part of my mind understood these were my accomplishments too. But gaining strength every day was the other version of me, the one who prevailed when I was alone. She had a mind and a voice of her own.

Away from Corky, I had nothing to still the vile voice rising inside me. *"You're a worthless, ugly, stupid, horrible person."* To question the cause or the source of the negative voice and the emotions it elicited was not even a blip on my radar. It became so much a part of daily life that I could seldom tell where it ended and I began. And I believed every single word of it. So much loathing and self-hatred permeated every part of me, I felt like a dead, rotted branch, just waiting for a strong wind to come along, snap me at my base and send me crashing to the ground. When alone, it was easy to entertain ever-darkening fantasies of disappearing forever.

THE LAST SUMMER we had together before college was the best. We went on camping trips, on long trail rides, to dozens of horse shows, and to many other adventures. I raced him across open fields, feeling like the little girl of my daydreams on her magnificent black horse, thrilled at the sensation of wind whipping across my face and the sound of pounding hooves thundering beneath me. I didn't know what our future held or how my life would change in the next couple years, but it didn't matter—I knew we'd be okay as long as we had each other.

CHAPTER FOUR

"No." The answer was no. Sorry. Most definitely, no. Deflated.

In my preparations to move to Kewanee, Illinois, and attend Black Hawk College–East (BHE) in the fall of 1996, I'd been looking for a place to board Corky. I visited the town that spring to see the college and find housing for me and my horse. The folks at BHE had suggested I ask Danny Conner, a local horseman and business owner, if I could keep Corky at his nearby farm. Excited at the prospect of having Corky so close—I had found a crappy but affordable trailer at a park a few miles away—and feeling encouraged by the BHE faculty, I stopped in at Danny's hair salon.

"No. Sorry." Arms raised, a section of a woman's hair neatly tucked between the first two fingers of his left hand, Danny glanced up at me briefly. "I used to allow Black Hawk students to board at my place, but it turned out to be too much trouble. Never met one I could trust." *Snip-snip-snip*, the small section of hair fluttered to the floor. My heart sank with it. Difficult to hear, harder to accept.

I wound up keeping Corky at a stable almost an hour away. The less-than-ideal location meant I would not be able to see him every day. On an oppressively hot August day, about a week into my move to

Illinois, I visited Corky and found him in a stall with no food and a bucket half-full of blackened, stagnant water. His nostrils flared, breathing hard, Corky looked at me weakly, his dark eyes full of confusion. Furious with the barn staff but mostly with myself for being so naïve to trust anyone to care for Corky in my absence, I went back to the salon to beg Danny to reconsider. This time he reluctantly said we could give it a two-week trial. Corky could come live at Conner Equine.

Situated on five acres of land surrounded by corn fields, Conner Equine provided a picturesque setting for the Conners' lovely two-story home and a plain but functional fourteen-stall barn with a small sixty-by-seventy-foot indoor arena. A large pasture took up most of the southeast corner of the property. There were also four smaller paddocks.

The pasture and paddocks were fenced with hedge wood, a strong wood that gave the property a rustic look. Hedge-wood fencing did not make for straight, clean lines but rather a twisted, gnarled look, as each pole had a slightly different shape—twisting up or down, out or in, creating a unique structure, with each post having three rows of hedge-wood poles wired to it.

Danny raised American Paint horses, a breed characterized by their colorful coat patterns and stocky quarter horse-type build. In 1996 he stood one stallion, a four-year-old sorrel tobiano called Tagit Delux (a.k.a "Tag"). A dozen or so weanlings and yearlings meandered in and around the barn when Corky and I arrived. I had little interest in the Paint horse breed beyond my love for horses in general. That would soon change, but for now I was content to have Corky close to home as we both settled into new lives and new routines.

A few weeks after Corky moved to Conner Equine, Danny showed interest in the way I worked with my horse, often taking time to watch our sessions. He was a kind man and a talented horseman, with sandy-blond hair and a face that appeared much younger than his fifty years. Charismatic, funny, and personable, I was drawn to him as a father figure and friend.

One day while I worked with Corky in the indoor arena, Danny called me over. I walked across the arena to the gate where Danny stood, Corky following close behind.

"I love the way you work with him," Danny said. "You have such a quiet and gentle way about you. He is so relaxed around you." He glanced at Corky. "Have you ever worked with foals or yearlings?"

I hadn't, but Danny didn't seem to mind. He asked if I would like to start working with a couple of his horses in exchange for Corky's board. I accepted my first official job as a horse trainer.

"Hey, little guy." The palomino weanling looked up from his hay, a small mouthful sitting between his lips. He seemed to size me up as I entered the stall, this seven-hundred-pound colt just about eight months old, aptly named Moose. He towered over the other weanlings from his crop and outweighed them by a couple hundred pounds. He now chewed the hay thoughtfully, perhaps deciding if he could squish me into the wall and therefore avoid any training for the day.

I grabbed the catch-lead on his halter and brought him to the wall. Looping the lead around the center support—a beginning step in teaching him to stand while tied—I picked up a curry comb and started grooming his soft yellow coat.

"Step over, Moose." I touched the colt's side and made a clicking sound with my mouth. *Click-click-click.* "Step over." The big yellow colt instead stepped toward me and leaned, pressing me into the wall. I pushed, and Moose leaned harder.

"Get OFF me!"

He wouldn't budge. I pulled Moose's head toward me and pushed my weight against his hip. The colt stepped away from me. Leverage. Worked every time.

Moose, a black colt named Magic, and a little tobiano filly named Scooter were the first three foals I worked with for Danny. I soon discovered I had a talent with youngsters. My quiet ways, designed to avoid drawing attention to myself, comforted the foals. It was a natural fit.

While settling in as resident horse trainer at Conner Equine, I was already well into my first semester at Black Hawk East. I loved BHE from day one. It was like 4-H for adults. I immersed myself in horses all day, every day, taking courses on horse training, horse health, horse nutrition, farrier science, horsemanship, business, and more.

In high school I'd felt useless and stupid. I didn't fit in with the popular kids, which seemed to be basically everyone but me, and several had made sure I knew it—kids can be so cruel to the misfits among them. I didn't have the right clothes, the right interests, the right hair, the right makeup, or anything else that would make me interesting to them. I was just weird, fat, and ugly. By then that inner voice had me convinced of my worthlessness.

BHE was different. For the first time, I experienced joy when going to school. I had horses as a common interest with my cohort and more experience than several classmates. This gave me confidence I'd never felt before, like I almost had some tangible, recognizable value. At the same time that inner voice kept reminding me to be careful what I believed about myself. *"Don't go thinking too much of yourself, you ugly cow!"* The negative inner monologue was incessant and exhausting, each word cutting me down a little more like so many hatchet chops to an already weakened and swaying tree. I so badly wanted to be taken seriously as a horse trainer. The dream felt unobtainable. So long as I was fat, flawed, and stupid, I could never truly see any value in myself at all, let alone believe any other person could.

I managed to make some friends, though a part of me didn't trust that the people around me were really who they appeared to be. I often believed they were talking about me behind my back and thought myself ridiculous to believe someone as fat as me could ever be a good horse trainer. Mostly I tried to keep a safe distance, carefully selecting the social situations I engaged in. I always needed an out I could rely on in case the situation became too uncomfortable. Needing to care for Corky or go to work were ready-made escape excuses.

I found it safest to decline offers to go out except for one-on-one situations. Eventually friends became discouraged and stopped asking altogether. This was both good and bad. I felt safe but lonely.

My college years were my first away from home. Moving away from everyone and everything I knew was an avenue of forced self-discovery. I had to figure out who I was, as I no longer had family around to suggest my identity—I wasn't Louise's daughter or Andrea's sister. No one in Kewanee knew my family—I was just that girl from Michigan. What I presented was their only reality. It is a common rite of passage many young people go through when they learn to navigate the world on their own and soon realize the ideas and "truths" they grew up with actually belonged to their parents.

This forced self-discovery left me insecure and unbalanced. The negative inner voice that had plagued me for years was now taking on a personality and identity all its own. The voice was mine, but it wasn't. She was me, but also something … darker. She'd drawn a heavy black curtain across my mind, deep in my subconscious. Behind the curtain, a little girl hid from a *monster*.

CHAPTER FIVE

On a warm fall evening at Conner Equine, Danny approached me while I brushed Corky in the barn aisle, preparing for a ride.

"I have something to show you," he said with a boyish grin. "Here, come with me." He laughed. "You're going to love this!"

I followed Danny across the street to a pile of what looked like scrap metal dotted with parts of old appliances. Perplexed, I wondered what this man I barely knew was up to. Danny knelt in the grass and reached into the pile of twisted, rusted scrap metal. He slowly withdrew his arm, and his hand emerged from the opening holding a tiny, fluffy puppy!

Handing me the puppy, Danny grinned. "Here! This one matches your shirt!"

I held the little ball of black-and-white fluff close to my chest. The little puppy grunted and squirmed before settling into my arms. I then held his little body out before me, one hand under each tiny foreleg, oversized white paws dangling in the air above my folded legs. A wide smile crossed my face. I brought the puppy close to me. He crawled up toward my shoulder, pressing his furry body against my neck. My heart melted.

"There are six more in there." Danny pointed at the opening in the junk pile.

"Where did they come from?"

"You wouldn't believe it if I told you." He explained that a few weeks earlier he had noticed a pregnant stray dog sneaking into the barn early in the morning, eating the food Danny left out for his dogs. Danny called to the stray, but wary, she growled, barked, and ran away, disappearing into the junk pile across the street.

For the next two weeks Danny watched each morning as the small black dog, her belly heavy with puppies, snuck into the barn to eat and drink, then scampered across the street into the junk pile on the neighbor's empty lot. The first morning she appeared at the barn no longer pregnant, Danny took the dog food away. After the stray had come looking for food a couple times and found none, Danny watched as she disappeared into the junk pile. Grabbing some chicken and a flashlight, Danny went out the door and walked down his driveway and across the street to the stray's junk den.

A low growl reached Danny's ears from somewhere beneath the twisted and rusted metal, old appliances, and long-forgotten auto parts. Kneeling in the grass near the opening of the makeshift den, he clicked on his flashlight and peered inside. The black dog crouched down in the small space facing the opening, her lips curled back in a snarl. Danny slowly reached his hand inside the stray's den, holding a piece of chicken out to the dog. The stray growled louder as Danny's hand advanced closer to her. When the chicken was in reach of the black dog, Danny stopped and waited, holding the meat out for the stray to take. Finally the growling subsided and the black dog snatched the chicken from Danny's hand.

For the next two weeks Danny repeated this process. Each day the stray growled a bit less and took the food more readily, until finally she allowed Danny to touch her. A few days later, the stray allowed him to see and count her puppies.

"Can you believe that?" Danny chuckled after he finished his story.

A few days later, with Babe (as the stray was named) now able to trust Danny and reasonably tame (though still timid), Danny and I scooped up her puppies and moved them and her to a comfortable, clean stall where they would be safe and warm. I could only imagine what the fate of Babe and her puppies would have been if Danny had chosen to ignore them and let them grow up wild, eventually killed by coyotes or crushed under the tires of a car on the nearby highway. Instead, as he did with so many dogs, Danny welcomed Babe and her seven puppies into his barn, where he would raise them and care for them until he found a home for each one.

Four puppies looked like they had an Australian shepherd father. They all had the gray-and-black-spotted coat known as blue merle, with varying amounts of white markings and tail lengths, which ranged from barely a nub to full length. One puppy had half a tail. The others appeared to have a different father. Two were fluffy like sheepdogs, another slick and black. All were adorable. I had always wanted a dog, and soon my heart latched on to a beautiful blue merle puppy with white hind paws; white front legs, chest, and shoulders; and a white stripe down his face. The puppy had a naturally docked tail an inch or two in length. He had one blue eye and one brown eye and the black-and-pink-speckled nose common to Aussie puppies.

"I want this one," I said to Danny one evening, my favorite puppy squirming in my arms.

"That is the one that matched your shirt!" Danny laughed.

I gave him a knowing smile. When the puppies were six weeks old, I took mine home.

I'd never owned a dog before, let alone raised a puppy, and soon learned I was not prepared. I did my best to overlook the path of destruction my puppy left in his wake as he chewed his way through the house, opting for furniture and carpet over toys and rawhide.

The destructive little ball of fluff with a stump tail needed a name, but nothing I tried fit him. I finally settled on the name Diefenbaker (DEE-fhen-baker), the name of a character (a wolf belonging to a Canadian Mountie living in Chicago) on *Due South*, a favorite TV show.

It wasn't long before Dief and I became an inseparable duo. He came with me to Danny's farm every night and occasionally came to school, where he was a popular distraction. Seeing so many people, horses, and other animals helped Dief develop strong social skills. He was confident and comfortable in new surroundings, but our constant togetherness eventually led to issues with separation anxiety for Dief.

One evening I returned to the old, decrepit trailer I called home. Darkness had enveloped the land hours ago, and the late hour had me looking forward to bed. I slipped the key into the lock of the back door, which opened into the kitchen with a squeak and a groan. Reaching inside the doorway, I flipped on the dim light, and it spilled onto the floor, illuminating the room like dull candlelight. I gasped at the sight.

Napkins, aluminum cans, empty food containers, and various other bits of trash were strewn all over the floor near the door. The path of destruction continued into the kitchen, where the trash gave way to torn strips of cabinet wood, chewed bits of linoleum, diced telephone cords, bits of cardboard, and dozens of unused napkins. I stood shaking my head at the destruction and wondering what my roommate would say, when the sound of plastic bumping against linoleum drew my attention to the trash can lying on its side, facing the door.

For a moment, silence, and then the trash can wiggled, whined, and eventually produced a puppy with a bit of napkin stuck in his sharp little teeth.

"Oh, Diefenbaker!" I closed my eyes and produced a sound similar to what I imagined my mom had made on numerous occasions. With a deep sigh I closed the door, turned, and strode back to my truck. I drove to the local twenty-four-hour big-box store and purchased a plastic dog crate, as a friend of mine had suggested a couple weeks before.

That blessed crate, just what we needed! Dief adapted and soon voluntarily spent time in his new crate. It became his bed of choice, and before long I didn't even have to encourage him to enter it when I left home. The mass destruction stopped, and Dief was house broken in a matter of days (although prior to purchasing the crate, I'd been trying for weeks).

At the end of freshman year, I moved out of the trailer and into a one-bedroom apartment in an old house. Technically, Dief was not allowed in this apartment. But a cleverly placed tablecloth, lamp, and a few books on top of his crate, plus the fact he seldom stayed home alone, made for a satisfactory arrangement. If we were quiet and kept a low profile, surely we could avoid being caught.

"We'll be ok, buddy." I scratched the fuzzy pup behind his velvety ears. Dief picked up his rope bone and offered it to me. I grabbed the end and tugged. Hiding Dief would be the least of my worries in the year to come.

PART II
DIVIDED MIND, STOIC SMILE

CHAPTER SIX

"I hate you!" I screamed through my tears.

There was a sharp pain in my head each time I screamed. It started in the center of my forehead and radiated out and all the way around my skull, finally dissipating after it shot down my neck. The pressure was so great, sometimes I felt like my head would explode.

"I hate you!" I screamed again. My body shook. "You are a worthless piece of shit! I hate you so much! You are useless! You have never been any good for anybody! You have no real friends. People just pretend to like you because they feel sorry for you! They can't stand to be around you any more than I can! I hate you so much!" I cried, the tears coming ever faster, each sob shaking my body while the pain and pressure built inside my head. "Why can't you just die? Please, God, why? Why can't you just die?"

I turned away from the mirror and slammed my head against the jamb of the bathroom door. Again and again I bashed my head until I was lightheaded and seeing stars burst before my eyes.

"Please, please, why can't you just die?" I whimpered, turning back to the mirror. "I hate you so much. Please die," I cried to my reflection and slowly crumpled to the floor, my rage finally spent.

Exhausted, a small part of me wondered if the people in the next apartment had heard me. I tried to be careful about my surroundings when I unleashed on myself. *Jeez, I hope you didn't screw up.* I slowly stood, remembering hitting my head against the jamb. "I hope there is not a mark," I mumbled, not wanting to explain any injuries to anyone, should they ask. My face still held a deep reddish-purple tint, but I saw no mark on my head. *Good.* But just as suddenly as I had that thought, the negative voice in my mind shot back, *"Way to go, dumbass! You can't even do that right, you pathetic loser!"* I nodded my agreement as I weakly walked to the couch and sank into the old gold-colored cushions. Propping myself up on a pillow and drawing my knees toward my chest, I reached for the remote and flipped on the television.

I must be crazy. Do sane people really behave this way? *Surely not*. Normal people didn't behave this way. "Why, God?" I prayed aloud. "Why do you keep me here? Why do you allow me to live when so many good people die? Please, God, can't you just take me?" The tears came again, slow and soft this time, trickling in a single-file line down my cheek and onto my shirt.

"Toughen up, you loser!" I hissed at myself, angrily wiping the tears from my face.

I dug my fingernails into my forearm until I drew blood. Small cuts on my arms and legs were easy to explain away. I worked with horses, and cuts and bruises were a daily occurrence in the barn. No big deal.

I turned my attention to the television. My insides felt hollow, cavernous, and mercifully numb. This self-inflicted abuse was nothing new but had escalated in recent months. I could not identify any particular trigger for the self-harm, not that I really thought on it in those terms. I felt more like a victim of something outside of me, or perhaps more accurately, something *inside* of me. The negative self-talk had been there for as long as I could remember—an angry, hurtful voice filling my mind with constant reminders of my uselessness, pointing out all my faults and bad choices while ridiculing me on a daily basis.

But it was changing—*she* was changing, taking on an identity of her own. Increasingly I felt like more than one version of me resided inside my head. Both were me, but both were different. I eventually named her, the voice, "Mean Cheryl," because she was me but she was also someone else, or something else. *My God, she is so mean.* She didn't feel like something I had any control over. Like an abusive partner, I both feared her but also felt I needed her. A cold shudder raised goose bumps on my arms. I squeezed my knees closer to me.

"Welcome to your new normal, you crazy bitch."

CHAPTER SEVEN

"Arooowoooo!" Dief yodeled as he trotted into the barn.

"Is break time over?" I placed my ice water on the table in the barn aisle.

"Oooo-oooo," Dief replied, his voice trailing off. I'd yet to hear my nearly two-year-old dog bark, but he often communicated with a bark-howl I referred to as his yodel.

Dief had a strong, natural herding instinct, and I'd been working on channeling this energy so he could help around the barn, though I had no idea how to train him to use his innate talent. Despite this, after a year and a half together, Dief had become a valuable working dog. A simple voice command of "hold," and Dief would stand guard at an open stall door, not allowing the horse to exit. He also watched me closely and would help keep a foal with the dam, by coming around behind and bumping the foal's lower legs with his closed teeth.

Conner Equine was a small operation, oftentimes having a staff of only one—me. I frequently found myself handling mares and foals on my own. Most of the time, the foals followed their mothers from the indoor arena, where they were turned out for exercise, back to their stall without incident. Occasionally, not unlike a child who doesn't want to come in for dinner, a foal would take the scenic route, checking out empty stalls, cats, or other foals as he ever so slowly returned to his mother's side.

One day I was moving a mare and foal from the arena to their stall just a short distance away—it should've been easy. I watched over my shoulder while the foal slowly stepped up to the open gate. His mom, already in the aisle, stood just outside their stall door. All the foal had to do was turn to the right and enter the stall.

The little foal looked to his right, at me, and at his mom, and then he looked to the left, where Dief guarded the aisle. I stood quietly, watching the foal while his mother waited patiently by my side.

"C'mon, baby. Let's go!" I muttered.

The foal took a long, slow step to the left. Staring down at Dief, he flared his little nostrils and snorted. Dief responded by taking a herding stance, preparing to turn back the foal if it took another step in the wrong direction. For a brief moment, neither foal nor dog moved. I held my breath, watching the standoff. The foal took another cautious step toward the dog. Dief sprung forward and bumped the foal's front shin with his closed teeth. The foal squealed, leapt in the air, and inexplicably bolted toward Dief. The dog narrowly escaped being trampled and quickly ran after the truant foal as he exited the barn. I yelled after Dief, not wanting him to inadvertently chase the foal into the road. My call went unanswered—Dief had a job to do, and he was not about to quit now.

Oh God . . . oh shit. That familiar hollow feeling returned, my stomach sank to the floor, and my anxiety rose. *Please, God, I can't screw this up.* To make a mistake felt like a death sentence. My memories were filled with incidents of sheer terror at messing up, letting people down, not being good enough. Now I had a loose foal running around by the road. *My fault if he gets hurt or killed.* I took a deep, shuddering breath.

The mare at the end of my lead shank no longer stood quietly. With her foal out of sight, she panicked, becoming dangerous to handle. Trying to swing her big body around in the narrow barn aisle, she shoved me into the wall with her head. I had to either put the mare in her stall and go after the foal or try to use the now half-crazed mare as bait, hoping the colt would find his mom more interesting than whatever outdoor adventures he'd discovered.

I had been pondering my choices for less than a minute when I heard the clicking sound of galloping foal feet on the cement aisle of the upper barn. The deviant foal burst into the lower barn with Dief hot on his heels. He tore down the aisle, turning the corner at the end and bolting past me and his mom right into his stall. Dief stood in the doorway of the stall, staring down the foal, daring him to make a move toward the door. I quickly put the mare inside and shut the door. I had no idea what happened between Dief and the foal outside, but my dog had saved my butt and possibly the life of that foal through his quick and exact actions.

I crouched and hugged Dief, thanking him for his help and breathing a deep sigh of relief. There would be no punishment for me today.

"Aaaaroooowoooo!" He wagged his little stump tail.

LATER THAT SPRING, I picked up a second job. I still worked for Danny, my job at Conner Equine becoming a breeding internship for school, in addition to my work training the young horses. A friend of Danny's found herself in desperate need of help. One of her employees had been kicked by a horse and had to be off work for several months. Dief and I moved to the friend's farm, located in Brimfield, Illinois, a small town about an hour from Danny's farm in Kewanee. I lived in an apartment above the barn and worked five days a week at the Brimfield farm from 7:00 a.m. to 1:00 p.m. I then drove to Conner Equine and worked from 2:30 until 9:00 or 10:00 p.m., at which point I drove home to Brimfield for the night. Saturday and Sunday were my days off at the Brimfield farm, but I still worked at Danny's seven days a week.

Late one morning while working at the Brimfield barn, a huge thunderstorm whipped up hard and fast, as they so often do on the edge of tornado alley. The sky turned black, and a cold wind chased the heavy, humid air from the barn. Lightning flashed and thunder rumbled in the distance. Leaves swirled around in the barnyard, caught in a mini twister that lifted them high and then blew them out of an invisible volcano.

Finishing up cleaning the last stall and hoping to stay dry, I wanted to dump the manure before the heavy rains reached the barn. As I exited the stall, Dief snuck in and cowered in the corner.

"It's not safe for you to be in here with this horse," I said to Dief.

He looked at me with trepidation and stayed put.

"C'mon, Dief. Out you go!" I motioned toward the stall door.

A loud clap of thunder shook the air. Spooked, the young horse in the stall spun rapidly and bolted for the partially open stall door. I threw my hands up and yelled, "Get back!" The horse stopped abruptly. I'd narrowly avoided a dangerous escape attempt.

"C'mon, Dief!" I grabbed the dog's collar and pulled him out of the stall just as the horse lunged again for the door. "Get back!" I slammed the door just before he reached the opening. Black clouds blotted out the sun, and the now cold wind tore around the barn, howling through the eaves and blowing leaves down the aisle. Eyeing the sky warily, I hopped on the four-wheeler and rushed out to dump the manure.

The sky opened up above me, releasing a torrential downpour. I'd made it back just in time. The wind ripped at the trees and blew dirt and debris down the lanes and into the barn, where it swirled around my feet. I heaved the heavy doors shut against the wind.

Walking across the long indoor arena to the other side of the barn, I'd expected Dief to come running toward me at any moment, but he didn't. Assuming he had found another place to hide, I walked up and down the barn aisle, calling his name and looking in the stalls and the feed and tack rooms. No Dief. I poked my head out the barn door; cold rain pelted my face. I screamed Dief's name into the wind. Nothing. I had been gone less than ten minutes. *Where could he be?*

A thorough search of the upstairs came up empty. Dief, always right on my heels, followed my every move and took his job seriously.

He seldom went off on his own and always came when I called. That familiar hollow, stomach-dropping panic crept in.

The storm blew full force now. Lightning tore across the sky, briefly illuminating the landscape in a surreal white light. I walked out onto the porch of the loft apartment. The cold air pulled at my clothes, sending a chill up my spine. I squinted into the whipping onslaught of the storm, calling out to Dief once again. The wind captured my voice, blowing it uselessly away. I called him again and again. Pointless. No one could hear me over the storm's wrath.

I had to leave for Kewanee. Reluctantly, I headed down the stairs to my truck, not wanting to leave without Dief. *I have to go to work*, I told myself. Surely Dief had hidden in the woods somewhere. He would come home and be waiting in the barn when I returned that evening. I looked up at the blackened sky. The storm, finally blowing itself out, had left as quickly as it had come. Hopping into my truck, I shouted out for Dief one last time, glancing around the barnyard, my hope waning like the energy of the dying storm. I steered my truck slowly down the long driveway and through the back-country roads, continuously calling for Dief out my open window, hoping I would see him somewhere along the road. I never did.

It was well after dark when I returned home to the barn in Brimfield. A new storm brewed in the distance, still too far away to hear, but I could see the lightning streak across the sky. The wind howled eerily through the trees. I fully expected to find Dief waiting for me when I walked into the barn. I stepped across the front entry and flipped on the lights, but only the soft nickers of horses hoping for a midnight snack greeted me.

An intense pressure grew in my chest. I sucked in a deep breath, holding it for a moment before releasing it with a loud whoosh through tense lips. My eyes filled with tears, and panic gripped my heart, the gravity of the situation finally sinking in. Dief was really gone. I had lost my dog and didn't know if I'd ever see him again. Unaware of how close I'd become to Dief in the short time we'd been together, the onslaught of such intense emotion took me by surprise. It scared me to be so attached to something I could lose so easily. But more than that, I felt vulnerable and out of control at the realization I hadn't understood that my love for Dief held such power over me. Staying in complete control of everything that could hurt me was part of my survival mechanism. I lost control when I lost Dief.

Tears flowed down my cheeks. I walked frantically through the barn, searching all the stalls, the feed room, tack room, and lounge. No Dief. I stumbled up the stairs to my apartment in a stupor, dumbfounded by the fear, pain, and loss. I had been so certain Dief would return while I was at Danny's. Now I didn't know what to do. I prepared to go to bed, feeling empty and lost without my friend but also unsettled by the strong emotions surrounding his disappearance.

Unable to sleep, I grabbed a flashlight and went out into the black night, searching the property while calling Dief's name over and over. Crying into the blackness of the night air, I prayed to God to help me find my friend. The only response I heard was the howling wind and the sound of trees bending and cracking under the relentless strain of the coming storm.

Reluctantly I turned and headed back to the barn, stopping and calling for Dief every few yards. My legs felt like heavy logs as I trudged up the steps to my apartment, still in utter disbelief. *How could Dief be gone?* My mind reeled, trying to grasp the reality of those words. Once again tears stung my eyes and rolled down my red and weary cheeks.

Just a few hours remained before I had to get up for work. I fell into bed, eventually drifting into a restless slumber. I woke frequently, climbing out of bed and walking outside onto the porch to call for Dief. Each call drifted off into the night, unanswered.

Dawn broke over the silent paddocks while I dressed for work. Maybe Dief would be in the barn when I went down to feed the horses. Holding on to that last bit of hope, I walked down the stairs. "Please, please let Diefy be there when I open the door," I prayed, my voice a trembling whisper. I turned the knob, and the hinges creaked as the door swung open. I cautiously peered out into the barn aisle. Dief was not there.

"Dief! Dief!" I cried. "C'mon, buddy! Dief! Come!"

I looked around and listened, not really believing I would see him when I called. It had been more than eighteen hours since he'd disappeared. I drifted to the feed room and started my morning barn chores

The morning marched on relentlessly, the hours of being a dog-less dog owner quickly approaching an entire day. I moved through my tasks in a haze of distracted grief. Having pretty much given up on Dief returning on his own, I barely reacted when I heard the jingling of dog tags late that morning. Another dog, Shep, also lived on the farm, and I had already mistaken his jingling tags for Dief's about two dozen times that dreadful morning. Each time my heart had leapt with hope and anticipation, only to have the hope stomped under the boots of cruel reality when I realized yet again it was only Shep I'd heard walking down the barn aisle.

"Oh, Shep," I grumbled under my breath, "you and your tags are making me crazy."

Jingle, jingle, jingle. The sound slipped down the barn aisle and slithered into my ears. "I'm not falling for this again," I said to myself. Hope was no longer a part of my day. *Jingle, jingle, jingle.* The sound taunted me.

"Oh, fine," I said aloud, leaning the manure fork against the wall of the stall I was cleaning. Peeking around the stall door, I glanced down the barn aisle. Nothing.

"Diefenbaker?" I called out to the empty barn aisle. *Jingle, jingle, jingle.*

"Dief?" I called again, stepping out of the stall. *Jingle, jingle.* The sound reached my ears from somewhere just out of sight. I took a couple steps toward the taunting jingle, then stopped, my mouth dropping open with disbelief. Dief drifted listlessly around the corner and stumbled into the center barn aisle. The dog turned toward me on shaky legs, took a few more steps, and collapsed in a heap. Dief lay flat out on his side, his tongue hanging out of his open mouth as his sides heaved with the effort of his panting. He looked as if he had just sprinted for miles with the devil on his tail.

I ran to Dief and fell to the floor next to his prone body, hugging him and crying into his fur.

"Where were you?" I asked. "I was so worried about you!" I sat on the hard cement barn aisle and told Dief how scared I'd been and how I thought I'd never see him again. Tears streamed down my face, but this time they were tears of joy and relief. My friend had come home.

I checked Dief over for injuries. He appeared to be unhurt, though exhausted. I sat on the cool cement watching Dief closely as his breathing slowly returned to normal. Aside from the massive heaving of his sides, the dog lay motionless. Gently stroking his soft coat, I wondered where he had been for the past twenty-two hours. I concluded from his utter exhaustion that he must have run a great distance at a high rate of speed to find his way home. Perhaps he had hidden from the storm in someone's garage and gotten trapped until this morning. Or maybe someone had picked him up along the road and taken him home, only to have Dief run off when the well-meaning individual let him out.

I shrugged and let the questions slip from my mind. I would never know where Dief had been, and it really didn't matter. He was here now, and I would not, *could not* allow myself to lose him again. Dief took in a deep breath and released it as a long sigh. He lifted his head off the cement and looked up at me before rolling from his side to his belly and crawling onto my lap. I wrapped my arms around my dog and gave him a gentle squeeze. Placing my index finger on the white stripe near the tip of his nose, I slowly traced the stripe up to where it ended on the top of his head. Then I brought my finger back down toward his nose, against the hair, making the stripe wide and rough before tracing it back toward his ears, making the stripe narrow and smooth once again.

CHAPTER EIGHT

"*They're all going to find out!*" Mean Cheryl taunted. "*They're going to find out who and what you really are!*" The now familiar guilt and anxiety rolled in my belly, and I sucked in a short breath, releasing it sharply between my pressed lips. I counted the horse and rider pairs lined up ahead of me and Corky. One, two, three, four ... Time was running short before our turn came to navigate the next jumping obstacle.

My time at Black Hawk College neared an end. After this last semester, I would graduate with two degrees in horse science. One degree with a training focus, and the other with a management focus. For my last couple semesters, Corky lived at school, and I used him in class. Despite the improvement in my riding from my course work and time spent on Danny's stallion, Tag, I still lacked confidence in myself and my ability. This went double for work over fences (jumping). A course called Hunt Seat Equitation, where the majority of the work focused on jumping, stood between me and graduation. Corky and I had jumped before, many times—I'd even shown him over fences a couple times—but none of that mattered. I knew I wasn't any good at anything.

Corky loved to jump, and he was quite talented, but due to my extreme insecurity in myself and my riding, I did more to hinder rather than help him with our jumping efforts. On this day in class we were working on a jump configuration called a bounce—two fences placed close together so the horse must jump the first fence, land, and immediately jump the second fence, as there is no room to add a stride. The bounce petrified me.

The horses and riders were all lined up along the arena fence, head to tail, waiting for their turn to attempt the bounce. A familiar fear festered in my belly, growing with each step moving Corky and me closer to the head of the line. I knew my horse could jump the bounce easily. I had seen him do such a jump before with my former 4-H leader in the saddle. I also had far more experience than many of my classmates and a kind, honest horse to ride but ...

Far too soon my turn came. With all the confidence of a guppy surrounded by hungry piranhas, I took up contact with the reins until I could lightly feel Corky's mouth. Just barely squeezing him with my lower legs, I gave a scarcely audible click-click sound with my tongue and cheek. Corky, having already seen the fence, readily moved forward into a bold trot. With mild panic gripping me, I quickly shortened the reins, slowing Corky to a dawdling jog.

"Let go of his face, Cheryl. Move him forward a little faster," the instructor cautioned over the loud speaker. I knew Corky didn't have enough momentum to successfully navigate the bounce. Fully aware I was setting us up to fail, still I couldn't make myself *ride* the horse. I hung on like a useless passenger, bracing myself for a disaster of my own making.

Corky slowly jogged toward the fence.

"Give him more gas!" the instructor yelled.

I can't. I knew she was right—Corky needed to go faster—but too afraid, I did nothing. Being the kind and honest horse he was, Corky tried to make up for his lack of momentum by rocking back and leaping straight up and over the fence in a deer-style jump. My body snapped back, then forward. Completely out of sync with the motion of the horse, I slammed back into the saddle, unprepared for the second fence. Corky stopped abruptly, hurling me over his shoulder. I landed painfully in a heap on the ground between the jumps.

Shame burned my cheeks a fierce red. Uninjured, I forced myself to get back on and try again. For a moment, saving face trumped my fear. I pushed Corky forward toward the bounce. *What have I got to lose? I've already made an ass of myself.* I held my breath on the approach (*breathe, stupid*) but kept my leg on, keeping Corky's forward momentum. Jump-land-jump-land, canter off. We did it.

But Mean Cheryl wouldn't allow me to feel victorious. *"You should have done it right the first time, you stupid cow."*

Interestingly, or perhaps tellingly, I approached most challenges in life much like I approached the bounce that day—knowing I wasn't giving myself every (or any) chance to succeed, but unable to do anything about it. Accepting defeat without trying—not out of laziness but from a deep knowing that I would never be good enough, never amount to anything, never matter to anyone.

I successfully finished my course work for the final semester and graduated with two associate degrees—equestrian science and horse science technology.

"I hope you go on to more schooling, Cheryl." My instructor placed her left hand over my right, giving our handshake a final pump. I turned my face away slightly but held her eye contact, as any adult is expected to. "You're very smart." She smiled and turned away to greet other students milling around after the graduation ceremony.

Confusion. Her words made me feel good about myself, like a tiny slice of hope peeking through a barely open door. Then, *bang!* Mean Cheryl slammed it shut in my face. *"She's just saying that because you're no good with horses. She's trying to be nice. You're so damned gullible."* She was right, of course. Not smart, not talented, not anything. Defeat. *Will I ever be enough?*

Mentally spiraling downward at an ever-increasing pace, for the first time I went beyond considering suicide and started making plans to end my life. Guilt and shame gripped me. I didn't deserve to live.

"You are worthless garbage!" Mean Cheryl hissed in my head. *"You don't deserve a horse like Corky, you worthless waste of space!"*

This was new. I didn't *deserve* Corky. I let the thought roll around in my head until it made sense. Losing Corky would be the greatest punishment of all. I don't recall when this need to punish myself began. Was it after the I burned my hand with the hot water? The clarity and sense of control that accident brought was almost liberating. I remember locking myself in my car with the windows up on a sweltering hot day, but that wasn't the first time the part of me that became Mean Cheryl tried to hurt me. Peering further back into my memories—deliberately banging my head on the cement driveway. Was that third grade? Fourth? Biting myself so hard the mark lingered for hours. Of course, there were the more recent hitting and screaming episodes. *I really am crazy.*

No part of me wanted to sell Corky, but shortly after graduation, I put him up for sale. Mean Cheryl had made it quite clear—I didn't deserve Corky, and I'd be selfish to keep him. I justified my actions by telling others that I was too busy working Danny's horses to give Corky the time he deserved or that I didn't have the money to keep him. Neither statement was entirely true—I was pressed for both time and cash, but I could have made it work. If only I had tried. A battle raged in my mind and heart. I didn't want to sell my horse, but Mean Cheryl relentlessly reminded me that I had no right to keep him.

"You don't deserve Corky," she'd rant on endlessly. *You are a horrible, selfish person to even consider keeping him."* But I didn't want to sell him. I struggled against Mean Cheryl, and for the first time I questioned her. I kept Corky for sale halfheartedly for several months. I sabotaged the potential sale of my horse several times, telling buyers he could be spooky or pointing out (sometimes manufactured) imperfections. With no buyer, I let myself believe maybe it was OK to keep him. I stopped advertising and no longer mentioned he was for sale. Had I finally defeated Mean Cheryl?

A COLD, harsh rain pelted my face. Bitter wind pulled at the few remaining leaves on the autumn-bare trees. A woman I'd never met had come out to Conner Equine to look at our foals and yearlings. I took her around and showed her the horses for sale.

"There are a few more out back." I waved my arm in the direction of the rear barn door.

The woman followed me outside. Our feet made sucking noises in the mud as we headed around to the rear of the barn. Two of the lots out back contained young horses for sale. In the middle lot, standing among the yearlings, was Corky.

"Who is the gray horse?" the woman asked.

"That's Corky," I replied. "He's my Arabian gelding."

"He's beautiful." The woman moved closer to the hedge-wood fence.

"Thanks." I stared at the mud around my feet.

"Is he for sale?"

My heart sank into my stomach. I glanced at the woman.

"Well, sort of, yeah, I guess," I stammered.

"You don't sound sure." The woman's eyes searched mine.

"I don't really want to sell him, but I have to." The lie pierced my heart, and hot tears stung my eyes.

"How much?" the woman asked.

I blurted out a reasonable but high price, hoping it was more than she would pay.

"OK," the woman replied. "I have a client who might be interested in him."

Oh hell. I just lost my horse.

I MADE little effort to complete the sale of Corky. I failed to return calls and avoided discussing sale details with the prospective buyers. The woman brought her client, a middle-aged lady named Ronda, out to see and ride Corky. Torn between the pride of showing off my horse and the desire to sabotage the sale by riding him poorly, I ended up giving a halfhearted display of Corky's skills, not challenging either of us to be our best. My plan half worked, as Ronda seemed less interested in Corky after our ride.

"Maybe he's not the right horse," she said. "He looks a little green to me."

A tiny bit of hope crept into my heart.

"Can I ride him?" the trainer asked.

"Um, sure." I slid off my horse and handed her the reins.

The trainer mounted, soon demonstrating Corky's multitude of talent. Ronda seemed impressed, and I could see she wanted him. About to lose my best friend, I felt helpless to do anything about it. Mean Cheryl's endless monologue reminded me I didn't deserve to own such a wonderful horse. In reality, I held all the power. All I had to do was say no. But I couldn't. Mean Cheryl manipulated my mind. I was powerless to stop the sale of Corky.

I felt like a little kid losing a favorite toy as a punishment for lying or getting a bad grade. But Corky, so much more than a toy—he was my heart. Mean Cheryl would never allow me to stand up for myself and express my true feelings. Losing Corky certainly would be a just punishment for the horrible things I had done. I deserved to live with the pain and the guilt.

"Oh, grow up and quit whining!" Mean Cheryl's voice, cold and cruel, echoed in my head.

Ronda was speaking now. I returned from the depths of my mind, working to focus on her words.

"… yes, I'm interested in Corky. Let me go home and speak to my husband. We'll be in touch."

"Sounds great!" The lie curdled like rotten milk on my tongue. Inwardly I gagged. Outwardly I forced a smile, extending my hand for the obligatory handshake. "Thanks for coming. I'm glad you like him."

Still holding Corky's reins, I led him while I walked Ronda and her trainer to the barn door, which led out to the driveway. Waving goodbye, I closed the door behind them. The barn seemed particularly damp and cold that evening as I stood in the aisle facing my friend.

"I'm so sorry," I said to Corky, burying my face in his mane. Tears ran silently down my cheeks. My hand shook as I stroked Corky's neck. I thought of all the adventures we'd had together. I had always imagined I would have Corky forever. We would grow old together, and I would care for him until the day he died. He was only eight. I had missed forever by at least twenty years.

Slowly, I removed Corky's saddle and bridle. I ran a soft brush over his gray coat, smoothing the fine hairs, which possessed a subtle silver glow in the dim lights of the barn aisle.

Danny entered the barn as I was finishing up. "How did it go?" he asked, knowing Ronda had come to see Corky that night.

"It went well," I whispered. Pausing, I took a deep breath and added, "I think he's sold." I choked back more tears.

"That's good," Danny said. "It's the right thing to do."

Later that week, Ronda's husband called to finalize the sale and set a date to take ownership of Corky. Just like every other part of my public life, I pretended to be happy. I pretended to be excited about the money. I told family and friends it was the right thing to do. I told them I'd made the best decision for Corky. I lied to everyone, and soon I almost believed it myself.

Several weeks after Corky moved to his new home near Davenport, Iowa (a little over an hour from Kewanee), I went to visit him. Corky nickered when he saw me enter the barn. I opened his stall door and was immediately attacked with Corky kisses. The gelding ran his lips up and down my front, searched each pocket for treats, and then nuzzled each cheek as he ran his soft muzzle over my face and through my hair. I hugged him and cried with my face pressed into his neck. Corky stood silent and still, his warm breath tousling my hair.

"I'm so sorry. I'm so sorry I let you go. I love you so much, Corky. I'm so sorry." I spoke softly into his long mane. Would he ever forgive me? Could I ever forgive myself? Wiping the tears from my face, I reached into my jacket pocket and retrieved a treat. Corky accepted the gift graciously.

"I miss you." I ran my fingers through Corky's mane. He pressed his muzzle against my cheek—the feeling was mutual.

CHAPTER NINE

The trees around the farm swayed with the fall breezes, their branches ablaze with flickering flames of red, orange, and yellow. Fall was a busy time at Conner Equine. Spring foals were weaned from their mothers, young horses were prepared for the major fall futurities, and Danny selected some of the best foals sired by his stallions to come to his farm for training and showing.

Dozens of attractive foals had come through the barn that year, but I had a definite favorite—a wildly marked, leggy colt named Farley. I buzzed with excitement when Danny chose him to return and placed him on my training roster. Unfortunately, a respiratory infection sidelined the young colt for the big shows that fall. No worries though—Farley would be a star the next year, I felt certain. There was something about his personality, his enthusiasm to learn, his bravery, and his ability to trust so freely that really made an impression on me.

Unlike me, Farley seemed made for the limelight, comfortable and sure of himself. He reminded me of Corky. Perhaps that was why I latched on to little Farley so quickly. Farley had natural talent and took to each new phase of his training with the ease of a much-older, more-experienced horse. Now a two-year-old, I introduced the colt to the feel of a training surcingle around his body and a gentle bit in his mouth. I taught him to drive from the ground so he would learn rein pressure and how to respond to voice commands, asking him to travel at different gaits in a circle around me. After mastering ground driving, I introduced Farley to the saddle and, later that year, to the weight of a rider on his back.

Never a buck or any objection, Farley took to being ridden as if he'd done it his entire life. Truly an exceptional animal, the colt had become the star of my training string, well on his way to a stellar debut in the prestigious fall futurities—a sort-of year-end championships for young horses.

"You've done a great job with him."

I looked up, not realizing Danny had come into the barn to watch me work with the colt.

"That's a real feather in your cap, what you've accomplished."

I looked at the dirt around my feet, then back up at Danny. Compliments made me feel so uncomfortable. But I also felt a tinge of pride. Someone had recognized my talent.

"Um, thank you. He's such a good boy." I deflected the attention back onto the horse. Pride always came with a dangerously sharp edge. Allowing myself to feel pride in my accomplishments risked awakening Mean Cheryl. She would certainly tear me back down again. Only horrible, self-centered people felt good about themselves. Feeling good about myself meant letting my guard down, which opened me up to ... I shook my head. I would never follow that thought to its conclusion.

Late that summer Farley developed a severe gait irregularity. After a thorough work-up at the vet, the colt was diagnosed with a debilitating neurological disease called equine protozoal myeloencephalitis (EPM). At the time of his diagnosis in 2000, EPM was usually career ending and often a death sentence. Vets understood little about the parasite that attacked the EPM-afflicted horse's spinal cord and central nervous system. Treatments were expensive and seldom effective. Farley's long-term prognosis seemed guarded at best. Even if he did recover, the gait irregularity might not disappear. EPM also had a high incidence of relapse.

The young stallion went through six months of difficult treatment. By the spring of his three-year-old year, he had beaten the odds and was free of EPM. However, the treatment had taken a toll on his young body, and the gait irregularity remained. The nerve damage he'd suffered meant Farley could not feel, and consequently could not properly use, his right hind leg.

Unacceptable. Determination settled deep within me. I would not allow Farley's story to end this way. I had an idea. What if I could find a way to make Farley use his hind leg properly again? He couldn't feel it, but due to the placement of a horse's eyes, I knew he could see it. Perhaps with enough repetitions of correct movement, his muscles would *remember* how to move correctly once again. "Muscle memory" describes how a complex physical activity that requires intense concentration to learn can eventually become an automatic response—something one can do without thinking about it. Kind of like learning to ride a bike—once you learn it, your body never forgets. Certainly worth a try.

I used what I knew about influencing a horse's gait to develop a physical therapy program for Farley. I had to find a way to make the colt pay attention to the leg he couldn't feel. Finding some long pieces of hedge wood outside, I placed them in the round pen, lined up parallel to each other, like widely spaced railroad ties. Farley trotted over the makeshift ground poles, stumbling on each one with his right hind leg.

"C'mon, Farley. You can do this." After a couple more trips over the poles, the colt tipped his head slightly to the right, putting him in position to see the poles. This time he didn't clip a single one.

Next I moved the poles farther apart to encourage the horse to take a longer step. Farley attempted to go through them the same as he had before, but due to the changed distance between poles, he stumbled over them, stepping directly on the final pole.

"You have to pay attention Farley. You can do this." After a couple more unsuccessful trips through the poles in this new configuration, Farley figured out if he took a longer step, he could move through them without hitting a single one.

I now had a plan for Farley's recovery. I would use the poles in a constantly changing configuration to encourage Farley to pay attention to where he was placing his right hind foot. As Farley improved, I elevated one or more of the poles, while other times I arranged the poles so they were at different distances from each other. By constantly changing the height and distance between the poles, Farley learned to use his eye to tell him how high to lift or how far he needed to reach his right hind leg. Before and after his workouts, I stretched Farley's hind legs forward and backward, trying to increase his range of motion. I massaged his back, loins, and hips, hoping I could somehow stimulate his nerves. After several months, he took noticeably longer steps, *and* his short-stepping right hind leg moved better than ever!

Spring of 2002 blossomed around me. A stronger and healthier four-year-old Farley had reached the next stage in his recovery. The time had come to ride the colt. I used the ground poles as I had before, this time riding him over the obstacles in various configurations. From the saddle I could use my leg and seat to guide Farley into a long and low frame, asking him to lift his back to round and strengthen his topline. Some days I had Farley drag some heavy tires around the arena to build strength in his hind legs and quarters. By late spring, a year since Farley's EPM treatment ended, the young stallion had no trace of asymmetry remaining in his gait. As long as I kept his hind end engaged and his back lifted into a proper frame, Farley appeared normal. I had accomplished what others said could not be done.

Victory.

"You're too fat to even think you'd be allowed to show Farley, you stupid cow! Seriously, who do you think you are, you fucking moron!"

Defeat.

Mean Cheryl's words were jagged claws tearing at my heart and mind. I would ruin any chance Farley had of winning. Horse show judges didn't look at fat girls. Still, I so badly wanted to show Farley— we had worked so hard for this chance. A chance no one thought he'd ever get. I'd started the year weighing more than ever before. I'd managed to lose around fifty pounds by walking daily and watching my fat intake—the diet trend of the era. Now I'd plateaued but still had so much weight I *needed* to lose. Mean Cheryl constantly berated me for my size, my disgusting rolls of fat, my horrible, ugly, fat face. Perhaps if I could be thin, I could silence her. Maybe I could even learn to love a thin version of me. *Is that even possible?*

Obsession. I stopped eating anything with a measurable amount of fat. In addition to working two physical jobs totaling over seventy hours a week, I also walked miles a day, often into the wee hours of the morning. Finally, completely and utterly exhausted, I'd return home and collapse into bed. Too tired to hear Mean Cheryl any longer, sleep would mercifully claim me for the few hours remaining before the alarm would ring to start another day. During the year I worked on Farley's recovery, I lost over one hundred pounds.

"You're still fat!" Mean Cheryl reminded me. True. I knew I'd never be attractive or thin, but I did earn the right to show Farley—the only thing I cared about. I spent the summer of 2002 showing Farley at the schooling shows, while showing his half brother, Magic, on the American Paint Horse Association circuit.

By early fall, his recovery completed, the stage had been set for Farley's first big competition. The colt handled himself beautifully at the show, the picture of a well-behaved young stallion. Pride in Farley filled me, so wonderful it was how hard he tried for me. The judge was impressed as well, placing us first in all four classes, against several nice horses.

Pride in my accomplishments was stilted and fleeting. I'd lost a ton of weight and received numerous compliments on my training ability and accomplishments with Danny's horses. I felt oddly unsettled. The compliments made me feel both good and somehow terrified. I *did* want to hear praise from others. The accolades allowed me to briefly feel pride and something I could only guess was similar to self-worth —a foreign concept to me.

Still, self-loathing burned within. Mean Cheryl had not been silenced. On the outside I appeared successful and happy, well on my way to the horse training career I'd dreamed of. Inside, the part of me that was not Mean Cheryl gradually dimmed like a candle flame robbed of oxygen. I would never defeat her, only struggle with my last bit of sanity to hide her from the rest of the world.

"*You stupid idiot!*" Mean Cheryl screamed. "*What makes you think you're anything special? A stupid cow to think for a second anyone would ever want you to train their horses if* anyone *else were available!*"

Her words cut through me like a dull table saw ravaging a piece of soft lumber. I nodded in agreement, a hammer clutched in my hand, swinging the tool repeatedly, hitting my thighs and forearms.

Icy-cold fingers closed around my broken mind, pulling me ever deeper into darkness.

CHAPTER TEN

Constant, obsessive movement increased my already substantial weight loss. I became fanatic watching the numbers go down on the scale, often weighing myself four or five times a day. When I plateaued again, panic. The pounds refused to budge, so I decreased my already minuscule food intake while increasing my exercise. I lost a few more pounds, and then my hair started falling out. I'd periodically feel disoriented and lightheaded. Finally, one evening while walking Farley back to his stall, I collapsed in the barn aisle. My muscles twitched. Gripped with spasms, I could not control my arms or legs. I floundered there in the dusty barn aisle, unable to get back onto my feet.

I landed in the emergency room three times over the next couple weeks. Each time for the same reason: collapsing, unable to control my body parts, unable to get up. Danny and my friends at Conner Equine were understandably concerned. Normal people didn't just fall down for no apparent reason.

The ER doctors seemed stumped. "Have you been drinking? What drugs did you take?" The doctor's voice sounded accusatory.

"No, nothing. I don't drink, I don't do drugs. I don't even smoke!"

They don't believe me. They think I'm faking. They think I'm a pathetic, attention-seeking loser.

"*They're right, you know,*" Mean Cheryl's sneering voice broke in. "*You knew that all along. You're a terrible, selfish, attention-seeking, pathetic excuse for a human being. You know it. Now they know it too!*"

Oh God, now everyone would know.

I received drug tests, the nurse forcing urine out of me with a catheter. No drugs in my system. *Duh.*

"Are you pregnant?" the doctor asked.

"No, not a chance."

The nurse drew blood anyway. I received two pregnancy tests from the same ER doctor in the space of four days. *No one believes me.*

The collapsing episodes continued. I saw a neurologist. More tests. A new neurologist. More tests. CT scan, echocardiogram, sleep testing. Nothing. No one could figure out why this kept happening.

In the meantime, I kept going to work. I tried to appear normal—the only card I had left to play. There seemed to be no reason for these episodes of collapsing and temporarily losing control of my body. One might think it'd be terrifying to experience this, to not know what was going on. But I didn't feel scared, only ashamed.

"*You are crazy. Now you can't hide it anymore. Everyone knows.*"

When no explanation could be found for my collapsing episodes, Danny became apprehensive having me around the horses. Fearing injury or liability, he wanted me to leave Conner Equine. After six years of employment, I couldn't believe Danny would give up on me. I took my dismissal quite personally.

"*Obviously he's finally discovered what a stupid, crazy, useless bitch you are.*" Mean Cheryl would not allow me to see Danny's concern for my safety as a valid reason for asking me leave. I felt only shame, frustration, and sadness. Without my work at Conner Equine, I had no reason to remain in Illinois. The decision felt both difficult and obvious. It felt like someone had torn out the last dozen or so chapters from the story of my life, then shoved in some blank pages and tossed a dried-out ink pen in my general direction.

Danny gathered our mutual friends and clients together—a

group we called the Tag Team, since they all owned horses by Danny's stallion, Tagit Delux—and gave me a lovely going-away party. We shared stories of our years together, the horses we'd known, the long horse show weekends, and the hours we'd spent together in Danny's barn. The party softened the blow from the loss. I would be forever grateful for that get-together, for all the years I spent working for Danny, and all the experience I'd gained through his mentorship.

Tears filled my eyes as I said goodbye to each of the horses I'd grown to love. The most difficult, of course, being Farley. I stroked Farley's winter-fuzzy neck. "You be a good boy." Warm tears trickled down my frozen cheeks. Would I ever see him again? "I sure wish I'd be around to see your and Gypsy's first foal," I said, referring to a breeding I'd recommended between Farley and a favorite training client's mare. The mare was due to foal in just a few months.

Farley nuzzled my shoulder, then my cheek. "I love you, too buddy," I said, backing out of the stall.

The door closed with a definitive *clank!* Nothing left for me to do but walk away.

"YOU'RE A JOKE!" Mean Cheryl's words cut deeply. *"No one would ever hire a fat cow like you as a horse trainer."* I agreed, her logic obvious—I would never amount to anything trying to follow this ridiculous pipe dream of having a career working with horses. I could start over. Do something new. Move to where nobody knew me, where nobody knew I was crazy. Just push the reset button. Drop into the game with a new life.

There were few universities I could transfer to with my credits from Black Hawk. I chose the one farthest away, Middle Tennessee State University. There, I could start fresh with a new career path. Why I chose a major in advertising, I had no clue. Except that it sounded like a "real" job, something adults had been telling me I needed since I'd first told my high school guidance counselor I wanted to work with horses for a living. I had to do something. So I headed south.

In the stifling heat of early summer, I packed up my life and moved to Murfreesboro, Tennessee. The town still bore scars from the Civil War, both in the hearts and minds of many residents and on the facings of the ancient downtown buildings. I ran into more than a few folks who seemed to genuinely despise my obviously Yankee accent and mannerisms. Most people were kind, or at least indifferent. However, a few made it clear they didn't want me there.

"You Yankees don't belong down here in God's country," a customer at the cafeteria-style restaurant I worked at told me. He fixed me with a stony glare before tossing his money across the counter. I picked up the bills and coins spread across the surface between us and placed them into the cash register.

"Um ... thank you?" I handed him his receipt. He walked off without another word.

Mean Cheryl thrived in Tennessee. She had me right where she wanted me—alone, far from friends and family, and not a horse in sight. My self-destructive behaviors and suicidal thoughts escalated after the move. Something new came too—deep, debilitating anxiety. My heart raced as the cold, bony fingers of anxiety circled around my throat. At night I paced my tiny apartment, tears erupting from each eye and slowly creeping down my face. *I am certainly going crazy.*

"Not going. Gone," Mean Cheryl corrected.

The collapsing episodes continued in Tennessee, although less frequent. I saw another doctor, who had no diagnosis for me. *"Faker, faker, you're a big fat faker."* Finally I was referred to a neurologist in Nashville. He took one look at me and said my problem wasn't neurological; it wasn't even physical. He said I had an emotional problem. Stress, severe depression—sure, why not? He said my extreme dieting, stress from relocation, and obvious depression had caused my body to basically shut down—hang the out-of-service sign on her; she's broken. The doctor prescribed an antidepressant and sent me on my way. No instructions, no follow-up appointments, nothing—just drugs.

I took the new meds as instructed, and Mean Cheryl thrived. My anxiety shot through the roof. I couldn't sleep. I couldn't even sit down. I paced my apartment, crying constantly, my stomach tied in knots. The collapsing episodes did indeed disappear, but after a week of sleeplessness and being unable to work or even relax for a minute, I called the neurologist.

"It's not the meds," he said emotionlessly.

"But something is wrong! I can't sit still. I cry all the time. I pace. I want to hide. I feel anxious and scared all the time. This is not normal for me!" Tears welled.

"It's not the meds. Keep taking the meds."

"But what am I supposed to do? I can't live like this! Please, can't you help me?" Silence on the other end. The doctor had hung up. I crumbled to the floor, crying and then screaming uselessly into the phone. I threw the phone across the room. It hit the wall with a loud *smack!* and fell to the floor. Balling up my fists, I hit my thighs and body over and over again.

"I can't do this anymore!" I screamed, "Please, God, kill me, please!" I lowered my face to the carpet, banging my forehead rhythmically on the floor. Thump, thump, thump, thump … the sound of insanity.

Later that night, still lying on the floor in the darkness, I thought about a place I'd recently discovered while hiking with Dief. One of the trails ended on a large rock ledge jutting off a cliff. A couple hundred feet below the cliff, old-growth pines reached up from the forest floor. *It would be so easy. There are no guard rails or barriers, nothing to stop me.* I imagined what it would feel like to step off of the ledge and plummet to the earth below. Would I be scared or elated? I pictured myself flying head first off that cliff, a broad smile creasing my lips as my body, finally released from the torturous presence of Mean Cheryl, plummeted blissfully toward the earth.

CHAPTER ELEVEN

Call Sarah. The voice, like that of a timid little girl, sounded barely a whisper in the darkness of my mind. *Call Sarah? Why would I call Sarah?* We hadn't talked in months.

Call Sarah, the whispered voice came again. *She knows about this.*

It had been almost twenty years since I'd met Sarah at the beach party. We'd remained close friends, growing up together in Kalamazoo. Through phone calls and meet-ups when I visited Michigan, we'd stayed in touch when I'd first moved away from home. In later years, Sarah visited me in Kewanee, and I visited her when she lived in Minnesota. But by the time I'd relocated to Tennessee, Sarah and I had not spoken in several months. It had happened slowly, often the case when two adults live different lives in different parts of the country. Sarah now lived in northern Ohio. Calls and emails went unreturned on both ends. We'd drifted apart but had never truly lost track of each other.

My hand shaking, I pressed the buttons on the cell phone to ring Sarah's number. I stood on the corner, staring at the sidewalk beneath my feet. Dief and I had walked many miles from home, through the antebellum neighborhoods of the onetime Civil War–ravaged Murfreesboro. Some of the old brick homes still bore the scars of gunfire. The phone rang once, twice, a third time and then ... voicemail.

"Sarah?" I began after the tone, my voice trembling. "Um, it's me, Cheryl. Um, I have a question for you. I, um ... thought you knew someone, maybe knew something about antidepressants? I don't know who to talk to. I feel ... weird. I just want to ask you about it ... or something ... Sorry. Weird message ... Bye."

I clicked the red End button on my phone and let the tears flow. My body shook with the rush of the pent-up anguish exiting through my tears. Dief looked up at me, his one blue eye standing out in sharp contrast against the black-and-gray fur on his face.

"What is wrong with me?" I asked Dief.

He wagged his stump tail and took a few steps closer to me, never taking his eyes off mine. I knelt and hugged him, crying into the soft fur of his broad shoulders. Still kneeling, I straightened my upper body and lifted my right hand to scratch Dief behind his velvety-soft ears. Placing my index finger on his forehead, I traced the thin strip of white down the center of his face. First toward his nose, against the hair, making the stripe wider. I then traced back up from his nose to the top of his head, making the stripe sleek and narrow again.

After a while I stood up and looked around the quiet neighborhood. "Which way should we go?" I asked Dief.

He didn't move but continued to look into my eyes with his stump tail wagging hesitantly. I didn't want to go home. I didn't want to do anything. I didn't care. I crossed the street, wondering what I'd do if a car were to drive by. I could step in front of it, but it might be going too slow on this residential street to do me any good.

"I don't want to be maimed," I said aloud. "I want to be dead."

Those final words stung my ears before they sank into the pit of my stomach. I'd never said it aloud before.

"Hmmm," I said to the empty street. "Interesting."

I walked on across the blacktop and continued down the sidewalk. My phone rang. I looked at the display—Sarah. Suddenly afraid to talk to her, I let the call go to voicemail. The phone screen lit up briefly, backlit with a soft blue-white light. The tiny speaker above the display emitted three short, sharp beeps. *Beep! Beep! Beep!* Sarah had left a message.

My right thumb hovered over the Talk button with the image of a green phone handset emblazoned on it. My stomach flipped and rolled in an odd little anxiety dance, just under my racing heart. My chest tightened, stealing my breath. What would she say? Would she have some good advice? Would she totally dismiss me? Would she call me crazy and tell me to never call her again?

I didn't have the presence of mind to feel bad for thinking Sarah would ever be anything but supportive. The depression-fueled self-hatred, loathing, and whatever (*secret?*) hid behind the dark curtain in my mind wouldn't allow me to draw logical conclusions. A warm breeze swirled around my feet, blowing tiny bits of dirt and leaves around my legs. The air felt thick and heavy, like a dampened, musty old woolen coat. I looked up at the darkening sky. Storm clouds gathered, danced, and swirled. I was still several miles from home.

"We should get going," I said to Dief.

He looked up at me. His stump tail, tucked against his bum, moved ever so slightly from side to side. He could feel the storm coming too. I looked back at the phone still in my upturned hand. *Listen to the message. Do it now.*

I took a deep breath, then released it forcefully through my parted lips. My right thumb descended on the Talk button, connecting me with my voicemail.

"You have one new message," the robot voice said into my ear. The phone let out another short, sharp beep, and then Sarah spoke.

"Cheryl? It's Sarah. I got your message. Are you OK? You don't sound OK. Please call me back! I'm really worried about you. You sound terrible. I'm here. Please call me!"

Oh crap, you made her worry. Way to go, dumbass. I dialed Sarah's number. I hadn't wanted her to worry.

"Hello?" Sarah's voice came through the tiny phone speaker.

"Hi. It's me ..."

"Cheryl! Are you OK? You don't sound OK. What's going on?"

"I'm OK." *Liar.* "I'm just having some weird, um ... problems. I remembered you had some experience with a friend with depression, and I just feel so out of control, anxious all the time. Is this ... am I ..." My voice trailed off. I did not want to say what I was thinking, fearing, aloud.

"*Craaaaazy,*" Mean Cheryl sneered in a drawn-out, cackling voice. "*She's going to find out you're craaaaazy!*"

"Do you want me to come?" Sarah asked. "Because I'll come right now. I can leave here in about an hour and get there tonight."

I was shocked. "Oh, um ... no, no. That's not necessary. I'm fine. Thanks though."

"You don't sound fine. I'm coming."

"No. You don't have to ..."

"I'm coming. I'll be there tonight. Just hold on. Don't do anything. Wait for me."

She sounded worried. I was perplexed. *What did she hear?* I thought I sounded fine. *Did she know something I didn't?* Tears silently crept down my cheeks.

"OK," I whispered. "I'll be here."

"Good!" Sarah sounded relieved. "I'll be there as soon as I can. Call me if you need anything. Bye. I love you."

"Bye. I love you too." My last words were barely above a whisper. I clicked the phone off.

"C'mon, Dief." I crossed the road, my loyal friend walking beside me. Thunder rolled in the distance. We had miles to go before we'd find shelter from the storm.

Sarah dropped everything for me, even risking her new job, which she had waited two years for—jeopardizing a tremendous opportunity that would not come again should she lose the job because of me. But she came anyway, making the trip from northern Ohio to central Tennessee in record time. What did she see in me? How did she find value in my life when I could find none? I'd felt this way in all my relationships. Like somehow I'd fooled everyone—they didn't know what an awful person I truly was.

"*But they'll find out. Sarah will find out.*" My heart sank at Mean

Cheryl's words. I had to keep her a secret. I couldn't let anyone know about my burgeoning insanity.

Sarah arrived at my doorstep late that evening.

"Aroooo-ooooo-oooooo!" Dief yodeled his greeting, wagging his tail emphatically. He was thrilled to see her. So was I.

I hugged my friend, wetting the shoulder of her T-shirt with my tears. "I'm so glad you're here."

"Me too," she said.

"Thank you for coming. Thank you so much."

Sarah stayed with me for a couple of weeks. The only person I would trust and the only one I would talk to, Sarah helped me find my way out of the black hole I'd fallen into. With Sarah advocating for me, I found a therapist and a new doctor, who prescribed different medication. I eventually recovered enough that I returned to school and work. Both were things I'd been unable to do for many months.

"What are you passionate about?" my new therapist, Paula, asked.

I furrowed my brow briefly, then brought my eyes up to meet hers. "Horses."

"What are you doing to follow that passion?" Paula's deep-brown eyes seemed to search my soul.

"Nothing. I gave that up."

"Why?"

"Because I ..." I couldn't decide how much I wanted to tell this woman. I'd had others in my life who'd been less than supportive of my "childish" passion. "It's not ... real. It's not a real job. I just ... can't."

Paula looked at me as if she expected more words to spill from my mouth. I looked down at my feet.

"If you could do anything with your life, what would it be? What is your dream job?"

"I don't ... I ..." I took a deep breath and held it.

"You don't have to tell me," Paula said gently. "But I want you to think about it. Maybe journal about it."

"OK."

"What can you do to let horses back into your life again? It doesn't have to be as a career, but I can see you are miserable without them."

Paula was right. I knew this.

"Maybe I could buy some horse magazines? Or a book?"

"Yes. That sounds like a wonderful idea." Paula smiled.

A tinge of excitement ignited within me. Subtle and weak, but present. The first positive emotion I had felt in a long time.

CHAPTER TWELVE

Paula's advice to buy a couple horse magazines and start journaling not only reawakened my horse passion but also helped me realize what a monumental mistake moving to Tennessee had been. I remembered the trip my 4-H group had taken to Kentucky years ago and recalled the dream I'd had as a young girl. I wanted to work on one of the famous Thoroughbred farms in Kentucky's famed Bluegrass Region.

I dropped a few résumés in the mail and soon received an interview and then a job offer caring for the mares and foals at Claiborne Farm. Packing up my belongings, I bade Tennessee farewell and good riddance to a terrible part of my life. Kentucky would certainly be much better. I'd be living my ultimate dream. Perhaps I could even get rid of Mean Cheryl.

I'd never seen anything like Claiborne Farm—three thousand rolling acres of Kentucky bluegrass enclosed by miles of black, four-board wood fencing. Claiborne is probably most famous for being the home of 1973 Triple Crown winner Secretariat, from the time he retired from racing until his death in 1989. In their more than one-hundred-year history, Claiborne has raised and raced numerous champions. Home to generations of horse racing's elite—both human and equine—the historic farm held ghosts of legends and glimpses of greatness around every corner.

January 2006, twenty-nine years old and thinking I'd finally figured life out, I started work at Claiborne Farm. I truly couldn't believe I'd been hired, a fat girl like me, working for a famous horse farm. Soon my assigned barn filled with the high-pitched whinnies of little Thoroughbred foals. I'd handled foals at Conner Equine, but these Thoroughbreds were bigger, faster, and tougher. Living the dream of my childhood, I felt blessed each day I drove to work and saw the sun rise over the rolling acres of winter-brown pastures. Watching the foals discover their legs, and then their speed, brought joy to my heart. They galloped around their dams in ever-widening circles. Their exuberant actions mirrored my own inner happiness.

In the afternoon, the foals napped in the sunshine, the wintertime pastures a canvas of brown-green grass dotted by glistening bay, brown, and chestnut bodies of sleeping foals and watchful mares. Later in the day the horses returned to the barn, and I'd spend time with each foal, handling their feet and introducing them to brushes and rub rags.

Winter gave way to spring, and the days grew longer and warmer. Foaling season neared the end, and everywhere I looked mares and foals peppered the landscape. The pastures turned from brown to green, and the trees awoke from their wintery sleep with thousands of tiny green buds poking out from wandering gray branches. The older foals now bravely ventured away from their mothers, racing each other along the vast expanse of never-ending green. They bucked and kicked and played, thrilled at the sheer joy of being alive.

I longed to feel what they felt, but the darkness had returned. Mean Cheryl had come back. The honeymoon over, I realized all the beauty of Kentucky and a dream-come-true job could not save me. An intense battle raged within me each day. I tried desperately to maintain my facade of normal. *Please, God. Don't let them find out I'm crazy. Please.* Desolate. Hopeless. Mean Cheryl continued her relentless monologue.

"*You're a worthless, ugly, horrible person. Everyone is going to find out what you really are. It's just a matter of time before the truth comes out. Just die, you piece of garbage. I hate you so much. Everyone does."* Mean Cheryl went on and on. Each word cutting deeper, confirming what I already knew—everything she said was absolutely true.

My journal, once filled with explorations of finding my purpose and living my dreams, increasingly housed entries that reflected deep hopelessness and a quickening downward spiral into severe depression.

Journal entry— "A Letter to Myself," April 30, 2006

Cheryl-

You are no good to anyone. No one is glad to know you. You annoy all the people you know. No one wants to talk to you so stop calling. Everyone would be better off without you. I can't believe how fat you are. No one likes fat people because they (you) are slow and stupid and so very ugly with all your huge fat rolls hanging everywhere. You are not now and never were a good horse trainer. All you did was ruin the horses so someone else would have to fix them later. You are too fat to train them anyway and far too stupid. I hope you die soon; we all do. We're so tired of looking at your stupid, ugly face. You don't deserve to live; you never did.

Anyone who ever claimed to care about you lied. They never did and never would. Not someone like you. Do the world a favor and kill yourself right now you useless piece of shit. Go away! I hate you, everyone does. You are a failure, and I never want to see your fat, ugly face again! Please die soon, you fucking cow!

Die, die, die!!!

Signed,

You and everyone

THE NEGATIVE VOICE of Mean Cheryl made up the entirety of my reality. She'd taken over my thoughts. Her negative monologue, the only thing I could hear. Her words convinced me I had no one to turn to and that no friendship was real. I could see no value in my life. I had nothing to offer. No use in trying to fight it.

Try. The tiny whisper of a little girl interrupted my thoughts.

Who was she? This little girl, I heard her tiny whispers in the few quiet moments. My imaginary black horse flashed across my mind. *It's her.* The little girl that was me, the little girl on the black horse. I strained to hear her tiny voice.

Maybe you could—

"Shut up, you stupid bitch!" Terrified at Mean Cheryl's rage, the little girl scurried behind the black curtain in my mind.

I'd noticed the black curtain not long before, like a mental barricade. I could not see beyond it. Something lurked back there, something Mean Cheryl did not want me to discover. That little-girl voice, the tiny whisper, perhaps the last bit of my mind not overtaken by Mean Cheryl, tried to tell me I would be OK. She tried to tell me perhaps there was someone I could turn to, like she had in Tennessee. *Call Sarah*, she had said then. But no sooner would such thoughts enter my mind than Mean Cheryl would scream and spew her hatred, chasing the little girl back behind the black curtain. She could never come out ... She lived back *there* with the monster.

Journal entry—May 8, 2006

Okay—I would daresay there are still some issues to be worked out. I'm not sure what happened last week to bring on whatever happened to me. I was so angry and full of hate for myself. I thumped on myself with a hammer for a while, not hard enough to leave a mark though (I am such a wimp). Then I beat my fan to death with that hammer until it was in dozens of pieces. I remember wishing it was me.

What's going on? Things can be fine, but then I totally flip out. I changed my mind. I don't want to think about this. One thought keeps bugging me ... If I read this journal, I believe I'd think the author was crazy. I'm a little scared. God, help me ...

HAUNTED. Crouching down next to my bed was a demon. From the corner of my eye, the black form looked human in shape, though it had no features. I lay frozen in my bed, unable to move. The demon slowly reached his hand over my face and covered my mouth and nose. My chest tightened, and I tried desperately to get air, but I couldn't. Panic rose. The demon lifted his hand, and I gasped, gulping in air as if I had been trapped in a vacuum. He covered my mouth and nose again and again. I struggled to free my arms from invisible binds, desperately wanting to rise from my bed and run from the demon. My body wouldn't move, but suddenly I floated far above it. I looked down at the demon crouching next to me. A soft yellow glow cast from my bedside lamp lit my body. The demon crouched within a widening black shadow. He placed his hand over my nose and mouth again, then removed it. Over and over he repeated the action. The demon had no face, but somehow he conveyed a look of fascination at how easily he could snuff out my life. His red eyes glowed within deepening shadows. I drifted away.

The next morning my alarm woke me as usual. I remembered the demon and wondered if any of what I'd seen and felt could possibly be real. The sensation of the demon's hand covering my mouth and nose lingered on my skin. My chest tightened for a moment, then released. I looked over at Dief. *Had he seen the demon? Did he know what was going on? Was the demon real, or was it a dream?* Dief stared at me warily. His eyes held no fear, just a deep concern one wouldn't expect to see in the face of a dog. I called him over to me.

Dief rose in his little half-stretch style he'd developed as he'd gotten older, ambled over, and sat next to me. I placed my index finger on his forehead, tracing the thin strip of white down the center of his face. I traced it first toward his nose, against the hair, making the stripe wider. I then traced back up from his nose to the top of his head, making the stripe sleek and narrow again. I held his silky-soft ear in my hand, then scratched his head before returning to the stripe, tracing it once again.

"Am I crazy, Dief?" I asked my friend.

He looked at me with his compassionate eyes, one blue and one brown. I traced his stripe with my finger again before getting ready for my day. The demons, like every other dark, crazy thing that occurred in my life, would remain a secret between me and my dog. Time to put on my happy face, the face that projected sanity and normalcy to the world. Yes, I must put on the face of a normal person and go to work.

CHAPTER THIRTEEN

Mean Cheryl rose above me, victorious, as I stood at the edge of an enormous black hole. The edges crumbled beneath my feet. Icy gray fingers reached up from the dark depths, circling around my tortured mind, threatening to pull me in. Unstable, I teetered on the edge of my darkness, suspended precariously between the horror of life and the bliss of death. A sickly grin danced joyfully across my lips. I could fall or I could jump—it didn't much matter. Smiling into the darkness, a desolate cold wrapped around me. *I am the darkness and the darkness is me.* Anticipating the end, I felt relieved. Closing my eyes, I prepared to succumb to the cold, black oblivion reaching up to consume me.

I'D STRUGGLED through work that day, trying to hide my roller coaster of tears, despair, confusion, and anger from my barn partner. That afternoon, I drove home feeling numb. Rage rose violently within me as I walked up the stairs to my apartment. It dissipated when I reached the top, replaced by sheer exhaustion. I glanced at my cell phone, the little girl with the black horse hoping someone had reached out, but the display read "No missed calls."

"See?" Mean Cheryl sneered. *"No one cares, you worthless piece of shit!"*

"You're right," I said aloud. "Nobody cares."

"Exactly! You are such a piece of garbage. I can't believe you haven't figured out that no one cares. They all want you to die. No one will miss you. No one. You have no value. You are a waste and a disappointment. You have nothing to offer the world. You are nothing but a worthless, ugly piece of trash. I hate you. Everyone hates you. Just do the world a favor and kill yourself, you useless, stupid cow!"

Mean Cheryl had taken over. I felt like a scrap of paper caught in a tornado, a helpless victim, powerless against Mean Cheryl. Body sagging, defeated, I wandered into the bathroom. Standing at the sink, I lifted my face to look in the mirror. A sad and defeated woman looked back at me, her hollow eyes filled with despair. As I stared at my reflection, the face in the mirror morphed into something terrifying, like a face possessed. Her eyes narrowed. The look of despair turned to one of anger and hatred. She fixated me with a cold, stony gaze. One last word delivered with contempt and finality before she turned away.

"Goodbye."

I had the next day off, so I knew no one would miss me until I failed to show up for work on Saturday. "Miss me" weren't really the right words though— "notice my absence" seemed more accurate, in my current state of mind.

I set out several days' worth of food and water for Dief and let him out to relieve himself one final time. I shed no tears and felt no fear as I swallowed the pills. In fact, I no longer felt anything at all. I wasn't really there anymore. Only Mean Cheryl existed. The little girl with the black horse had disappeared. No longer an autonomous being, I had been completely consumed by Mean Cheryl. My body felt like that of a puppet, and she pulled the strings.

Long, dark shadows slanted across the kitchen floor, crawling up the cracked plaster walls, chasing the last of the sun's light from the room. I glanced around the antiquated kitchen, my eyes falling on the ancient faded linoleum. My gaze moved upward to the old stove, a monstrous structure with rounded edges and dials worn blank from countless meals prepared. This kitchen reminded me so much of my grandma's kitchen. Swallowing hard, I returned my attention to the letter on the table in front of me.

"I want Karl to have these books I told him about the other day. I think he'll like them. Tell Linda thanks for the horse—I appreciate the thought but ..." But what? The horse in question was the three-year-old daughter of Farley and Gypsy, the breeding I'd recommended, the one I knew would be my dream horse. Her owner, Linda, had offered to give her to me. I closed my eyes tightly and held my breath, clenching my body as if I were trying to keep something from escaping, some part of me I could never let anyone see.

It's too late anyway came the whisper of the little girl with the black horse. Her voice quivered with fear.

"Shut the hell up, you stupid bitch!" Mean Cheryl taunted, sending the little girl scurrying behind the black curtain in my mind.

I held the pen above the paper as I searched for the words to complete the sentence. "I never deserved her anyway," I wrote.

I turned my attention to the bottle of antidepressants on the table in front of me. I wondered how many it would take.

"Better take some more," Mean Cheryl hissed.

I swallowed the drugs obediently before returning my attention to the note. "Please give Dief to my best friend, Sarah. He loves her." I looked down at Dief lying on the floor at my feet. He looked up at me with questioning eyes, his stump of a tail tucked tightly against his rump. Tears stung my eyes. I made no effort to blink them back, yet only a single tear escaped. It slid slowly down my cheek, dripping off my chin and onto my shirt, leaving a tiny, inconsequential dot of moisture on the dark cotton. "I'm sorry," I whispered to my loyal friend.

I looked back at the note, wondering how I should end it. My pen circled in the air above the paper. Finally I lowered the point to the writing surface. "I'm sorry I'm such an ugly, horrible, worthless piece of garbage." I scratched my name at the bottom.

Holding the paper up slightly from the tabletop, I reread the short note that apparently summed up my final thoughts on the life I'd lived.

"Not much," I said aloud to the darkening kitchen.

"Not much to work with," Mean Cheryl sneered.

I set the paper back on the kitchen table and took a swig of the codeine-laced cough syrup I'd chased the pills with. Picking up the pen in my right hand, I scribbled the date at the top of the page. Who knew how long it would be before anyone actually came looking for me? They should have an accurate date of death. I looked at the date in the top right corner of the page, May 11, 2006. I was twenty-nine.

Feeling lightheaded, I wandered into the bedroom with Dief, as always, right on my heels. Sitting on the edge of the bed, I looked down at Dief's beautiful face. My dog stood in front of me, looking into my eyes with a questioning expression. I traced the stripe on his face with my index finger, first down toward his nose, against the hair, making the stripe wide and rough, then back up toward his ears, making the stripe smooth and narrow again.

"I'm sorry, Diefenbaker," I whispered to my friend. "I'm sorry I'm such worthless garbage. You'll have someone much better than me to love you. You get to go live with Auntie Sarah!" I tried to inject some cheer into my voice.

The tears trickled down my face one by one, weaving a wet path toward the corners of my mouth. "I'm sorry," I said again, giving Dief a final pat on the head. "I love you."

Dief stared at me as I lay down on the bed, pulled up the covers, and prayed I would never wake up.

A SOFT WHIMPER reached my ears, but I pretended not to hear as I drifted over the gaping black hole. I did not want to come back. I was ready to go. I had come this far—much too late to drag myself back now. I needed only to let go and it would be done. There would be no more pain, no more hate, no more rage. Only cold, black peace, and I welcomed it.

The whimper grew more intense, more demanding. It pulled at me. Reluctantly I listened. I felt as if I were rapidly floating backward, away from the black hole, away from the only place I would find peace. Grasping at the air in a feeble attempt to stop my backward motion, I hurtled back through space and time. I could not escape my personal hell. Riddled with guilt and shame that had no face, I simply wanted to die. I *needed* to die. But once again, the whimper ... It drew me back from the darkness.

"No," I groaned. "Please, no." My eyes fluttered open. I was back in my apartment. Deep sadness enveloped me. Failure. This was not what I'd planned. *Why am I still here?*

A soft whimper reached my ears from the hallway. Dief. I staggered from the bed.

Night had fallen, and its blackness filled my apartment like the darkness that gripped my heart. I stumbled into the inky-black hallway following the sound of Dief's whimper. The streetlights cast a small sliver of light into the passageway, and Dief's white fur on his chest and legs seemed to glow in the darkness, like a distant beacon on a foggy night. My dog stared up at me, his blue eye catching the small amount of moonlight, while his brown eye seemed to disappear into the black fur on the left side of his face. Dief whimpered again, and his body shuddered. He watched me closely. Slowly he turned away from me, taking a few steps toward the stairway, which led down to the exterior door. Dief turned his head, beckoning me once again before turning back, taking a few more steps toward the stairway. I stumbled after him.

Staggering down the stairs, I followed Dief through the hall to the door to let him out, wondering how he could have to go out again already. It'd only been a few hours. I was mildly aware that I felt fairly normal, just a little sleepy.

"*Did you manage to screw up your suicide too?*" Mean Cheryl wanted to know.

The heavy, old wooden door creaked as I opened it toward me. I pushed the storm door open for Dief to go out. He stood there silently, refusing to move.

"C'mon, Dief! Go!" I yelled.

He looked over his left shoulder, as he had before. His eyes showed deep concern and sadness.

Suddenly, cramps gripped my stomach and waves of nausea washed over me.

"Go!" I croaked.

Unable to hold the door any longer, I clutched at the wall, desperately trying to keep my balance. The world twirled around me. Dief reluctantly went out the door, which closed behind him. He turned and sat on the step, looking back at me. I stared at him incredulously … What was his *problem?*

"Why did you drag me down here, Dief?!" *Oh God, why? Why can't you just let me die?*

My head spun. I felt as if the floor and walls lurched and pitched like those in the horror house at an old carnival. The world spun wildly. I couldn't tell which way was up. *Where is the floor? Where are my feet? Why is this wall moving?* Sweating heavily, I tried desperately to focus my vision enough to see where my dog went. I caught a glimpse of Dief in the yard as he slipped into the shadows just outside the circle of yellow light cast by the bare bulb hanging from the porch roof. He headed toward my truck.

"No, Dief." I groaned. "Come back. Come!" Dief did not return, lost to the shadows of the yard. The hallway pitched and spun. I reached for the storm door, and then everything went black. I was nowhere, nowhere at all.

I OPENED MY EYES. *Am I standing?* I wasn't sure. I couldn't feel my legs. The skin of my arms and face burned, as if the fires of hell were escaping through my pores. I looked down, still figuring out if I was standing, and vomited on my shirt. The house spun and tumbled, distorting the floors and walls like powerful winds twisting sheet metal. I held tightly to the doorjamb, feeling as if I would slide down the steeply sloped hallway and crash into the wall at the far end. My skin burned, and my head felt as if it were no longer connected to my body, floating and spinning somewhere just above my neck.

Finally, panic set in, and I screamed. I didn't know what was going on anymore. I was supposed to be dead. *Why won't the room stop moving?* With a fierce grip on the doorjamb, I tried not to fall off the slanted moving floor. I screamed again and again. Then, blackness.

A VOICE CAME to me from outside my darkness.

"Can you let go of the wall?"

I opened my eyes but saw nothing.

"Miss? I need you to let go of the wall so we can help you."

A man's face materialized in front of me.

"I can't let go," I whispered.

"Why not?"

"I'm afraid I'll fall."

The man's brow furrowed. "Do you know you are sitting on the floor? You won't fall—you're already down."

"I am?" I did not believe him. *This is a trick.* "I don't feel like I'm sitting."

"Trust me," he said. "You are sitting on the floor." He touched my left hand. "Here, can you feel this hand? It is touching the floor."

"It is?" I asked, dumbfounded, certain I'd been holding the jamb with both hands. I concentrated on my left hand.

"Yes," he replied. "Can you let go with the other hand now? I promise you won't fall."

I WOKE up at the local hospital later that same night. My skin burned, and sweat covered my face. A police officer stood by my bed, his face a mix of concern and uncertainty. Apparently my landlady had called 911 when she'd heard me scream and fall in our shared entryway.

"Do you remember me?" the officer asked.

I shook my head. "Am I in trouble?" Suicide was against the law, wasn't it? Did they arrest people for that?

"No, you're not in trouble. It's just part of my job to stay with you for a while."

"Why?" I felt small, like a shamed little girl.

"Don't worry—you're not in trouble," he reassured me.

Just then a nurse walked in, a white Styrofoam cup in her hand. "Here, drink this." She handed me the cup, which held a vile-smelling black liquid.

"What is it?" I eyed the cup suspiciously.

"It will make you feel better." I naively took a swallow and gagged.

"Keep going," the nurse said.

I took another swallow and gagged again. I looked at the nurse. She nodded, pointing at the cup. One more swallow, gag, and it all came up. The nurse stood ready with a bedpan. *Liar*, I thought, eying the nurse. I looked down at the bed pan, pill fragments, and black liquid floating in the plastic container. Now I understood—they were trying to undo what I had done.

I awoke the next morning feeling physically exhausted but not much else. My mind held a complete absence of emotion. No sadness, no fear, no anger—just vast nothingness. I remembered parts of what happened the night before—grabbing at the floor, which had seemed to twist and roll beneath me, making a complete ass of myself instead of dying, agreeing to allow a police officer to take Dief to the animal shelter but only if they promised to hold him, not adopt him out—I frowned at that last memory. Deep shame washed over me when I realized what I'd put him through.

A nurse walked into my room through the open door. They always left the room doors open in the psych ward. They also took your shoelaces and cut the drawstring out of your shorts. I eyed my laceless tennis shoes on the floor near the bed.

"Who can we call for you?"

I stared at the nurse blankly. *Who can you call? No one, that's who.* It dawned on me that my suicide failure had opened up a whole can of worms I was absolutely not prepared to deal with.

"No one." I looked at the floor.

"Don't you have any family or friends? Anyone we can call?"

"No, no one. They all live out of state anyway." I could not let anyone know what I'd done. No one could learn my secrets.

What would happen if they knew about the self-inflicted abuse, my own private hell, my suspicion of insanity? Already a hellish nightmare, how much worse would life be if my family or friends knew what an utter lunatic I really was?

The nurse looked at me, her eyes searching mine. "OK, well, let us know if there is anyone we can call for you." She turned and exited the room.

Dodged that bullet.

I had a more immediate problem to deal with—I was due back at work the next day, and it appeared there was little chance they'd let me out of the hospital anytime soon. Through all of the deep depression, anxiety, and self-abuse, I'd always kept one thing constant: I showed up for work. The one strength the part of me that existed outside of Mean Cheryl held was the ability to push through and maintain some semblance of normal by showing up for work, school, or any other responsibility every day.

My needs were unimportant and certainly no excuse for letting anyone down. Missing work for a sick day or something as ridiculous as a personal day was unacceptable. Self-care did not even register a blip on the radar screen. My needs didn't exist. How could they? Mean Cheryl had nullified and invalidated them years ago. In my perception, self-worth could only be found in what I could do for others and therefore was deeply intertwined with my ability to work. I had *no value* if I could not be productive. This had been true for as long as I could remember. Quite obviously this was the best way to keep myself out of trouble, and consequently safe. Anxiety gnawed at my belly. I so feared sharing my secret, but I feared being perceived as a bad employee even more. After agonizing over this conundrum for hours, I finally opted to call my sister, Andrea.

I squirmed in the seat of the open phone booth a few feet from the nurses' station. You get no privacy in the psych ward. No shoelaces, no drawstrings, no razors, no privacy. *You're such an idiot! Look what you've gotten yourself into!* The phone rang once, twice …

"Hello?" Andrea answered, her voice coming across the few hundred miles from Michigan.

"I did something bad," I whispered into the phone, in one short sentence summing up the screwed-up societal view of depression and suicide.

As quickly as I could and with as little detail as possible, I explained to Andrea where I was and that I needed her to make a phone call for me. I asked her to call my manager first thing in the morning and tell him I was really sick and in the hospital and wouldn't be to work for a few days. I couldn't make the call myself—I felt I would crumble under the pressure and start crying, or worse, tell him what I'd done. I also asked her to call the shelter and make sure they knew Dief had not been abandoned. She agreed.

Thank God. Relief swept over me. I had bought myself a few days to get myself together. I could then return to work as if nothing had ever happened, and only Andrea would know the truth. I could live with that

I'd felt certain my story of being sick in the hospital and unable to come to work for a few days would be enough to keep anyone at work from giving me another thought. But my feeling of success soon deteriorated into utter shock, then shame, followed by despair. I hadn't succeeded at all. It seemed my boss, Karl, did care about me.

I hadn't told Andrea the name of the hospital where I'd been admitted. I wasn't sure where I was, and I'd given as little detail as possible regarding what I'd done. Unable to get the information from my sister, Karl called all the hospitals he could think of, looking for me. He had no luck though, since a hospital could not confirm the presence of an individual residing in the psych ward. Andrea called me back, telling me what Karl had done. She encouraged me to allow her to tell Karl what had happened. Could I let one more person in on my secret?

"Please tell him the absolute least amount of information." I wiped tears with my free hand. "Please, promise me. Tell him not to tell anyone else." My stomach flipped and sank like an incapacitated submarine. I deeply feared the stigma of depression and suicidal tendencies. They'd treat me like a crazy, fragile woman on the brink of insanity. They wouldn't trust me. My career at Claiborne would be over. I might never work in the industry again with that stigma following me around. I had worked so hard to hide my crazy self from those around me. Nothing was more important than appearing normal.

I hadn't anticipated failing my suicide attempt or any of the shame and embarrassment that came with that failure. In high school, a student had committed suicide. The reactions of teachers and students that day and what I observed and read in the years that followed had shown me the societal view of a failed suicide is to invalidate the illness that brought the victim to that point of utter despair in the first place. The victim is called selfish, their illness dismissed as imaginary (why can't you just be happy?). The seriousness of the disease of which suicide is a symptom is frequently discredited by saying the attempt was simply a "cry for help," as if the person were only seeking attention. There was no national movement toward suicide awareness and prevention when I was in high school or when I attempted to take my own life over a decade later. Nobody talked about it, like a dirty little secret, to admit you were having thoughts of suicide made you appear weak minded, unable to cope. *Crazy.*

How could I explain that I felt I had no control over what happened to me? How I'd literally felt like a victim trapped inside a Cheryl-shaped body with a lunatic called Mean Cheryl trying to murder me? I'd felt possessed that day, like I no longer had control over my own body. I'd felt like a little girl, unable to escape her abuser. At the same time, I knew that part of me that felt like Mean Cheryl's victim couldn't stand up to her anymore, and I had felt relief knowing I'd reached the end. Except I hadn't reached the end. I'd *failed*. Mean Cheryl still occupied my mind, the little girl with the black horse still held a secret, and I was still utterly crazy. My confusion compounded and at times enveloped me. At least a part of my mind understood these three "people" were all versions of me. But I couldn't always access this knowledge, and when I could, I didn't understand why I had divided myself up in this manner. What the hell was wrong with me?

CHAPTER FOURTEEN

*A*fter five days in the hospital, I managed to convince the staff it was safe to let me go home, and they released me. I had to get Dief, and I had to get back to work. I had to reclaim *normal*. Outside, a cold rain fell. I had been wearing my pajamas the night of the suicide attempt—a T-shirt, shorts, and no bra. Now, five days later, I still wore the same clothes. I had no one to bring me a different outfit, like the other patients in the ward. The shame of wearing the same clothes for almost a week, surrounded by strangers, dug into me deeply. I'd been forced to go to group sessions and meals with both men and women, wearing no bra, feeling more vulnerable than I could have imagined, and also feeling like I deserved every agonizingly embarrassing moment.

Karl drove me home from the hospital. He also saw me in my ratty old T-shirt and shorts. Not the way I wanted my boss to see me. He offered me his jacket, and I took it gratefully. Finally able to cover myself, I zipped it up clear to my chin.

Dief had been taken to the local animal shelter the night of my suicide attempt. My sister called the shelter the next day, telling them Dief had not been abandoned and explaining how his owner was in the hospital and there was no one to care for him. They assured her theirs was a no-kill shelter but refused to hold him for me. If I did not come to claim my dog within five days, he would be put up for adoption. The shelter refused to believe there was no one to care for Dief while I was unable. They insisted my sister should drive down from Michigan and pick him up if we didn't want to lose him. The staff at the hospital also tried talking to the shelter for me, but they received the same response. I felt so stupid, ashamed, helpless, and utterly alone. The thought of my loyal friend sitting alone in a shelter, not understanding what had happened, tore at me like a thousand raking claws.

"Demon claws," Mean Cheryl hissed. *"There's a special place in hell for people like you."*

The cold rain continued when I drove to the animal shelter to rescue Dief. Excitement welled up as I entered the small office area and rang the bell at the desk. I couldn't wait to see my friend. When the shelter volunteer came out from the animal holding area, I explained to her how I'd been in the hospital and was here to pick up my dog. She reminded me it had been five days and that my dog had been put up for adoption.

"Yes, but I'm here now to pick him up. I didn't abandon him. He's not a stray. I was in the hospital, and there was no one to keep him for me."

"He didn't have a collar on. We had no way of knowing who he belonged to," the volunteer replied flatly.

"That's because he was in the house, I don't make him wear his collar when he's inside!"

My voice turned frantic. "I didn't abandon him. I had to go the hospital. There wasn't anyone to take him!"

I tried to hold myself together, not wanting to cry in front of this woman.

"My sister and the nurses at the hospital called you every day—they told you where I was. They told you he wasn't abandoned!" What was going on? I knew Andrea and the nurses had called, but they had also said the shelter refused to hold him past five days. Had Dief been adopted? Had he been … I shook my head to erase the thought before

I completed it. Panic slid an icy hand around my heart, then squeezed. The blood drained from my face. *Oh God, they're not going to let me have Dief back!* I looked down at Dief's collar in my clenched fist. His collar!

"Here!" I held up the collar, the tags making a faint jingling sound. "Look. Here is his collar with his license and his name tag! See?"

The volunteer looked up without interest. "Mmm-hmm. His adoption fee is seventy-five dollars."

"Adoption fee?" I asked incredulously.

"Yes. Any stray can be adopted if the owner doesn't claim it within five days."

"But I *am* the owner."

"Nobody claimed the dog," she repeated. "He is available for adoption."

I finally realized I could not win this argument. "Um"—I couldn't believe what was happening—"well, I'd like to adopt him."

"Okay!" Her face brightened with a smile. "We've just got some papers for you to fill out."

I spent the next twenty minutes filling out Dief's adoption papers.

"You've got his breed wrong." I pointed to the line that read "Catahoula mix." "He's an Australian shepherd mix."

The woman glanced up at me but said nothing.

After completing the paperwork and accepting my payment, the woman disappeared through the door to the holding area. A few minutes later she emerged with Dief pulling at the end of the leash. A smile spread across my face, and I knelt and hugged my friend.

"Thanks," the woman said as we walked to the door. "Good luck with him."

"Yes, thanks," I replied, feeling as if I were now exiting an episode of *The Twilight Zone*. What a strange experience. Dief raced out the door to the nearest patch of grass and relieved himself for what seemed like several minutes.

"Didn't they let you out?" I asked him.

"Aaaroooooo-ooooo!" Dief yodeled in reply.

"Poor buddy. I am so sorry about this."

"Ooooo-ooo," Dief whispered, wagging his stump tail.

"Let's go." I pointed to the truck.

"Oooooo." Dief hopped into the front seat.

I COULDN'T REALLY CALL the period following my suicide attempt a "recovery period" because no real recovery took place. My new therapist was a heavyset middle-aged woman with limp mousy-brown hair, an expressionless face, and thick-rimmed glasses of the sort my mom used to wear in the 1970s. She looked positively bored with her life, and I wondered if she was as unhappy as me.

"What brings you here today?" she asked.

What brings me here? Did you read the referral notes from the hospital? I tried to kill myself. I failed. Now I'm here. I shrugged.

Therapist Lady tried again. Monochrome words fell from her mouth, scattering uselessly onto the dirty carpet at my feet. She looked at me blankly. I took a deep breath. I had to try.

"I can't sleep. I feel anxious, ashamed, guilty all the time. It's like horrible butterflies in my stomach, constantly, for months now." I looked at her expectantly. I'd just shared more with Therapist Lady than anyone else.

"Why do you feel guilty?" she asked.

"I don't know. I just do, all the time." I stared at the ugly brown carpet under her chair.

"You should just stop then," she said, her face vacant behind the lenses of her 1970s eyewear. "If you don't know why you feel guilty, that is called an irrational fear, an unfounded fear of something that does not exist. We know it does not exist because you cannot name it."

The words fell from her mouth like jagged boulders tumbling down a mountainside, with me standing frozen, vulnerable in their path of destruction. She droned on, but I had tuned out, still trying to process the news that my guilt and anxiety were irrational and I should just stop feeling that way. It really was my fault.

"... you also probably have a personality disorder." She paused after that last bombshell.

I snapped back to attention. A personality disorder? Was that serious? Was that why no one liked me, because there was something wrong with my personality? Quite distressing news—as if being insane wasn't enough, now I had a defective personality.

"How do you fix that?"

"You don't, really," Therapist Lady replied with her perpetually expressionless face. "There are drugs that help though."

Oh perfect. More drugs for the next time I tried to kill myself.

Convinced Mean Cheryl was an auditory hallucination, the psychiatrist at the hospital had already started me on a powerful psychotropic drug. I'd tried to explain repeatedly that I didn't actually *hear* a voice. I knew what I heard came from within my own mind. The doctor should have recognized this as negative self-talk, but obviously he'd heard nothing I'd said once he'd decided I was hallucinating. It's amazing how quickly a person loses all credibility once they exhibit any signs of mental illness. It's not unlike trashing an entire car because the fuel pump has gone bad. The car obviously needs some help, but the bad part doesn't mean the whole thing is junk. I never saw the hospital psychiatrist again after I my release. I wondered if he would care to know his psychotropic drug did nothing to silence Mean Cheryl?

Nothing had changed. Nothing had gotten better. If anything, post-suicide-attempt life was an even bigger disaster than what I'd tried to leave behind. Therapist Lady had completely invalidated my anxiety, told me I had a personality disorder, and recommended more drugs. Despair engulfed me. Mean Cheryl didn't even have to tell me what a loser I was—I wore it like a shroud.

The heavy wood door creaked in protest while I pushed it open and went inside. Like my soul, the apartment was dark and empty. I ambled partway down the hallway before crumbling to the floor. Dief sat down next to me, watching me closely. I wrapped my arms around his body and held him tightly, my tears wetting his soft fur.

"What is wrong with me, Dief? I'm sorry I'm so crazy. I know I don't deserve you." My tears came more rapidly, and my body trembled.

"Why do you love me?" I asked my friend, looking into his eyes.

Dief stared back at me, one blue eye and one brown eye searching my face. Could he see into my soul?

I scratched behind his ears and rubbed his neck. Placing my index finger on his head, I traced the white stripe on his face. First downward, against the hair, making the stripe wide and rough, and then back up, making the stripe narrow and smooth.

"What will I ever do without you?" I asked. "Promise you will never leave me."

PART III
FOLLOW ME, FRIEND

CHAPTER FIFTEEN

The large trailer door swung open, rusted hinges protesting with squeaks and groans. Rain pelted my face. A cold, sharp wind blew through my too-thin hooded sweatshirt. The damp air seeped into my body, where it would linger for hours, keeping me chilled well after I returned home and changed into dry clothes. Unusual weather for late spring in Kentucky, but I did not want to be anywhere else. Indeed, today was a big day.

I peered inside the cavernous stock trailer parked outside the repurposed tobacco barn at Sunland Farm, a boarding stable located on the west side of Paris. Large enough to hold several head of cattle, its size made the tiny brown-and-white mare tied inside seem all the smaller. She stood looking at me, a curious expression on her face. Having come from northern Illinois, the mare still held on to her shaggy winter coat, while the horses here in central Kentucky had already let go of theirs. Soaking wet from the rain splashing through the ventilation slats on the upper portion of the trailer, her thick coat formed tiny rivulets of muddy water that ran in dark streaks down her spindly legs. Much smaller than I'd expected, the mare looked more like a yearling than the three-year-old I knew her to be. She stood quietly at first, taking in her surroundings through her limited view out the trailer door. Then she lifted her dainty head, and her little body shook as a high-pitched whinny erupted from deep within her. Her patience wearing thin, she shuffled back and forth, her hooves making hollow *clonk-clonk* sounds on the hardwood floor.

I stepped cautiously into the trailer, talking to the little mare. Eyes wide, she watched me closely but did not show fear. I spoke softly, approached slowly, and placed my hand on her neck.

"Easy, girl. This is your new home."

The mare pushed her muzzle toward me, and I let her sniff my hands. Seemingly satisfied, she took a half step back and waited for me to untie her. Together we stepped off the trailer into the cold wind and driving rain.

Dief came out of the barn from where he had been intently watching my interactions with the little mare.

"Aahroooo-wooo-oooo!" he yodeled, greeting the new horse, hanging back to assess the situation.

With the mare safely off the trailer, Dief trotted up to greet her, maintaining a respectful distance.

"What do you think?" I asked him.

"Aaahrooooooo-woooo!" Dief answered, wagging his stump tail slowly.

"I think so too."

Together we walked to a small paddock with a run-in shed. Spying the pile of fresh hay in the corner of the small three-sided building, the little mare went right to it, eagerly lowering her head to have a taste. I could see her ribs under her wet coat. Her shoulders and hindquarters were slab sided and underdeveloped for her age. I suspected winter had been tough on her and her previous owner, with hay shortages and a floundering economy, especially in rural Illinois, from where she had come. After eating a few mouthfuls of hay, she walked over to me, stretched her neck, and lifted her muzzle up toward my face.

"Hello, beautiful." I breathed softly into her nostril. Gazing at her, I listened to the *crunch-crunch-crunch* of her grinding hay stems between her teeth, a sound I loved. She was really mine. The first daughter of

Farley and Gypsy, the foal I thought I'd never meet after things fell apart in Illinois. Now I owned her. The rain let up, and a ray of sunlight poked through the heavy gray clouds.

"Hey you," I whispered softly. "I like you."

She lifted her head and looked at me. I patted her on the neck.

"I'll see you soon, beautiful." Stepping out of the shed, I turned toward the gate, where Dief waited patiently.

"Aahrooo-ooo!" he yodeled.

"Yeah, I'm ready," I said. "Let's go."

Dief fell in line at my heels, and we walked across the barnyard to my truck.

"Oooo-oooo," Dief yodeled softly.

"I agree," I said with a smile.

The next day, the dark clouds and icy rain had disappeared, and the sun shone brightly. I walked from the barn to the paddock. A new leather halter and a black-and-gray braided nylon rope, which had belonged to Corky, dangled from one hand.

"Hey, little horse," I said when I reached the paddock gate where the tiny mare waited for me. "How was your first night?"

"Aaarooooo-woooo!" Dief yodeled, looking up at me.

"What do you think, buddy?" I asked him. "Do you like the new horse?"

"Oooooo-oooo." Dief's yodeling bark-howl softened to a barely audible rumble. He wagged his tail briefly before he sat down just outside the gate, knowing he wasn't allowed in the paddock with the horse.

A warm spring breeze had replaced the blustery, damp winds that had greeted the new horse the day before. Without lifting her head from the soft green hay, the mare watched me enter the paddock. I walked slowly toward her, whistling softly. She lifted her head. Soft strands of grassy hay fell from her mouth as she chewed.

"You are a tiny thing, aren't you?"

She blew a sharp snort through her nostrils and lowered her head to take another mouthful of hay. She didn't move when I stroked her neck and ran my fingers over her slightly protruding ribs. Leaning over, I reached around her neck and slipped the new leather halter over her head and buckled the crown piece. Much too big, the halter hung loosely on her small head.

"It'll have to do, mare." I eyed the poorly fitting halter.

I turned and walked toward the gate. The little horse followed me obediently through the opening onto the soft grass of the barnyard.

"Aaaroooo-oooooo!" Dief took his customary horse-leading position on my left side. The three of us walked together into the barn. I felt light and happy, like I hadn't felt in a long time. The new horse gave me something to focus on. Training her, bringing her up to a healthy weight, and caring for her on a daily basis were all things that forced me not only to get out of the work-is-my-only-value mindset, but also to look into the future. Perhaps most importantly, concentrating on the new horse's future gave me a reason to want to live long enough to see it. The little mare needed me, but I needed her more.

Retrieving a tote with Corky's old brushes in it from the tack room, I looked at the new horse, wondering where to start. Thick, shaggy brown hair covered her head, making her eyes look sunken into the pile of a buffalo skin rug. She stepped forward, shoving her head toward my chest in an attempt to rub her face on me. I scratched her forehead.

"Does your face itch?"

She responded by shoving me with her muzzle.

"That'll be enough of that." I gave her muzzle a sharp shove.

The mare's eyes widened. She lifted her head, as if trying to look directly into my eyes.

"You weren't expecting me to shove you back, eh?" I said with a smile.

The mare lifted her nose toward my face, stretching her neck as she deeply breathed in my scent.

"Yes," I said to her, gently blowing into one nostril, "that is a much nicer way to say hello."

I gently pulled at some of the thick hair on her jowl. It came out in a clump between my fingers. "Perhaps we should start here." I looked more closely at the spot from where I pulled the clump. It ... *moved*. I'd discovered the source of her itchiness—lice! *Oh, gross!*

An hour later, her face freshly clipped, cleaned, and deloused, I marveled at how much the little mare resembled her sire. Her eyes, the shape of her head and ears, and her gentle personality all reminded me of Farley. She was dark bay like her mother, but like her father, she had a loud tobiano pattern with large patches of white over her neck and shoulders. Now clean, I could see her legs were white with several Dalmatian-like spots sprinkled down each one. The white from her hind legs extended all the way up one side, creating a wide stripe on the back third of her hindquarters, over her rump, and down the other side. From the rear she appeared to have a brown bullseye in the center of her bum. A solid black tail grew out from her rump, nearly reaching the ground. Her mane, half-black and half-white, hung long and stringy down her skinny neck.

"I knew there was a beautiful horse under that buffalo-hair head." I stroked her face.

"So did you think of a name for her yet?"

I hadn't heard anyone pull up. Startled, I looked up and recognized a fellow boarder entering the barn.

"Not yet." The mare had come with the name Star, but the moniker didn't work for me. She didn't look like a Star. The blaze-faced mare didn't even have a star. I thought for a moment. When Farley's first foal crop came in 2001. I'd called all the colts "little Farleys" and the fillies "little Farlettas." *Hmmm ... should I?*

"Farletta," I said aloud. Never one to be fond of common names, it sounded good to me.

"What?" the boarder asked.

"I'm going to call her Farletta."

The woman looked at me, as if waiting for the punch line. "At least until I think of something better," I added quickly.

CHAPTER SIXTEEN

On my days off from Claiborne, I frequently took Dief for a truck ride. We explored the beautiful Kentucky countryside of Bourbon and Fayette Counties, driving past the miles of limestone walls made from stacked flat slabs of the gray rock. Dark-green moss grew from the cracks and crevices between the stone slabs, some of which had been stacked over 150 years ago as land borders were marked between the now historic horse farms. Sometimes I'd still picture myself, the little girl on her black horse, bounding across the green fields and leaping over the stone walls. Driving allowed me to isolate my mind just enough from outside worries to find the peace and safety that little girl felt.

I pulled into the long gravel driveway leading up to Farletta's Kentucky home, the circa late 1700s homestead known as Sunland Farm. Farletta thrived on the acres of lush green pastures surrounding the historic brick home. Aside from the approximately forty fenced acres, the farm also boasted two hundred acres of adjacent pasture to ride in (although we had to share it with several dozen head of cattle), a large galloping field with cross-country fences constructed of the trunks of fallen trees and other natural objects, a small outdoor arena, and a converted tobacco barn with seven airy, comfortable stalls. The farm manager, an extremely talented woodworker, had done amazing restoration work on the old barn and outbuildings. The old farm felt like a safe haven, a place I could go to escape Mean Cheryl, even if only for a brief time. I'd always felt more peaceful outside, more able to connect to the part of me that wasn't Mean Cheryl.

"Hey, pretty girl."

Farletta waited at the gate. She must have heard my truck pull in. That little girl in me constantly reached out to connect with Farletta, but I felt wary of allowing this. I'd intended Farletta to be a project horse—a horse I planned to train and then sell, putting the money I received toward a new horse. I would then repeat the process. I intended to be business minded in this endeavor, flipping horses like people flipped real estate. No way would I get sucked into the emotional attachment of horse ownership again. I wouldn't risk letting Mean Cheryl use Farletta against me as she had Corky. Determined to remain emotionally detached, I built a fortress around my heart, resolute to never let Farletta in. But that little girl, so persistent, her heart leapt and her eyes lit up each time she saw Farletta. I quickly squashed the sensation. I knew becoming emotionally attached would be dangerous.

At three years old, Farletta appeared to have the education of a weanling. She liked attention but hated work (in her case, work was anything I asked her to do that she didn't want to do—a.k.a, *stupid stuff*). Being tied to the hitching post was stupid; learning to lead, stop, back, and turn was stupid; being in her stall when she wanted to be outside was stupid; being outside when she wanted to be inside was stupid; having protective boots and wraps applied to her legs was stupid; having a bath was stupid; and shortening her mane was borderline torture and, therefore, undeniably stupid. She loved being loose in her paddock and having me pet and scratch her—not stupid. Eating grass at the end of a lead rope held in my hand—also not stupid. Actually, any form of eating could be described as acceptable. Anything beyond those activities landed on Farletta's *no* list.

Farletta gained weight and grew quickly on the lush green pastures of her new Kentucky home. I worked with her slowly, taking her through all the steps of training a weanling—brushing, lifting her feet for cleaning (which she hated!), leading, and tying. Farletta fought me about handling her feet—she seemed convinced she could not stand on three legs and often reacted violently to my attempts. *What am I missing?* I wondered each time she flipped out. It made no sense. I could handle her feet with no trouble for several days, then one day some switch would flip and she'd panic, flying backward, eyes wide, like she was trying to escape a dangerous predator. But she didn't seem to truly be panicking. I didn't feel fear from her, but resentment, or perhaps frustration. Like a person who keeps repeating themselves because no one is listening.

Aside from her occasional temper tantrums, Farletta was everything I'd dreamed she'd be when I suggested the pairing of Farley and Gypsy while still working at Conner Equine in 2002. Although smaller than I'd imagined, standing only about 14.2 hands, though her sire and dam were 15.2 and 16 hands respectively, Farletta had the big, flowing gaits you'd expect from a much taller horse. This made her quite suitable for training and showing in hunt seat or lower-level dressage, my two favorite disciplines.

Through the remainder of spring and into the summer, Farletta grew and blossomed into the beautiful, healthy horse I'd known I'd find under all that wet hair and bones when she'd arrived at Sunland. Her hind quarters were a full three inches higher than her withers—a good indication she had at least three more inches to grow as her withers caught up. She had put on a couple hundred pounds in fat and muscle, mostly in her hindquarters, over her back, and filling out her belly. Her neck and shoulders were still slight and underdeveloped, but the change was already impressive.

As we were working on resolving the great hoof handling fiasco of 2006, I continued Farletta's lessons, teaching her first to lead quietly at my shoulder while walking and trotting, to stop and stand quietly, and to move backward willingly. Leading lessons eventually became an acceptable use of her time, and she soon seemed to enjoy the work. I took her for walks far out in the back fields and let her graze in the long grasses and clover there.

Soon she was ready to learn about the longe line. Longeing involves having the horse walk, trot, and canter around the handler in a circle at the end of a long rope (usually twenty-five to thirty feet in length). It is easiest to teach a horse to longe in a small, circular arena called a round pen. Unfortunately, Sunland not only didn't have a round pen, but the riding arena, surrounded by low wood planks and built on top of a steep hill, was also less than ideal. It did not have a proper barrier to help Farletta understand how to stay on the circle. It took several attempts over the course of a few days, but eventually Farletta understood the concept of longeing. She soon traveled around me in circles at a walk, trot, and canter.

Incredibly intelligent like Farley, Farletta differed from her sire in that she disliked work and used her intelligence to produce nefarious outcomes. One such outcome took me quite by surprise. Trotting in a leisurely circle around me, I missed the meaning of a side-eyed look. Next thing I knew, she threw her head in the air, snatched the line out of my hand with a strategic jerk of her nose, and leapt over the arena barrier. The errant mare landed on the other side and ran away with her nose in the air and her tail flagged victoriously behind her. Many horse owners will appreciate my mental conundrum—that of being impressed with her graceful athleticism, while also being irritated with her problematic behavior.

"Well, that's new," I said to the empty arena. "Have you ever seen anything like that?" I looked at Dief, standing dutifully outside the enclosure.

"Aaarooooo-oooooooo!"

I took that as a no.

I trudged down the hill and found Farletta standing along the fence line, grabbing large mouthfuls of grass with a look of satisfaction on her face.

"What was that all about?" I grabbed the rope attached to her halter. Farletta lifted her head and snorted in my face before grazing again. Nice. Wiping my face with my shirtsleeve, I tugged the rope, asking the mare to lift her head and follow me back to the arena.

Farletta came along willingly, and I naively thought perhaps this was an isolated incident. It was not.

Farletta became adept at snatching the longeline from my hand and leaping out of the arena. She did it over and over, sometimes several times a day. I knew getting mad, yelling, and hitting would do nothing to stop her behavior and would result in her distrusting me. I had to outthink her, but for many days she proved too smart for me.

Interestingly, Mean Cheryl stayed remarkably silent during these training trials. My moments of training ineptitude were such perfect ammunition for her, why didn't she say anything? Although I felt peaceful at the barn with Farletta, my anxiety often bubbled out of control at home. Many sleepless hours were spent watching old DVDs or walking Dief late into the night.

STILL BEING OUTSMARTED by my horse, one evening I decided to take Farletta out in the big open field behind the barn for her longe lesson. She couldn't jump out of an arena if she wasn't in one. At worst she could drag me around the field for a while (which she did). However, soon she traveled in a circle around me at the walk, trot, and canter. Success!

Farletta willingly accepted the saddle and bridle and did beautifully with ground driving—a technique where the trainer builds on the voice cues learned in longeing while teaching the horse rein cues from the ground (versus while mounted).

Farletta's first ride was virtually the same as Farley's first ride—completely uneventful. Standing on the tailgate of my truck parked in the driveway, I maneuvered Farletta so she stood with her left side against the edge of the open tailgate. Placing my right hand on the front of the saddle and my rein hand on Farletta's neck, I carefully lifted my right leg over the saddle and slid on. Farletta stood stock still, as if she'd been ridden a hundred times before. I touched my legs to her sides and gave the verbal cue to walk. Farletta walked off willingly, quickly adjusting to my weight in the saddle. I carefully steered her around the parking area, making large circles and figure eights, using the rein commands she'd already learned from her driving lessons and adding soft leg cues, which would eventually become our primary form of communication. Farletta did everything I asked without objection and remained relaxed throughout our short ride. I slid off the little mare, satisfied and proud of her.

Farletta chewed her bit thoughtfully and twitched her ears backward and forward, listening to the summer evening sounds of the farm. I scratched her neck just in front of the withers, a favorite spot. Farletta stretched her neck forward and twitched her lips, demonstrating her enjoyment of the neck scratching. She opened her mouth and stretched her lips toward the sky, tilting her head from side to side. Three small wrinkles appeared under her left eye, and she seemed to smile. I marveled at the appearance of the wrinkles. I had never seen a horse make a face like that. Really quite adorable.

A twinge of sadness crept across my heart, interrupting our joyful interaction. I could feel myself growing attached to the little horse, and it scared me. I'd justified accepting the gift of Farletta by taking her on as a project with the intention of selling her. I couldn't possibly keep her. How could I even consider it after what I'd done to Corky? I didn't deserve another horse to love.

If Farletta continued to ride as well as she had this first time, it wouldn't be long before she was ready to sell. Her weight was good, and she looked healthy. No longer the skinny, scraggly little horse I'd pulled out of the trailer on a wet, cold day months before, she was now beautiful and fancy, with striking good looks and an adorable baby face. The more rides I put on her, the closer we came to the day I'd officially list her for sale.

"It's stupid to be sad," Mean Cheryl taunted. *"You knew she was never going to be yours. Toughen up and quit being a baby about it! This is how the horse business works, dumbass!"*

Oh God, she was back. I nodded my agreement. Farletta and I turned together and walked back to the barn in silence.

The next several rides went as well as the first. Farletta picked up on her lessons quickly and finally seemed to enjoy having a job. Easy to ride and never fearful or apprehensive, with a soft mouth, light sides and a willing attitude, Farletta would make somebody an awesome horse.

"*But not you,*" Mean Cheryl chimed in.

Right. Not me. A strange mixture of pride in my work and deep sadness for what I was about to lose came over me.

CHAPTER SEVENTEEN

"OK, sweet girl" I lifted my reins, asking Farletta to stop. The mare turned her head and touched her nose to my left foot, resting in the stirrup. She blew a breath on the toe of my boot, then nudged it with her upper lip. "Yes, a walk sounds like a fine idea." I leaned forward and rubbed her forehead, then swung my leg over her back and dismounted.

The sun slowly dropped behind the distant westerly tree line, casting a soft yellow glow across the barn yard and riding arena. A lovely pink hue tinted the sky as the sun crept ever lower on the horizon, preparing to disappear altogether. The evening flowed peaceful and quiet. Farletta, Dief, and I had the farm to ourselves.

I removed Farletta's tack and slipped on her halter. The three of us headed out to the back field, where the sweetest clover grew. Dief ran ahead of us, nose to the ground, inhaling the wonderful scents of the farm. The soft green grass made a whooshing sound as my boots moved through the long blades.

"Why can't it always be like this?" I asked my four-legged friends.

"Aaaroooo-ooooooo!" Dief replied. Farletta twitched an ear in my direction as she grabbed mouthfuls of the long, lush grass.

"I don't know either." I sat in the cool grass, then leaned back to face the sky. Fluffy clouds danced across a blue canvas. I relished the peace and solitude of these quiet evenings with just the three of us. Dief flopped down next to me, and Farletta grazed a short distance away When we were out together, away from everyone and everything, I almost felt like a normal person. Farletta had the power to silence Mean Cheryl. The mare's quiet energy filled me with peace.

I remained there in the grass until the first pink streaks of the setting sun appeared in the darkening sky. *Time to go back now.* The thought brought feelings of resentment and … fear? Anxiety coiled within me like tightly wound rolls of razor wire. Rising to a seated position, I looked at Dief and touched his soft ear. Dief said nothing. His stump tail drooped, no longer wagging and animated but now seemed to be a reflection of the tension rising within me. I placed my right index finger on his head, slowly tracing the stripe on his face. First, I traced it down toward his nose, making the stripe wide and rough. Then back toward his ears, making it narrow and smooth again.

I rose to my feet, picked up Farletta's rope, and started back across the field, Dief following close behind. I could feel my body tense and my face tighten with each step bringing me closer to the barn.

Arriving home, I switched out my barn boots for some sneakers and took Dief for a long walk. We'd recently moved into our own house on Claiborne Farm, another part of living that childhood dream. I walked the quiet farm roads, Dief running ahead of me. How could I want more? But still, the anxiety grew, gnawing at me relentlessly. This had become a nightly ritual: barn, walk dog, shower, and pajamas. Then I sat alone with anxious thoughts I'd been holding off all day. It felt like being in a constant state of fear, how one might feel walking alone through a dark alley in the bad part of town late at night. The dread built within me, a terrible fear of … what? I didn't know, but I couldn't deny the existence or intensity of the emotion.

"I hate you! I hate you! You stupid, fat cow! I hate you!" I punched my arms and legs hard enough to raise hard lumps, which would later turn into deep purple bruises. "Why am I alive? Why, God? Why?" Tears streaked my face. I screamed until my throat burned.

Deep, guttural screams that sounded like the cries of demons erupted from within me. I collapsed onto the floor, my body shaking with sobs. I would never be normal. I would never feel OK again. Life felt like a cruel joke, and I was the unwitting target. Rising to my hands and knees, I crawled across the floor and into my bed. This couldn't continue forever, could it? Why did I go on?

"Why do you keep me here?" I asked God angrily. "Why? Why can't you just let me die?" Then the tears returned, flowing down my face and wetting my pillow, waiting for sleep to come.

JANUARY SWEPT IN, cold and wet. The change in season brought with it new responsibilities in my work at Claiborne. Despite that oppressive, hateful voice of Mean Cheryl shredding my mind and crushing my self-confidence, occasionally a piece of what I considered the real me came forward. It was the part of me that wasn't afraid to move far from home for college in Illinois and Tennessee, or to take off for Kentucky to capture the dream of the little girl I had once been. I asked to be placed in the foaling barn that season, where I would care for the broodmares and hopefully deliver foals, something I'd wanted to experience since reading Walter Farley's book about the famous racehorse Man o' War. Karl granted my request, and I felt elated. I had done it, one small step up the ladder of success.

Not long after I started my new position, my anxiety worsened. I worried about everything: messing up at work, having Karl regret his decision, what the other people at work thought of me getting a house after less than a year of employment. They would find out what a crazy, messed-up disaster I really was. I'd moved myself under a microscope, and like sunshine magnified into a laser beam of fire, I felt ready to combust.

Farletta still provided a respite for me, even as the anxiety surrounding my work life intensified. I continued her training with the intention of selling her. I not only covered the basics thoroughly, but I also exposed her to as many new experiences as I could possibly think of—exploring the fields and sagging barns beyond the farm, trekking over new and different terrain, even walking her down the road by the barking dogs, excited children, and cars driving past. I marveled at her confidence and quiet demeanor. Considering how green and uninterested in learning she'd been just the year before, I was impressed at the effort she now put forth.

A cool spring evening found me sitting astride four-year-old Farletta as she walked through the cattle pasture near the back of Sunland Farm. Cows and calves dotted the open field, grazing silently as the sun dropped slowly behind the trees. I'd never ridden Farletta with the cattle before, and I felt apprehensive. A new experience on a young, green horse could always go south in a hurry. The presence of Angela, a friend from Claiborne, on her older, more-experienced mare bolstered my confidence. Safety in numbers, right?

Dief trotted along in front of Farletta, while my friend's two dogs, Micky and Petunia, ran farther ahead, chasing each other around in the emerald-green grass. Distracted, Micky broke away from his play with Petunia and ran toward the herd of cattle, scattering them in all directions. A small brown calf darted out from the spreading herd, with Micky hot on his heels. The little calf ran, yelling for his mother, while Micky chased him straight toward me and Farletta—a terrifying sight for a green horse that had never encountered cattle.

I froze in the saddle. There was no point in trying to get out of the way in the second or so of time I had to make a decision. I figured we'd be safer if Farletta faced the calf. If I tried to move her, who was to say the calf wouldn't follow us? I'd rather risk having Farletta rear or spook backward than have her skitter sideways or bolt on the slippery, uneven ground. Steadying myself, I gathered up the reins and braced for impact. The calf continued at a full run, unaware of the horse in his path. In the split second I had to think on it, I imagined if I survived the impact and resulting fall, the calf's mother would come charging out of the herd to finish me off.

The calf ran full tilt right at Farletta's front legs. A stride or two before impact, he attempted to turn sharply. His tiny hooves slipped on the wet grass, sending him sprawling onto his side. The calf's forward momentum allowed his now horizontal body to continue on the original path, and three hundred pounds of wet, scared calf slid across the rain-soaked grass, stopping at Farletta's feet. Seemingly perplexed by the little calf, Farletta took a single, slow step backward and stared down at him. The calf scrambled to his feet and ran back to his mother, unharmed. Given her age and level of experience, Farletta's reaction was as unusual as a bank teller waving a robber over to her window saying, "Hey, rob me first." She should have been terrified, but she wasn't.

Well, color me amazed.

A realization dawned. There was something special about this horse. There was something *safe* in Farletta's presence—somehow she helped me recapture the way I felt as a child, sitting under the huge raised hoof of the larger-than-life Clydesdale statue.

You need her. The voice came from somewhere deep inside me. I listened closely, hoping the thought would repeat. *You need her.*

"I need her." I said the words aloud, letting them swirl around me as I contemplated the meaning. I'd had Farletta halfheartedly for sale for a couple of months and had some interest, even though she was priced high. I didn't really want to sell her. Despite my intention to guard my heart, I had become attached to the little mare.

Mean Cheryl rolled her eyes. *"You don't deserve that horse, you stupid bitch."* But this time, I turned away from her and toward Farletta. A small voice rose from somewhere deep inside, the voice of the child with the imaginary black horse. *You need her,* she whispered again. I thought back on the months we'd spent together and how Farletta had become a refuge for me, like a warm, safe place I could hide. Not only calm, Farletta also seemed immovably centered, very much in her own body and confident in herself, opposite of me in that respect. I felt comfortable in her presence. With Farletta I came the closest to silencing Mean Cheryl's painful and destructive rant.

I need her. My spirit lifted ever so slightly. I chipped away at the barricade around my heart. Piece by piece it fell away, and I finally allowed myself to love Farletta. *My* horse. The decision would change my life forever.

Although not the sixteen-hand jet-black Arabian of my childhood imagination, Farletta still more than fulfilled the dreams of that little girl inside me. Made up of the best parts of her sire and dam, a measure of Corky's heart, spirit, and personality dwelled within her as well. We connected deeply, quickly, and thoroughly. She settled into the role of my heart horse with ease.

Suddenly a brave rider, I routinely pushed myself to try new things with Farletta. Taking off through the open fields just the two of us, exploring the back roads around the farm, and even wandering into town for a run through the Starbucks drive-thru—nothing was off limits with my new horse. *My* horse. I'd climb on the fence to hop onto her bareback with just a halter and lead, or sometimes I'd ride her with no equipment at all, marveling at how a simple shift of my weight, or even visualizing a task, could direct her movement so effortlessly. I didn't second-guess myself when riding. I not only trusted Farletta, but I trusted my ability to keep myself safe on her. Could it be that the difficulties I had early on in her training were a result of that barricade I put around my heart? The one I'd finally torn away when I decided to keep her for my own personal horse. I suspected it must be true, since it seemed each day Farletta showed even greater willingness to learn and work with me.

I had given myself permission to love another horse, and we thrived in each other's company. Farletta made me feel amazing, a sharp contrast to the anxiety-filled hours of insomnia I experienced each night at home, a victim of Mean Cheryl's hatred and angst. Guilt of unknown origin tore at my insides, grinding away at my sanity until I could no longer lie in bed, waiting, praying for dawn in the blue light cast by my alarm clock. Mean Cheryl became an increasingly violent companion, tormenting my existence, making my private life a pure hell filled with self-inflicted injuries *(never let anyone see them)*, screams of rage, and sorrow that consumed me like a vacuous black hole. She bludgeoned me with thoughts of suicide, horrible verbal and physical abuse, and anxiety that erupted into uncontrollable sobs so violent, I'd cough and gag as I tried to catch my breath.

Even as parts of me flourished when I spent time with my horse—I played the part of happy, normal human well—the darkness in my heart devoured me. Mean Cheryl, increasingly difficult to subdue in public, threatened daily to destroy my outward appearance of sanity. Soon, all that remained would be a fluid divide between the person I was in private and the person I presented to the world. No one would know which version they would get at any given moment. Not even me.

CHAPTER EIGHTEEN

"Arroooo-ooooo!" Dief trotted into the barn. The hot, humid air clung to me as I walked along behind my dog. Dief, now eleven, had developed an arthritic limp sometime earlier in the year, but it didn't slow him down much. He gimped along nonchalantly, always eager to get up and go. What he lacked in speed and grace, he made up for in unquenchable enthusiasm. However, the stifling summer heat elicited a cruel reminder of Dief's advancing age. We could no longer go on long hikes or trail rides on a warm summer day, as we had just the year before. Dief's heart longed to join Farletta and me as we rode through the grassy fields, but his body would no longer allow him to romp alongside in the scorching Kentucky sunshine.

The hot summer sun slowly dropped from the sky, taking with it a portion of the stifling heat of the day as I led Farletta to the mounting block. Dief followed along closely, his stump of a tail wagging in the heavy late-summer air.

"You have to stay here, Dief," I said to the expectant dog.

His tail drooped pitifully at my words. Dief cocked his head to one side. His single, bright-blue eye seemed to search my soul.

"I'm sorry, buddy," I continued. "It's just too hot and humid for you to come along."

Dief lowered himself to the ground, never taking his eyes off me as I turned back to Farletta and climbed onto the mounting block. Placing my left foot in the stirrup, I swung my right leg over Farletta's back, my seat landing softly in the saddle.

I reached down and stroked Farletta's neck, tracing the line between her bay and white markings with my outstretched fingers. That peaceful feeling I could only find when with Farletta and Dief enveloped me. I breathed in the scents I loved: horses, earth, fresh grass, and clean air. Gently touching my calves to the mare's sides, I guided her toward the gate leading out to the field behind the barn. Dief followed us.

"No way, buddy." I glanced over my shoulder as Farletta continued forward. "Still too hot and humid. You stay here." Dief stopped and stood where he was. The look of sadness and confusion on his beautiful face pierced my heart like a thousand jagged daggers. A breeze ruffled Farletta's mane and drifted across my summer-tanned arms. She lifted her head, body tense, and stared into the distance. Her nostrils flaring wide, Farletta breathed in deeply and then let out a sharp snort.

"What are you looking at?" I asked. "Silly girl." I smiled and redirected Farletta's attention to our ride. *Unusual for her to lose focus like that.* I shrugged, and the thought fell away. We trotted through the gate at the far end of the field. It stood open, inviting. The cattle had moved to another farm, so now the field sat empty, beckoning riders to enjoy the wide expanse of open territory.

Farletta walked on around the perimeter of the grassy space, the rhythmic *clop-clop, clop-clop* of her unshod hooves soothing, like the babble of a secluded stream. I could detach myself from those feelings of self-hatred and worthlessness, at least for a moment, while I focused on the sights, sounds, and smells of our little piece of Kentucky. Mean Cheryl, like a true bully, waited for a chance to pounce at any sign of vulnerability. She would find me when I left the farm, perhaps even as I walked away from the gate after returning Farletta to her pasture. Always there, like a cloying shadow, ready to suffocate me.

Trying to outrun the dark thoughts, I nudged Farletta into a canter. She took off in an awkward and unbalanced gait, cantering a few strides before slamming on the brakes, throwing me onto her neck and nearly unseating me.

"What the hell was that?" Anger burned at the outermost edges of my patience. With a squeeze, I again asked Farletta to canter. She took a few strides, then stopped abruptly and backed up a few steps. Scrambling to stay topside, I regained my seat and then kicked her into a canter. Farletta balked but then cantered off in response to my increasing demand. Again, a few strides and then *boom!* A screeching halt. This time I came close to falling off, and my anger turned to fear.

"*You stupid idiot! You thought you had her so well trained! Fucking useless moron!*" Mean Cheryl spoke with a hateful, sneering voice. I sat in dumbfounded silence astride my horse. Mean Cheryl had found a way into my sacred space, weaseling her way between me and Farletta. Numbness overtook me as the implications of this change sank in.

Nothing is safe. I slid off Farletta's back and started the long walk back to the barn. A dark cloud stalked me. I shivered inwardly, despite the warmth of the summer evening.

Now she had taken everything.

CHAPTER NINETEEN

My downward spiral, rapid and demoralizing, threatened to rob me of my ability to keep Mean Cheryl a secret. I hardly slept anymore. Every night my stomach lurched and churned as I was crushed by guilt and shame, their presence validating Mean Cheryl's every negative, painful word.

I barely held myself together during work, frequently retreating to the privacy of the bathroom to cry for some reason I couldn't identify. I put extraordinary, exhausting effort into appearing normal, and consequently avoided people as much as possible. I covered miles a day on foot, walking during my breaks and into the late hours, until so exhausted I felt there might be hope of getting to sleep. No matter what I did, I found no escape from the constant feeling of dread that some horrible secret was in danger of being exposed, and then everyone would know.

Would know what? I asked myself.

"*They'd know what a horrible person you are,*" Mean Cheryl replied.

I didn't want that. Life would be unbearable if people really knew who and what I was.

Winding my way up the drive of Farletta's boarding stable late one evening, I stopped when I spied a car in the parking area.

"Why is someone here?" I asked Dief.

He looked up from his place on the seat next to me.

"I don't want to see anyone tonight."

I felt emotionally out of control and on the edge of breaking down in tears. *I should leave.*

The little girl behind the black curtain tugged at my heart. I really needed to see Farletta. I hesitated at the curve in the drive, still several yards from the barn. Removing my foot from the brake pedal, I let the truck coast the rest of the way to the barn parking area. I could grab Farletta quickly and escape to the back fields before anyone saw me.

"Let's go, Dief." I threw the truck into park and flipped off the ignition.

The car in the lot belonged to Marianne, a friend at the farm. She and her gelding, Seven, had been riding companions the previous year when I started Farletta under saddle. I must have looked distressed when I walked into the barnyard, because Marianne seemed to know right away something was wrong.

"What's going on?" she asked.

"Nothing." I choked back my tears, staring at the gravel around my feet.

"Are you sure?" Marianne's eyes searched my face.

Searching for my secret. "Crappy day at work," I lied, ready to explode in an out-of-control flood of tears and raw emotion. All I wanted to do was run screaming through the fields and crawl into the cold, damp blackness of a secret cave where I could hide forever.

Marianne's brow furrowed. "Are you going to ride?"

"No, I don't know … maybe … probably not … I don't think I have time," I mumbled.

"I was going to ride Seven around the back field," Marianne said. "Why don't you and Farletta come with us?"

"Oh, no, I can't do that," I stammered. "I … I'm not …" I didn't finish. Tears stung my eyes. *Don't cry!*

"*Quit being a baby!*" Mean Cheryl added.

"Here," Marianne said, "why don't you stay here and watch Uncle Seven for me. I'll get Farletta."

I couldn't hold back the tears anymore, and they trickled down my face. Marianne went to fetch Farletta, leaving me there to cry on Uncle Seven's sleek black shoulder.

Farletta stood quietly while I climbed aboard, but as usual, she walked forward the moment my seat touched the saddle—a bad habit I'd let her get away with. I felt numb on her back, like a useless passenger. Farletta sensed my discomfort, and she became fidgety underneath me, shifting her weight from foot to foot, trying to snatch the reins from my hands by tugging at the bit in her mouth.

"I can't do this." I tried to hide the panic in my voice. Tears once again streamed down my face. "She's not ready."

"She's fine," Marianne said gently. "Bring her here right next to Uncle Seven. She'll be OK with him next to her."

I cautiously steered Farletta over toward where Marianne sat astride Seven. Farletta spied a bucket on the ground near the hitching rail and skittered sideways away from it. I clamped her sides with my legs, trying to catch my balance.

You're messing up! You better pay attention, or you will fall off this horse! I took a deep breath and let it out slowly, trying to relax into the saddle. Farletta settled down and walked quietly out to the back field next to Uncle Seven.

"Are you OK?" Marianne asked again.

I didn't want to answer. Vacuous silence hung between us.

"I can't relax." I choked back all the fear and anxiety threatening to burst forth from every fiber of my being.

"Farletta is fine. She's doing great." Marianne reached over to stroke the mare's neck.

I opened my mouth to speak but then closed it without uttering a word.

"Don't tell her anything!" Mean Cheryl warned.

I took a deep breath. "No, it's not her," I said hesitantly. "It's me. I can't sleep. I am so nervous all the time. I don't know what to do."

Sharing those first words with Marianne made it easier to let more out. "I don't know why I can't just relax! I'm so tired. I just want to sleep, but I can't. My heart races all the time. It never stops." The words spilled out quickly, like blood from a gaping wound.

My tears came faster now, and my body shook as I tried to hold them in.

"Have you talked to a doctor?" Marianne asked.

"No … Well, yeah, sort of." I was not about to tell her about the suicide attempt and Mean Cheryl and all the craziness that defined my daily existence. "I have a counselor I talk to, but she just tells me I shouldn't feel this way, that it's not rational. That doesn't make the feelings go away. That just makes me feel dumb for having the feelings in the first place."

"Can you see someone different?" Marianne turned in the saddle, concern etching her face.

"No." I took another deep breath and held it a moment, trying to loosen the wrenching tightness in my chest. "I don't think there is anyone else."

I hadn't yet met a therapist that didn't make me feel stupid for my so-called "irrational" fear and anxiety. What good would it do to try someone else? No one could help me. I knew my life would always be like this. At least until God mercifully decided my time was up and allowed my life to be snuffed out like an insignificant flame—barely visible as the cold, dark night closed in around it.

"You just need to see someone better," Marianne said. "I know of a doctor in Lexington who can help you."

"Will this doctor really do something the others haven't?" I couldn't believe there was actually any hope at all of improving my life by seeing someone else.

"Yes." Marianne smiled. "Definitely."

"OK."

I assumed Marianne would give me a name and number I could call, which I would promptly misplace because I still didn't believe a different doctor would make a difference. After all, I was hopelessly damaged. Mean Cheryl said so. That and Therapist Lady said I had a personality disorder. Double whammy.

"Great. We'll go after we get these guys put away." She nodded her head toward Seven and Farletta.

"Now? Tonight?" I asked, scared. No. No. No. Not ready to go anywhere tonight. "No. I can't go tonight."

Surely she didn't mean tonight. It was already after nine.

"Yes, tonight," Marianne replied. "They can help you feel better."

After we stabled the horses, she drove me into Lexington to a mental health clinic with a twenty-four-hour emergency office. Part of me did want help, but the rest of me feared if I sounded too crazy, the staff would admit me into their sterile little loony bin and throw away the key.

Having talked to many different therapists in recent years, I knew what questions they would ask and how to answer them if I wanted to avoid an undesirable label (diagnosis) or a one-way ticket back to the psych ward. I still wasn't convinced this place could help me. It seemed far more likely I was in danger of being trapped in a situation I couldn't get out of without spilling my secret life to half a dozen people, including family members and my employer.

After assuring me they would not interfere with my work schedule, the doctor I spoke to convinced me to attend group therapy meetings. However, after I signed the paperwork confirming I would attend the meetings (as condition of release that night), I soon learned I had exactly one option for attending meetings—ten to one every weekday.

"I can't do ten to one every weekday," I said to the receptionist. "I live and work in Paris! It will take me almost an hour to get here. I can't miss five hours of work a day—I'll get fired!" I was trying not to panic, but I had the sinking feeling I had really screwed up.

"Well, this is important," the receptionist replied in her "stay calm and we won't bring out the straight jacket" voice.

"I *can't* miss work," I said again, this time with as much calm as I could muster. "The guy I just met with said there were lots of time slots available and it would not be hard to fit one in without missing work!"

"There are other times," the receptionist responded, "but they are all between nine and five."

"I *can't* miss work!" I repeated. *Is anyone listening to me?* "What if I refuse all together?" *Careful, dum-dum, they can still admit you.*

"Then your insurance company won't cover any of your expenses today, since you agreed to the recommended treatment and are now backing out," she said unsympathetically.

Dammit! I'd been duped.

"*Idiot!*" Mean Cheryl snickered.

WITH KNOTS IN MY STOMACH, I explained to Karl what had happened and how I was stuck in this treatment group.

He was visibly disappointed. "I thought you were over this," he said, once again driving home the realization that the general public simply did not understand mental health issues. Would we ever get out from under the stigma that the sufferer somehow created their own symptoms? That depression was a sign of weakness or defect? I felt ashamed and terrified I'd screwed everything up, just as I feared all along. I explained about the insurance issue, as if I agreed with him (*I should be over this*) but was trapped by the system. I promised him I would get out of it as soon as I could.

I originally agreed to six weeks of group sessions, but after constant begging to let me out, they finally released me from my agreement after five days. I managed to keep my job but was docked five hours a day for the time I missed. If I had been suffering a "real" illness, I'm sure I would have been able to use sick days, but apparently this was considered personal time and not covered by my salaried position.

After being released from the program, I was referred to a new therapist, which turned out to be a great blessing. Despite the work-related stress of being stuck in the group sessions, I am grateful for Marianne's intervention. Because of her, I finally found a therapist I could talk to who didn't make me feel like a useless idiot for my "irrational" feelings and emotions. Working with Aaron, I finally made some progress as we peeled back layers of pent-up pain, torment, and anger.

I found a few safe subjects to talk about—childhood, work—those which tiptoed the line between "normal" problems and my actual reality. Although Aaron was kind and helpful, I didn't trust him with my secret. Our sessions helped some to identify behaviors that weren't healthy, such as spending so much time alone. But I never told him about how I screamed at myself and tore out my hair or about hitting myself with a hammer or bashing my head into the wall. I couldn't tell him any of that. Then he would *know* I was crazy instead of just suspecting it. I couldn't risk losing the one thing in my life that made me appear to be a normal, functioning member of society—my job.

THE HARD LUMP on my forearm felt warm and tender. I touched it gingerly with the first two fingers of my right hand. Hammer bruise. Long sleeves for the next few day—good thing cooling, autumn temperatures had arrived.

Finally cried out after this last attack from Mean Cheryl, I rolled over on my back and stared at the ceiling. What had set her off this time?

"Listen to you. Jeez, you are a lunatic."

I closed my eyes. The memory poked me. Something had happened the other night, when my mind hung suspended between light and darkness, between meditation and wakefulness. Farletta had come to me. Surely it had been a dream. What had she said? I focused on the image. She stood on a path that wound into darkness. I wanted to follow her. Afraid, I hesitated. She turned her graceful neck and looked back at me.

"Follow me, friend." Her words appeared in my mind. "Follow me. I'll help you through this." I looked ahead of her, the foreboding path twisting into darkness. I took a deep breath, and I followed her.

CHAPTER TWENTY

I arrived at the barn later than I'd planned the Thursday before Thanksgiving 2007. My long-sleeved shirt was the perfect weight for the cool and comfortable evening air. My friend, who was also a coworker, was out of town for a couple of weeks, so I had three dogs with me in addition to Dief. A couple of other boarders had also brought their dogs to the farm that evening, so we had quite a menagerie of four-footed friends romping around the barn. My friend's dogs took off toward the back fields to play, while the ever-loyal Dief stayed right by my side, following me dutifully as I grabbed Farletta's halter and headed out toward the pasture to retrieve her.

Taking a deep breath, I drank in the smells I loved—fallen leaves, damp clay earth, dew-covered grass, and, of course, the horses. The low-hanging sun cast a golden hue over the rolling green hills of the old farm. Farletta and friends grazed on the near side of the closest hill. I whistled to her and rattled the chain latch against the cold steel of the pipe gate. Farletta lifted her head and looked at me.

"C'mon, girl!" I yelled across the short-cropped field of green between us.

Farletta sauntered her way down the hill in my direction. A big bay gelding noticed her departure and trotted after her. Farletta took this as a challenge, so with a squeal and a buck, she took off galloping, clods of dark earth flying from her hooves. She sailed across the pasture, sliding to a stop directly in front of me. I reached out and stroked her soft muzzle.

"Silly girl."

I walked Farletta to the barn and saddled her up for a ride with a friend and her gelding. We rode around the back fields, chatting and enjoying the beautiful evening. The horses' hooves made gentle swishing sounds in the long, cool grass. Such a peaceful ride, contentment washed over me. I had Farletta on a loose rein, her slow, relaxed walk carrying us back toward the barn, just a little ahead of my friend and her gelding. We passed through a narrow area between the paddock and pasture on our way up the incline toward the barn. Just then, the young Thoroughbred in the paddock next to me bolted, galloping around his enclosure with a squeal and throwing in a buck for good measure. Farletta lifted her head, and her eyes widened. Her body tensed, and she took a few jigging trot-walk steps. She surprised me with her startle, as usually nothing bothered her. After all, this was the horse that had been nearly run down by a panicked calf the year before.

"Easy, girl." I picked up the reins to slow her back to a walk. She came right down, and assuming she was over her discomfort, I loosened the reins again.

Complacent in that moment of silence, I turned in the saddle, looking over my shoulder to talk to my friend. The Thoroughbred bolted again, charging toward Farletta from her left side, his hooves pounding the hard-packed clay, sending clods of dirt flying up behind him. At the same moment, five dogs came barreling out of the barn to say hello, and not to be left out, the four horses pastured to our right came charging toward the fence line. This sudden convergence of animals had taken place in the space of a few seconds and caught me unprepared. The intensity of all the animals closing in on us was more than Farletta could bear. She spooked and bolted, throwing me violently backward and off balance. I scrambled, grabbing at reins and leather, trying to regain my seat while my panicked horse galloped inexplicably right at the fence containing the young horse who had been the first to startle her. The gelding ran at the fence, and Farletta turned away sharply.

Suddenly, there was no horse beneath me.

I saw the hard clay ground spinning below. I saw the golden light of the sun reflected off Farletta's left shoulder. I saw my hands grasping at mane. I saw my feet above my head. I saw a wisp of cloud in the darkening sky. I saw the black board fence. And I heard a heavy, crunching thud as I made contact with the ground. The earth moved around me, as if I were watching a poorly recorded video of the grass and the sky, one where the person filming didn't realize the camera was still on as he traversed to his next destination. I lay motionless on the rock-hard ground.

I am dying. My air is gone. I can't breathe. My mouth opened and closed like a fish removed from the water, desperately gasping for life, but no air would come into my body. Panicked, I tried to move, as if getting off my back into an upright position would somehow allow the air to enter my lungs and make everything okay. Residual adrenaline allowed me to achieve an upright position, but I continued to fight for air. The world around me seemed surreal, the colors somehow too crisp. The angle of my view was all wrong ... I felt disoriented. *Am I still sitting up?* I looked at the ground and determined I was still sitting but somehow also floating above it.

Strange sounds originating from somewhere deep inside me seeped out from my parted lips. Short, croaking gasps escaped from me, like air from a leaky balloon. I desperately tried to pull air into my lungs. *How long can I go without breathing?* Finally, after what seemed like an eternity, sips of air moved in and out of my lungs. I fought for more air, and the panic set in more deeply. *I am really stuck here on the ground. I can't move. I can't get up. I can't breathe. I can't escape.*

The pain came slowly at first. A strong but bearable twinge from my left shoulder blade moved through my body. Despite the wisps of air, it was still difficult to breathe. I continued to gasp periodically—an eerie, hollow sound escaping from my throat. With each breath, the pain increased and spread until my insides were on fire. I had fallen off many horses. However, up until now the pain had never been severe enough to prevent me from moving.

Reality seeped in. I was really in trouble. Trapped on the ground, unable to get myself up, I understood how completely dependent I was on the actions of those around me. *Terrifying.*

I slipped out of my body. I could feel the pain, the panic, the fear and anxiety, but as if it were happening to someone else. Like a well-written story in which the author can elicit the same feelings in the listener as she describes in the character—I both was and was not this person lying on the cement-like earthen surface. I heard snippets of conversation, as if listening through a closed door:

"Did someone catch Farletta?"

"I got her. She's really worked up. I gave her some hay in her stall."

"Get those dogs away from her."

"I'll put them in the car."

"Dief won't leave her."

"He's probably OK. Let him stay."

"The ambulance is on the way …"

Someone took off my helmet. Someone else removed my half-chaps. Sirens wailed in the distance. The conversation faded. Darkness closed around me. I disappeared into the night sky.

CHAPTER TWENTY-ONE

My brief hospital stay was one of the most degrading and humiliating experiences I'd ever endured in my thirty-one years of living.

When I fell off my horse, I crash landed at an estimated thirty miles per hour onto my left shoulder blade. The force of the one-point impact resulted in severe damage to my left shoulder, seven broken ribs, and a partially collapsed lung. I was lucky I didn't land on my head, as I suspect I would have broken my neck—however, in my current state of mind, a broken neck would have been a positive if it had killed me. After being poked, prodded, pulled, and moved from gurney to gurney in the emergency room, I felt more pain than when they'd brought me in. Turned out you can't get pain meds until after they look you over so you are able to "tell them where it hurts," while well-meaning ER staff torture you with an examination. Good times.

When they were finally done inspecting, harassing, and radiographing the obvious injuries, I only wanted to be left alone. *Please, God, don't let them touch me anymore!* So when the doctors asked if anything else was hurting, I lied and said no, even though a dull throb pulsed in my right hip. The hip did not complain as loudly as the rest of my body parts, so I ignored the ache and hoped it would go away.

Disregarding the pain was the only way to get the doctors and nurses to stop touching me and was the fastest way to get pain meds.

At nearly midnight, the nurses settled me in my room. I'd needed to use the bathroom for several hours, but intense pain had prevented me from paying too much attention to that particular body request, until now. Lying on my back, unable to move, I realized this request had now become an urgent demand. I looked around for a nurse Call button. Every small movement sent new waves of pain and nausea through my body, emanating from my ruined shoulder and searing across my broken ribs. Taking a breath sent a hideously sharp pain through my chest and back, like someone dragging shards of broken glass through my muscles. The pain remained sharply present even after movement stopped, eventually turning to a burning sensation, which finally decreased to a dull throb. I moved my head carefully from side to side but was unable to locate the Call button. A feeble attempt to move my arm was rewarded by a new wave of burning, searing pain and rolling nausea, ending in a room-spinning sensation with my head threatening to float out the door.

A young nurse came in to check on me.

"I need to use the restroom."

"OK." She stood next to the bed, looking at me.

I soon realized she was waiting for me to get up and go.

"I could use some help getting up." I lifted my head slightly off my pillow.

"Oh, OK." She moved closer but still made no effort to help me move.

Great. I'd gotten my wish. No one was touching me. I tried to sit up, an action that resulted in pain shooting through my body, accompanied by a deep burning sensation in the muscles around my left shoulder, which then radiated down my left side. A sharp gasp was rewarded with daggers stabbing into my back and lungs.

Fuck me, I cried under my breath.

"I can't sit up on my own. Can you help me?"

"Yes," the still-unmoving nurse replied.

She appeared terrified of me. Slowly, like the last bit of ketchup sliding out of the bottle, I realized she wasn't going to help me get up. I wondered if she knew how to help someone in my position, as she seemed inexperienced.

"We're not supposed to pull on you," she said, perhaps reading the perplexed look on my face.

"How do I get up? I can't push with my arms."

"We're not supposed to pull on you," she repeated.

My God I am worthless. Obviously they think I'm overreacting or being a total wuss. Shame burned my face.

Through a series of painful and decidedly ungraceful lurches, grunts, and wiggling movements, I finally found myself perched on the edge of the bed with my feet resting lightly on the floor. I only needed to stand up and walk a few steps to get to the bathroom. I carefully slid off the edge and onto my feet. Pain shot through my right hip (the one I'd ignored), and for a terrifying moment I wondered if it would support me. I eased more weight onto my feet and straightened. Every part of me screamed out as intense, white-hot pain worked its way from my shoulder blade, winding around my ribs, eventually traveling through my hip and shooting down my leg. Still not touching me, the nurse stood by my left side with an utterly bored look on her face. I could almost hear her thoughts, as if they were seeping from her pores: *I hate my job. Why can't this idiot woman just hurry up?*

I reached for the unsmiling nurse's arm to steady myself. She allowed me to hold her, but she offered no support or resistance and therefore felt similar to trying to steady myself with the aid of a wet noodle. I staggered a couple steps forward, putting out my right hand to catch the doorjamb. The room spun and lurched like a carnival fun house. Beads of icy sweat appeared on my forehead. My palms were cold and clammy, and I thought I would vomit.

"I feel so dizzy," I said with a gasp.

She said nothing, her blank face told me she either didn't know what to do or simply didn't care. Fearing I might lose consciousness, I twisted and hurled myself toward the toilet, landing painfully half on and half off the seat. Thankfully, I'd landed in a sitting position, rather than on the floor in a dejected heap. At this point I checked out, and my mind drifted once again to that place just above my body.

I think the nurse helped me work my underwear down around my knees and pulled the hospital gown out of the way. She stood over me and watched as I relieved myself. Somehow I scooted myself off the commode and back to my feet. I stood swaying in the cold fluorescent light of the hospital-white bathroom, my underwear around my calves. I lacked the mobility to wipe myself or pull up my own underwear. I felt like a helpless and shamed little girl, a grown woman who couldn't even perform the most basic act of self-care. On the verge of tears, I looked at the unsmiling nurse.

"I'm sorry," I said to her blank face. "I can't wipe. This is so embarrassing. I can't move my arms like that. Can you help me? It's just urine. I'm so sorry."

A barely audible sigh escaped her tight lips, but she said nothing. She donned some latex gloves, wetted a washcloth with warm water, and without stepping any closer than necessary, reached her arm out and dabbed at my bum. Of course that was not the part that needed wiping, but I had endured as much humiliation as I could tolerate at this point, so I didn't press her.

"Thanks," I muttered.

The nurse stepped away, still silent, still unsmiling.

"I can't reach my underwear. I can't bend over. I'm so sorry. Can you help me?"

The unsmiling nurse halfheartedly tugged at my underwear until it was within my reach. The burning pain tore through my body as I bent and pulled my underwear into place. When the room spun again, I gave it up and lurched toward the beckoning mattress, somehow maneuvering myself into the bed. Out of breath and sweating, I gave up trying to find a comfortable position. The nurse retreated, and I was alone.

A few hours later I had to go to the bathroom again but decided to say nothing. I would hold it as long as I possibly could so as to avoid the physical pain and the emotional shame that had accompanied my previous trip.

My left arm was basically useless. It wasn't broken, but because of the broken ribs and the damage to muscles and tendons in and around my shoulder, it was painful to even try to move it. As a result, I could not work the bed controller, press the nurse Call button, reach the TV remote, or reach the water on the bedside table, because all were on my left side.

Around eight the next morning, a new, smiling nurse replaced the unsmiling nurse. This nurse was middle aged and had a kind look. She seemed chipper and energetic. What a relief! Someone who knew her job and liked it. Maybe she could help me.

"Here is your breakfast!" She placed a tray of food on my bedside table. She observed my full water pitcher and frowned. "You should really be drinking water!"

"I can't reach the pitcher," I said.

"Oh! I see." She poured a glass of water and placed it next to the tray on the side table.

"Thanks, but I can't ..."

"You're welcome!" the nurse chirped as she left the room.

I said nothing. Clearly I needed to toughen up. *Worthless garbage.*

I regarded the food on my side table. I couldn't reach it. I painfully attempted to lift my left arm, with no success. I found I could tolerate the pain if I only moved my arm from the elbow down, allowing my upper arm to remain supported by the bed and keeping my shoulder immobile. Carefully lifting my left forearm, I tried to hook my fingers under the edge of the side table. After several minutes I succeeded in moving the table close enough to reach the corner of the food tray. I then used my fingertips to bring the tray closer to the edge of the table. Finally, after about fifteen minutes, I secured my prize—a corner of toast was between my left middle and index fingers. I let my arm fall from the side table back to the bed.

It was then I realized I still couldn't reach my mouth with my toast prize. I flicked my left wrist and tossed the toast onto my chest, where I could reach it with my decidedly more mobile right hand and transfer it to my mouth. The toast was the only thing on the food tray I could reach and eat.

A couple hours later, the chipper nurse returned. She looked at my still-full food tray.

"You didn't eat very much." She frowned. "You must not be very hungry."

"Actually, I am hungry. I just couldn't reach the tray table. My left arm doesn't move very well."

"Oh! You should have said something! Why didn't you push the Call button?"

"I can't reach that either," I replied.

"Oh!"

The nurse moved the Call button closer to my left arm (but still out of my limited reach) and shoved the side table closer to me. "Call if you need anything!" she chirped over her shoulder as she darted out of the room.

With the tray table closer, I was able to reach the breakfast plate in the same manner as I had the toast. Using my grab-and-toss method, I managed to eat most of the now-cold eggs and sausage.

Eventually I dozed off.

Despite my negative experiences, I felt scared to leave the hospital because I worried that with my significant lack of mobility, I'd be unable to care for myself. Thankfully, my friend Mike (the manager at Sunland Farm) found someone to help me, a kind physical therapist, the only person I met outside the ER who actually took time to listen and try to understand what was going on with me. Given the nature of my injury (blunt-force trauma to my shoulder blade), she questioned why the nurses had me in a lying position in the first place, stating that was the worst position for me to be in, as it caused constant pressure on my injury. She helped raise the hospital bed to a sitting position. I felt immediate relief. She then showed me various techniques to help me rise from a sitting position with little assistance. Thanks to her efforts, I finally felt like I would be safe at home alone. Tears flowed down my cheeks when I thanked her for listening to and helping me.

Mike drove me home and helped me settle into my recliner, where I would spend the next few months. He left me with beverages and painkillers on a side table next to the remote controls for the TV and DVD player. Mike and Jess (a friend and coworker from Claiborne) came and checked on me periodically, and each brought delicious home cooking for me, a real treat. Mike also restocked my groceries when I needed them. Marianne supplied me with dozens of DVDs, and the boarders at Sunland took turns making sure Farletta had what she needed in my absence. Nothing for me to do but sit, recover, watch movies, and eat.

I had been active prior to the accident, working forty to forty-eight hours a week, walking several miles a day, hiking or visiting horse events on my days off, and spending time with Farletta every day. The accident ceased all activity. The lack of mobility in my arm and upper body made it unsafe to drive, so I was homebound for weeks, unless someone came for me. The sudden change from active and engaged in life—albeit superficially, for I never dared let my guard down enough to engage fully in anything—to an inactive recluse seemed to have no effect on me, at least none that I or anyone else detected. Vaguely aware of the nonchalant attitude I had regarding the accident, I talked about it matter of factly, without emotion. It was just a thing that happened, no big deal.

Before long the memory of the accident became like something I had read in a book. Indeed an unfortunate event, but it felt like it had happened to someone else.

Despite weeks of sitting alone, I didn't feel bored or depressed. In fact, I didn't feel anything. The part of me that felt fear, anger, sadness, frustration, or any other emotion had disappeared. I existed physically with just enough awareness to function, but emotionally I had checked out. *Cheryl has left the building.*

Dissociation is the psychological term for it—I was there, but I wasn't.

MARIANNE DROVE me out to visit Farletta two weeks after the accident. While I hobbled into the barn, carefully navigating the uneven ground, Marianne moved a soft chair in front of Farletta's stall and then went out to the pasture to get my horse. I carefully, painfully lowered myself into the chair and waited. Farletta entered the barn, her body silhouetted against the backlight provided by the sun shining through the open doorway. Tears immediately stung my eyes, the first emotion I'd felt in weeks. I'd missed her so much. Marianne led Farletta into her stall and released her. The mare nickered loudly and thrust her head over the half-wall to where I sat. She nuzzled my face and shoulders before moving her upper lip all around my head, tousling my hair and gently moving my head from side to side. I'd only had such a joyous greeting from one other horse—when I'd visited Corky for the first time after selling him. I had cried then too.

I sat with Farletta, talking to her and stroking her soft muzzle. Peace washed over me in her presence. I had missed her—my *soul* had missed her. I could have stayed for hours in the protective shadow of my mare, but it soon became difficult and painful to remain seated. I said goodbye to Farletta and told her I'd be back soon.

It took several weeks before I finally managed driving myself to the barn to visit Farletta. I had limited use of my left arm but was able to groom her and walk her around. I thought a lot about riding her during these visits. *I can't wait to ride again!* I'd say to myself, and I believed it. I didn't feel apprehensive. I felt confident I could avoid a repeat of the accident by being more mindful of what was happening around me and the signals Farletta gave me. The accident had happened because I wasn't careful enough. *My fault.* This was important for me to believe—if something was my fault, that meant I had the power to control and therefore prevent it.

The days and the nights ran together until I could hardly separate one from another. I drew pictures of Farletta, filling my sketchbook with images of me riding her. I looked ahead to an imaginary future, assuming everything would be the same. We'd pick up right where we'd left off. After all, Farletta and I were an unshakeable team. I would take her to shows, like I had Corky. She'd win awards, and we'd be successful. Everything would be great. Farletta would need to be registered with an official name if I wanted to show her. She would always be Farletta, of course, but she needed something fancier for the show ring. I scrawled a few names on the page beneath one of my drawings of Farletta. Looking them over, my pencil settled on one. I underlined her new name, made up of the three words from my dream: Follow Me Friend.

PART IV
PATH OF THE PEACE HORSE

CHAPTER TWENTY-TWO

Four months after the accident, I finally had enough mobility in my hip and shoulders to ride my horse safely, at least at a walk. My ribs still hurt (apparently broken ribs take forever to stop hurting), but I felt confident I could handle the pain. On a warm spring day, I saddled Farletta up for the first time since I'd fallen off her. I snugged up the cinch to ensure the saddle was secure before taking her to the arena to longe. I used longeing as a safety precaution, because if the horse had any surprises for me, I'd rather learn about them with my feet planted safely on the ground. Farletta obediently walked, trotted, and cantered around me. She seemed pleased to be working again.

Although I'd previously ridden her almost exclusively in her dressage saddle, on this day I decided perhaps the sturdier western saddle was a better choice, although I'd never ridden in it before. I bridled Farletta, strapped on my helmet, and led her to the mounting block. Carefully and somewhat painfully, I climbed up the two steps to the wooden platform. Farletta stood perfectly still as I put my left foot in the stirrup. *Deep breaths, Cheryl. You'll be fine.* I placed my left hand on the crest of Farletta's neck and my right hand on the saddle's pommel, just to the right of the horn.

"Whoa girl," I said.

Farletta stood like a statue. I was grateful for her unwavering stance as I prepared to mount. Taking another deep breath, I counted *one two three* in my head. On *three* I simultaneously pressed my foot into the left stirrup and pushed off with my right leg. The back of the saddle was much higher than I was used to, and I hadn't anticipated the lost range of motion in my injured hip. My thigh caught on the cantle as I attempted to swing my right leg over the saddle. *Oh crap. Not good.* Unable to bring my leg back to the safety of the mounting block, I attempted to throw my weight over the saddle in an effort to dislodge my hung-up leg. I succeeded in getting my right leg over the cantle but had put too much *oomph* into the motion and overshot the saddle. I found myself hanging off Farletta's right side in a general panic, followed closely by sheer terror.

Gripped with immobilizing fear, I clung to the side of my horse.

"I don't want to fall off. I don't want to fall off …" I whimpered over and over, tightly squeezing my tear-filled eyes shut. A fellow boarder standing nearby ran over and shoved me onto my horse. I sat in the saddle, trembling. Any and all confidence I had once possessed left me like a rapidly retreating army that just discovered they were devastatingly overmatched. I felt naked and alone. Like everything I knew, every fact I clung to, had suddenly been disproven.

I wanted to get off my horse. Right now. I had made a mistake. I wasn't ready. I couldn't do this. As much as I wanted to call it quits, a part of me needed to save face. Driven by that stubborn part that is a product of deeply held Midwestern work ethic—you must never, ever quit, and never, ever let them know something is wrong—I wouldn't allow myself to bail out. I sat up straight in the saddle, brought my legs under me, and pressed my heels down in an effort to give myself the most secure seat possible. Taking a deep, shuddering breath, I gently squeezed Farletta with my lower legs, asking her to walk. Farletta moved forward obediently, taking gentle steps, as if she understood just how fragile the tiny remnants of my destroyed confidence were.

After the first several strides, I relaxed. I hadn't forgotten how to keep my balance and move my body with the motion of the horse. I steered Farletta around the arena, making several large loops in each direction. After about ten minutes, I'd proven to myself I could get on the horse and ride—sufficient for one day.

Dismounting proved to be a daunting task because I had the same problem I had mounting—my right hip had poor range of motion. Fortunately, sitting astride Farletta had stretched the hip flexors and increased my mobility. My right thigh stuck for a brief moment on the back of the saddle when I swung my leg over to dismount. Panic seeped in. I hung suspended in this precarious position—my right leg stuck on the back of the saddle with my head pointing down near Farletta's right shoulder. The ground seemed to move back and forth beneath me, and I imagined falling head first onto the hard, crushed-limestone surface. If I was lucky, I'd break my neck and die. If I was unlucky, I'd only be maimed and useless. *More useless.* I shook the image from my mind. Taking a deep breath and holding it, I managed to jerk my right leg over the back of the saddle and slid safely to the ground.

"Thank you," I whispered to Farletta, stroking her neck. "Thank you for being such a good girl and taking care of me."

Farletta worked the bit in her mouth. Her face showed a sort of curious confusion. I was not the same, not the same at all, and she could feel it. My confidence had washed away, the tattered post-fall remnants being crushed to oblivion by the fiasco that had been my first attempt at mounting since the accident. I stood at Farletta's left shoulder, feeling alone and defeated. Tears silently crept down my cheeks. Farletta reached her muzzle around and gently touched my arm. My fingers traced the long, narrow blaze that ran down her face. We turned and walked back to the barn.

I erroneously thought getting back on Farletta would be the hardest part, as if conquering the fear once would disempower it. The first mounting experience wasn't liberation from fear but rather set the stage for what was to come—years of struggle, tears, heart-wrenching grief, and hopelessness.

I don't remember riding Farletta again after that first post-accident ride. I'm sure I did, but I have no recollection of ever riding her again in Kentucky.

CHAPTER TWENTY-THREE

Two months into my recovery period, Claiborne asked me to take a leave of absence (Karl stressed I was not "fired"). They had kept me on as an employee, let me stay in my house on the farm rent-free, and even paid me for the first six weeks after my fall. When it became evident I would not be able to return to work soon, they understandably wanted their house back, so I left. I temporarily moved in with Mike, who had a spare bedroom in his house at Sunland Farm, and found nonphysical work doing foal watch at a farm owned by one of Karl's sons.

During the time I was figuring out my next steps, my best friend, Sarah, was dealt a terrible and unfair blow that left her devastated and in need of a friend. Six months had passed since my accident, and my temporary foaling job was coming to an end, so I packed up everything that would fit in my Dodge Dakota, hired a friend to haul Farletta, and moved my little family to Ohio. Dief and I moved in with Sarah in her new house, and I found a boarding stable nearby for Farletta.

Although the circumstances that brought me to Ohio were unfortunate, my time living with my best friend was like a childhood dream come true. Sarah and I helped each other that summer, supporting each other through our own personal transitions. We spent hours talking about life, hiking with the dogs (Sarah had rescued a border collie puppy shortly before I arrived), cooking meals together, and just hanging out. That summer brought us closer together—now both in our early thirties, we'd been friends for twenty years. It was good to reconnect so deeply as adults. I was also glad I could take a step toward returning the gift Sarah had given me by coming to Tennessee when I needed support so badly a few years before.

It was during that summer in Ohio I have my first memory of riding Farletta a second time, although I can't recall any details. When I think of it, I see snapshots in my mind, tiny glimpses of me riding Farletta, as if I were viewing us from above. This is a fairly accurate description of how I lived my post-accident life, viewed from above. I had dissociated—not that I had any clue what was going on or even what it really meant to be disconnected from my body. My mind seemed to float far above me, in a place I felt safe, a place I had learned to go when … *what?* I still couldn't penetrate that black curtain in my mind. *You don't want to know what's back there anyway*, the little girl with the black horse said ominously.

I tried to return to my previous level of confidence and ability in the saddle. I did all right for a while, eventually taking Farletta to her first under-saddle show that summer in Ohio. But later, when I looked back on those memories, I could recall no detail, no sensation of my horse moving underneath me, no joy when I won a class, no elation at reaching new goals. I retained only those odd, disconnected memories made up of snapshots in time, viewed from some invisible perch above my head.

CHAPTER TWENTY-FOUR

I first realized the fall from Farletta might have impacted me beyond the physical realm the summer in Ohio after the accident. I was discussing it with Sarah, as always only disclosing the events as if recounting the plot of a movie rather than reliving a part of my life. I wasn't fully aware of what I was doing. I spoke about the accident as if it were no big deal, as if stuff like that happened all the time. In my mind I minimized the accident. This was doubly true when I spoke of it to others.

"But it *was* a big deal!" Sarah exclaimed, her voice rising in frustration.

I tried to understand the exasperated look on her face. Why did she care? What did she see? I half shrugged my left shoulder, made a "no big deal" face, and cast my eyes down at my feet. The tension in the air felt like it would crush me.

"We should get moving," I said. "It's getting hot in here for the dogs."

"They're fine," Sarah said sharply. "They have water, and we're parked in the shade."

I looked out the front windshield of Sarah's black Chrysler 300.

Sitting on my hands as I often did, I pulled my right hand from under my thigh.

"The sun is going to be below this tree soon." I motioned with the newly freed hand toward the sun dropping lower in the afternoon sky. "Then it will get hot in here."

Sarah rolled her eyes.

I turned to Diefenbaker and Sarah's dog, Red, in the backseat. "You guys don't want to get all hot, do you?"

They both stared at me, Dief wagging his stump. Thump, thump, thump, Red's fluffy, slightly curled border collie tail flopped against the smooth leather seat.

"Why can't you admit it?" Sarah asked.

"Admit what?" I pretended I didn't know what she was getting at.

Sarah was frustrated now. I could see it in her face and wondered how long I could dance around the subject before this escalated into a full-fledged argument.

Sarah's brow wrinkled with concern as her blue eyes stared into mine from the driver's seat. "You could have died. Can't you see that? It *was* a big deal. You could have *died!*" she repeated, emphasizing each word.

Tears stung my eyes, and I turned away from her, looking down at my feet resting on the gray floor mat.

"Say it." Sarah looked at me intently.

"Say what?" I whispered, still pretending I didn't know what she was getting at.

Sarah sighed and placed her hand on my left arm. "Say 'I almost died,'" she said softly.

"Why?" I questioned in a barely audible whisper. A single tear crept slowly down my left cheek.

"Because I don't think you know, I don't think you understand, just how serious it was."

I said nothing and continued to stare at my feet.

"Please." Sarah leaned in. "Just say it. Say it out loud: 'I could have died. I fell off my horse, and I could have died.'"

I looked at my friend, unable to speak.

"Say it," she repeated.

I took a deep breath. "I fell off my horse ..." I whispered.

"That's right." Encouragement rose her voice. "Then what?"

"I fell off my horse ... I *fell* off my *horse!*" I repeated, drawing out the word *horse*. More tears rolled down my cheeks. My shoulders jerked, and I gasped loudly.

"And ..." Sarah prodded.

"I could ... have ... died." My voice squeaked, then trailed off into a barely perceptible whisper.

Suddenly I catapulted back to that November evening in Kentucky. No longer in a car in Ohio, I lay frozen on the hard ground where Farletta had lost me. I couldn't breathe. I gasped for air, placing one frantic hand on my chest as the other grabbed at the dashboard. My chest heaved as I struggled for air, but I couldn't seem to will it into my lungs. Panic rose steadily.

"I can't breathe." My voice a jagged whisper, I lurched in my seat.

Only partially aware my body sat safely in Sarah's car, my mind had returned to the accident, and I felt as if I were living it all over again. I gasped for breath and cried while my body relived the sensations of the fall and its terrible aftermath. *What the hell is happening?* I wondered. *What is wrong with me?*

Sarah moved her hand toward me. I grabbed it and squeezed while my body shook. Together we sat while I relived those terror-filled moments. I struggled to push the emotions back behind the black curtain. *This is not safe*, I thought. *It's not safe to remember.*

"I USED TO BE A HORSE TRAINER."

The words scraped at my eardrums and tore at my soul. I hated the sound of them as they came out of my mouth over and over again.

"How did you go from *that* to social work?" would come the reply from the stranger, friend, or family member with the perplexed look, one I grew to hate as much as the grating "I used to be ..." statement.

With a deep sigh and a downward glance, I'd launch into a well-rehearsed series of reasons justifying my sudden about-face, which put me into the role of nontraditional college student as I navigated the path representing my early thirties.

The fall from Farletta made me seriously rethink my life as a horse professional. I was thirty-one and had been debilitated by a fall from my own horse, a horse I should have been safe on. Could I really expect myself to physically continue doing this work until retirement age? I explored other ideas, knowing from my experiences in Tennessee I had to somehow remain involved with horses.

I decided to go to school again. Perhaps I could work in a field where horses helped people in the way horses like Corky, Splatters, Farley, and Farletta had helped me connect to others and feel safe(r) in the world around me. I researched different schools and programs and determined my best bet would be a social work program, not because I wanted to be a social worker but because it provided an excellent skill set. I believed this would enable me to reach my new career goal: working in the field of equine-assisted therapies.

Sounds safe, right? No riding required. Not that I admitted that aloud or even to myself right away, but the no-riding-required part appealed to me. With this new goal, I moved Farletta and Dief from Ohio back to my hometown—Kalamazoo, Michigan. My stepdad, Rick, had recently passed away, and my mom was living alone for the first time in over twenty years. We agreed it would benefit us both if I moved back into the house I'd grown up in—Mom would have some much-needed companionship, and I would be able to keep my living expenses low while in school.

Mom was glad to have me back and to mother me. I easily slipped back into the role of the adult child I'd been before I'd moved to Kewanee twelve years earlier.

CHAPTER TWENTY-FIVE

Most people didn't know the truth about the terror I felt whenever I attempted to get on Farletta. I wasn't scared to *ride* her. My problem had to do with *getting on* her. The idea of mounting Farletta brought me to tears. I would stand on the mounting block next to her with one hand on her reins and the other on the saddle. Tears streaming down my face, body shaking, I teetered on the edge of panic as I placed my trembling foot in the stirrup, preparing to mount. Not surprisingly, Farletta reacted negatively to my behavior, which of course heightened my fear and in turn increased her anxiety—a terrible looping cycle, more dreadful with each pass.

Still somewhat green herself, she was now undergoing multiple new experiences—moving from state to state, learning new skills, attending horse shows. Now I was asking her, an animal with the instinct to respond to fear with flight, to stand quietly while I shook and cried and attempted to get on her. She'd jig and move back and forth, then step away from me when I put my foot in the stirrup and walk off as soon as my right foot left the mounting block. Her sudden and unpredictable movements turned my fear into panic-driven terror.

Still, I continued to push myself to ride Farletta, attempting to regain my former level of confidence, strength, and ability. However, it seemed the more I pushed, the more I withdrew. I'd been showing horses for nearly twenty years and had always enjoyed it, thriving on the competition and the thrill of connecting with a horse so completely that we performed in beautiful harmony as a single being. I showed Farletta in Introductory Level dressage tests, although I had shown at higher levels in the past. (Corky was two levels above Introductory.) I didn't feel capable of riding at a higher level. My confidence had been destroyed.

On the surface it probably appeared I had pretty much recovered from the trauma of the fall that had occurred less than two years before. Farletta and I did extremely well in our shows and took many first-place ribbons and championship awards. But each time I went to mount her—tears, anxiety, and body-shaking terror were my constant and unwanted companions.

"I CAN'T DO THIS ... I can't do this." My body trembled, my chest tightening with every shallow breath.

A kind stranger at the horse show had seen my distress and come over to help. "It's OK," she spoke soothingly.

"I'm sorry ... I can't ... I mean I can ... but I can't ... I don't know why I get like this." My stomach lurched and churned. Hot tears burned a path down my reddened cheeks. The kind woman rubbed Farletta's neck.

"She's OK. She's nice and quiet."

"I know. She's so good. I just ... we had an accident ... I can't ... I'm just not the same anymore ... if ... if I can just get on her, everything will be OK." My voice wavered and cracked. *You sound like such an idiot.*

"I'll stay here as long as you need me to," the woman said.

"Thank you so much. I ... I'm almost ready." I took a deep breath and held it a moment, trying to loosen the tightness in my chest. I let the breath out slowly. I placed my foot in the stirrup and swung my leg over. *I did it!* The anxiety flowed out of me, dissipating into the ground beneath Farletta's hooves. I took another deep breath and let it out slowly. The butterflies vanished. "I'm OK now. Thank you so much for your help. Thank you. It's really just the getting-on part. We ride fine. I just get so anxious about getting on."

"I know," the woman said. "I've watched you. You're really a great team. We all have our stuff, don't we?"

I nodded, grateful for her kind words and assistance.

"I'd better get her warmed up. Thank you again. I really appreciate your help."

"Any time," the woman said with a smile.

I squeezed Farletta's sides with my lower legs. She walked off as if nothing unusual had happened. We competed successfully all weekend, even winning the overall championship in our division. No one knew how much anxiety and difficulty arose each time I had to get on Farletta, no one except me and the helpful stranger. The show season continued on like this, my fear never lessening, only increasing until soon it became too much to overcome.

That winter I started my full-time schedule at Western Michigan University working toward my bachelor's degree in social work, and also worked full-time at Target. Naturally this took up much of my time, but it also became an excuse to avoid riding Farletta. I always found time to brush her, longe her, and do other unmounted activities with her, but I seldom found the time to ride her. When I did manage to get on her back, an event always preceded by the same crippling anxiety I'd experienced all summer, my rides were always short and within the confines of the arena. My adventurous pre-accident self was nowhere to be found.

Then it grew worse. Mounting became a huge production that required Farletta to stand perfectly still. The saddle had to be adjusted exactly right, with the stirrups in a specific position in relation to the mounting block. The block could not be too short or too tall, and Farletta had to be in exactly the right position with her feet squarely under her body. If anything changed, such as trying a new girth, a new saddle pad, or even new reins, my level of terror and apprehension compounded. Trying a new saddle or mounting from an unfamiliar block brought an almost crippling terror.

Farletta grew increasingly tense around me, constantly moving forward and backward within the confines of the rope when tied to the hitching post. She squirmed beneath my touch, no longer enjoying my brushing her or even scratching her favorite itchy spots. Much of the time, it seemed like all Farletta wanted was get away from me, as if she could hardly wait for me to put her outside. By winter of that same year, I could hardly bring her into the barn. She'd paw at the concrete aisle, raising her front hoof high in the air before lowering it to the ground and digging at the hard floor beneath her. She was clearly in distress, and I seemed to be the cause.

CHAPTER TWENTY-SIX

The sun shone bright, reflecting off a fresh blanket of powder with such intensity it hurt my eyes. January 2010 brought with it the usual subfreezing temperatures and several feet of snow. We tolerated the brutal weather in Michigan, justifying the frigid temps as a fair trade-off for the typically mild summers.

I stepped out of my truck into the shin-deep snow. The air bit at my face, and the moisture in my nostrils froze as I took in short, shallow breaths, not wanting to pull the frigid air too deeply into my lungs. I pulled up the hood of the sweatshirt I wore under my heavy winter coat and tied it snugly around my head so that it closed partway around my face. Now I looked like Kenny from *Southpark*. Pulling on my gloves, I trudged through the snow toward the barn door.

Turning the frozen knob, the door opened inward with a little shove. I stepped across the raised threshold onto the frozen cement of the barn aisle. The air seemed colder in the un-insulated barn. Frost clung to the metal siding, and I imagined for a moment the temptation for a small child to put his or her tongue to the frost only to discover it stuck to the cold metal. It's a lesson I learned—perhaps it is a temptation all kids growing up in a cold climate eventually give in to.

I walked across the barn to the large sliding door on the other side. Grabbing the frozen metal with gloved hands, I pulled hard against it. At first receiving nothing but a hollow creak for my effort, it eventually slid far enough to wedge my body into the small opening between the edge of the door and the jamb. Placing both hands on the door, I pressed my back against the jamb and shoved hard. At first the frozen door didn't budge, but finally, with a groan, it slid open far enough for me to bring Farletta in.

The sun sparkled off the snow, creating a blinding glare. I closed my eyes against it as I reached up for the sunglasses perched on my head, and I lowered them to my eyes. I looked out into the large field in front of me. The mares were huddled in a group, eating hay out of the large round-bale feeder. I whistled to Farletta.

"C'mon, girl!" I called over the frozen field.

Farletta turned her head at my call. She watched for a long moment, as if contemplating the value of coming to me versus staying with her herd and the hay. She turned back and took another mouthful of hay, chewing it thoughtfully before and making her way across the frozen ground.

I stood at the gate and watched her pick her way carefully through the minefield of frozen hoofprints. Due to the weather, I hadn't been able to get to the boarding stable for a few days, and I was anxious to see her.

"Hey sweetie," I called softly as Farletta approached the gate.

Her right eye was squinting, which was unusual, even with the bright sun. I unlatched the gate and went through the opening. "How are you, baby girl?" I whispered, reaching out with my gloved hand to stroke her fuzzy forehead.

Farletta lowered her head as I lifted the halter and slipped it over her ears. Together we turned toward the open barn.

I'd gotten used to Farletta dancing, pawing, and even calling out to her herd mates whenever I brought her into the barn. Such obnoxious behaviors seemed to be our new normal, but I hated it. Today Farletta was unusually quiet. She still kept a close eye on the herd, but she didn't seem anxious to get outside again.

Even in the dimly lit barn, Farletta held her right eye closed. Her eyelids looked puffy. Using my fingers to push her eyelids apart, I took a closer look. What I saw there was like nothing I had ever seen. My heart sank. Farletta's beautiful brown eye was a hazy greenish-blue color. Her pupil had virtually disappeared—her eye appeared completely made up of discolored iris. Floating along the bottom quarter of her eye was what looked like greenish mucus.

"Oh, honey, what is going on?"

After giving an anti-inflammatory/analgesic known as bute to make Farletta comfortable, I went home and spent several hours online searching her symptoms. The information pointed toward a disease of the eye known as equine recurrent uveitis (ERU), a disease the old-timers called "moon blindness," because it was once believed the symptomatic flare-ups coincided with various phases of the moon.

My heart sank as I read details of a typical ERU diagnosis: severe pain, inflammation, no cure, eventual blindness. I closed my eyes and was catapulted back in time, back to the day I received the news of Farley's EPM. The hopelessness and helplessness I felt then welled up in me again like a familiar, but unwelcome, visitor.

Upon examination, my local vet agreed it looked like uveitis but advised me to get confirmation from an equine eye specialist. She referred us to Dr. Brown at a clinic about an hour away. Farletta was officially diagnosed with ERU on February 3, 2010, her seventh birthday. I had no idea then what torture my poor, sweet girl was in for while Dr. Brown and I worked to preserve her diseased eye.

ERU cannot be cured, only managed. The goal of treatment is to minimize and treat flare-ups in an attempt to preserve vision in the eye as long as possible. You can't stop or reverse ERU, only try to slow it down. I was somewhat hopeful when Farletta was originally diagnosed, Dr. Brown thought she might only have a few flare-ups a year and we could preserve her vision through treatment for five to ten years. Unfortunately, this was not the case.

An ERU flare-up has been likened to a severe, unrelenting migraine headache. The eye experiences severe spasms as the pupil constricts, often to the point of invisibility. The eyelids swell, and the pink tissues surrounding the inside of the eye socket turn an angry red. Without treatment the constricted pupil can become permanently stuck, as it atrophies in place. Each time the eye experiences a flare-up, permanent damage is done and further vision is lost.

On Dr. Brown's recommendation, I started a journal, which eventually became a public blog and, later, a Facebook support group for owners of ERU horses. The purpose of the journal was an attempt to identify and avoid triggers, with the goal of preventing flare-ups. Farletta's primary trigger seemed to be sunlight, which I combatted by only turning her out at night and working with her either in an indoor arena or outside at dusk. However, as time went on, Farletta's list of triggers grew longer. Dust, wind, certain fly sprays, vaccinations, bug bites, and any stress could all trigger a painful flare-up.

Farletta did not do well on her ERU medications. She continued to have flare-ups, and the daily dose of bute Dr. Brown had prescribed soon led to a severe impaction colic, which very nearly killed her. After days of hospitalization and round-the-clock treatment, Farletta finally passed the impaction and returned home. She was skinny and weak but alive.

Farletta continued to have flare-ups of her uveitis throughout 2010, which kept me from riding her much. Due to my fears of mounting, it worked well to have a ready-made excuse not to ride. In September she had an experimental eye surgery in which a cyclosporine implant was placed into her diseased eye. Like her previous treatments, the surgery helped temporarily, but eventually it also failed to prevent flare-ups.

While Farletta and I continued to battle her uveitis, I studied my way through social work classes, which involved a great deal of reflective writing. You can multiply that times three for a master's program. I suppose you can write the papers without truly taking a look into your own life, but in order to get a perfect grade (my primary concern), be a good social worker (my secondary concern), and perhaps most importantly, learning to understand yourself (a concern not even on my radar), you must be willing to take a hard, honest look at what makes you tick. The only way to do this is to poke around inside the darkest parts of your subconscious, unearthing secrets, long-forgotten events, and the feelings those memories dredge up, as well as those deep, dark secrets you keep not only from everyone in your life, but even from yourself.

CHAPTER TWENTY-SEVEN

September is a month of transition. The days get shorter as the daylight hours slowly creep away, minute by minute, until we are left with only the cold, dark days of winter. The winds shift, and the air becomes markedly cooler in the evenings, foreshadowing the brisk October days ahead.

I longed for cool fall days when I could take Dief for hikes in the woods without worrying about him getting too hot. In two weeks Dief would be fourteen. No longer able to regulate his temperature in hot weather, Mom and I had even resorted to keeping the house a chilly sixty-four degrees so Dief would stay comfortable. The past couple summers had been hard for him, but I was sure the cool air of fall would make him feel young again. I'd always imagined he would slip away slowly as a gentle fall breeze carried the smell of burning leaves ever so subtly into the house through a forgotten open window. Instead it was more like a rock climber, grabbing a wedge of rock, only to have it slip from his grasp. He saves himself with a fresh hold, but this one crumbles and falls away. And so it was for Dief that September night, losing his grip only to regain it for a short time—just long enough to give me a false sense of hope, promptly dashed as he inevitably slipped further.

Evening blackened into night. Dief's waning life taunted me like a key clearly visible through the window of a locked car, something I desperately wanted and needed but could not hope to grab hold of. He whimpered on the floor next to me, breathing heavily. I knew it was time to take my friend to the vet, where, with assistance, he could pass peacefully.

I sat on the floor next to him, petting his soft fur as I'd done thousands of times before. I placed my index finger on his forehead, tracing the thin strip of white down the center of his face, first toward his nose, against the hair, making the strip wider. I then traced back up from his nose to the top of his head, making the strip sleek and narrow again. I wasn't ready. How could you ever be ready for something like this?

There on the floor, I cried, holding my friend. Dief's labored breathing quieted and slowed. He lifted his head and looked into my eyes with recognition and trust. His face changed slowly as a peaceful sensation washed over us and flowed between us. Dief shifted his body from lying flat on his side to upright, on his chest. Then he rose and weakly wagged his stump tail. It was as if he were suddenly all better, still an old man but no longer on death's doorstep. I don't know what really happened in that moment, but I am certain it was a gift from God. We were being given one last adventure.

The night was quite black, as it was still several hours before dawn. The air was brisk, as it should be on a perfect fall night, and it caressed my hot, tear-stained cheek as I helped Dief into my truck. Dief always loved to ride in the truck, right next to me in the passenger seat, my trusty copilot. I did not have a plan. We would drive—just drive with the night air blowing in through the open windows, swirling around us, breathing life into us.

I don't remember where we drove that night. Dief lay on the seat next to me, and I stroked his soft fur with my right hand, driving with my left hand, as I had done on countless trips before. He looked up at me, his blue eye clear and bright in the darkness, his brown eye hiding in the shadows. I absently traced the stripe on his forehead, then gently squeezed and stroked his soft, silky ears, only to return to the stripe on his beautiful face.

Suddenly I knew where we were supposed to go. I pulled into the McDonald's ahead on the right side of the road, pointing my truck to the drive-thru lane.

"Welcome to McDonald's," the speaker box crackled. "May I take your order?"

I requested a large order of french fries.

The smell of the fries immediately permeated the night air inside the truck. Dief picked up his tired head with a glimmer of hope in his eyes.

"Of course these are for you! You want some of these?" I smiled.

We drove on in the darkness of the night—it was nearly 3:00 a.m. now. We shared french fries, and I remembered the wonderful adventures we'd had. Dief eagerly accepted and devoured every fry I gave him. It brought me such joy to see him eat his special treat. There was genuine surprise on his face as I gave him fry after fry ... many more than I had ever allowed him before.

What did I do to earn such a wonderful treat? I imagined him asking himself.

"You were you," I answered aloud.

Too soon the fries were gone, and we turned for home. I mindlessly traced the stripe on Dief's forehead, against the hair, then with it, over and over again. It had been an hour, and he still seemed to be doing so well. I pulled into the driveway, parked the truck, and helped Dief out, allowing myself to believe that maybe this really wasn't our last truck ride. Perhaps we still had some time together?

Shortly after we returned home, Dief slipped again like the rock climber who'd lost his tenuous grip on the handhold when it crumbled beneath his fingers. I sat with him on the floor again, his body shaking with the effort of his breathing. It was time to go.

At the vet, I waited for the assistant to bring Dief into the euthanasia room after preparing and sedating him. I held him and hugged him, my tears wetting his fur. I gazed into his eyes. He looked at me blankly; he was nearly gone now. I held Dief's beautiful white paw as the vet injected the pentobarbital into my best friend.

"Don't go," I cried. "Oh, Diefy, don't go. I need you."

My body shook with the pain of loss. I looked down at Dief's paw in my hand. I could still feel his warmth, but my friend was gone.

I hugged Dief's body and buried my face in his soft fur. "I love you, Diefy," I said over and over through my tears.

I closed my eyes and saw Dief running through the fields, chasing rabbits, sleeping on the couch, curled up next to me in the truck, and yodeling his Aussie greeting as I walked into the house. It was all memories now. I kissed his head, touched his silky, soft ears, and traced the stripe on his forehead, first down toward his nose, against the hair making the stripe wide and rough. Then I traced it back up again, making it smooth and narrow.

Goodbye, my dear, sweet friend.

CHAPTER TWENTY-EIGHT

I wasn't prepared for what I would encounter when I opened the door that afternoon. I had survived my first night without Dief, my constant companion of nearly fourteen years. That morning I got up at five, showered, and dressed for work. I found myself ready to leave too early. I was used to allowing enough time to feed Dief and let him out, give belly scratches, and toss his ball a few times. I walked out the door into the crisp predawn air, numb.

When done with work that afternoon, I was feeling OK, at least for someone who had recently had her heart torn out and stomped on until it was tattered and bleeding, then stuffed back into her chest as if nothing noteworthy had happened. I tried to prepare myself for the empty house that would greet me when I opened the front door. I was ready to not hear Dief's "Aroooo-oooo-oooo!" greeting, to not see his stump of a tail wagging from side to side. I was not ready for the utter emptiness of the house.

I stepped sideways through the front door, deliberately keeping my eyes focused on the floor, not wanting to look at the vacant hallway. I faced the door as I closed it. There was no greeting, no clicking of toenails on the linoleum, no Dief. I took a deep breath and turned slowly to face the void. A wave a panic-driven emotion rushed down the hall and smacked me in the face. I gasped at the impact.

"He's not here … He's not here … He's not here … He's not here!" I cried over and over. "Dief isn't here! He's not here!"

I had a desperate urge to search for him. Look in the closets, the spare room, check his bed and the guest bed he wasn't supposed to sleep on but I knew he did anyway. I wanted to check the kitchen, the living room, the basement, the bathroom. I knew he wasn't in any of these places, but I felt like I had to check.

After searching all over the house for what I knew was not there, I finally fell against the door of the hall closet and crumpled to the floor.

"He's not here," I whispered through my tears. "He's not anywhere. He's gone, and I can't see him anymore. I can't hug him or pet his soft ears. My baby is gone."

I lay on the carpet and cried.

SEVERAL DAYS later I sat alone in my big green recliner when my phone rang. The display popped up with Marianne's name and number. I had not spoken to her since I'd left Kentucky over two years before. I was sorry we had lost touch, but we had maintained some contact through Facebook.

I clicked the Talk button and said hello. Marianne had seen my Facebook post about losing Dief and was calling to give her condolences. There was more to the call though.

"I'm so sorry about Dief," she began. "I know how much he meant to you. He was a special dog."

"Thank you," I squeaked.

"I want to tell you it's OK," Marianne continued. "It's OK to get another dog. Dief came to you for a reason. It is important that you were paired with him. It was part of a greater plan. You cared for him, and now you can care for another dog. There are more dogs out there that need you. It's OK to go help them. You will know when you are ready, but I just want to be sure you know it is OK to get another dog."

"Thank you," I squeaked again, wiping the tears from my eyes.

I needed to hear this. The emptiness in the house was unbearable. I didn't know how to be without a dog.

"I needed to hear that," I said.

"I know," Marianne said. "That is why I knew I had to call you."

A week or so later I learned of an adoption event at a local pet store. A new rescue organization called the Animal Rescue Project would be there with dogs to adopt.

The parking lot of the pet store hosting the adoption event was packed. The dogs were lined up in crates outside the storefront, and people were milling about, petting them and talking to the volunteers. I found a parking spot and walked toward the crowd hovering around the dogs, trying to choose a new furry family member. As I rounded the corner, I saw a cute tan puppy on a volunteer's lap. Next to her was a crate that held two mixed-breed puppies around six months old. One lay sleeping in the corner, and the other sat by the door watching the people. I knelt down to say hello. The puppy stood and wagged his tail excitedly. I smiled and, still in my kneeling position, turned to the next crate in the line.

I came face to face with two penetrating amber eyes surrounded by gray-and-black fur. I put my hand over my mouth. My heart leapt in my chest, and a smile spread across my face. This was the one. The dog held my gaze, looking into my eyes for just the briefest of moments before turning away when something else caught his interest. I spoke to him and whistled quietly, trying to get his attention, but the dog would not turn back toward me. I reached through the crate, trying to scratch his head. My finger just barely grazed the top of the dog's head before he moved to the back of the crate and lay down, still looking everywhere but at me.

Maybe I was wrong. I stood, shrugged, and kept looking. There were many more dogs to see, all types and sizes. Children squealed and pointed at a litter of beagle-type puppies crawling over each other in a small playpen. Many of the dogs were out on leashes, walking around and visiting with the prospective adopters. There were many wonderful dogs, but none felt like the right one.

From the corner of my eye I saw a young couple looking at the gray-and-black dog I had reacted to so strongly when I'd arrived. He had returned to the front of the crate but seemed intent on looking everywhere except at the people looking at him. The young woman said something to her male companion and pointed toward the dog. Taking out her cell phone, she knelt in front of the crate to take a picture. *Get away from him—that's my dog!* my mind screamed at the woman. The emotion was so strong I was taken aback by it. I tried to dismiss the feeling as I had before, but when it appeared the woman was looking around for a volunteer, I felt a sense of urgency.

I made my way to the adoption table. "I'd like to see the gray-and-black dog please," I said to the volunteer, pointing down the line of dogs.

"Oh, that's Blue," the woman said. "You want to talk with Mark." She pointed to a man in a red shirt. "He is fostering him."

"Thank you." I made my way over to the man in the red shirt.

Soon Mark and I were heading over to Blue's crate. He opened the crate and snapped a leash on Blue's collar. The dog walked out and stood in front of Mark. He was long and thin, with long legs and big feet. His coat was a beautiful blue merle color, a deep brown-tinged gray base with black splotches. The merle pattern was similar to Dief's, but this dog had no white markings.

Blue stood quietly with his tail tucked tightly against his bum. I spoke to him, called his name, and patted my thighs. Blue would not even acknowledge me; he was intent on looking at everything else. Despite his apparent lack of interest, I was still strongly drawn to him. I reached down to pet him, stroking him along his long back toward his tail. When I reached his tail, a smile spread across my face—there was only a stump.

"He has no tail." I looked up at Mark.

"He has a little tail," Mark answered defensively. "See?" He pulled the tail gently away from Blue's body. "It's just a couple inches, but it's there."

"It's just perfect." I smiled. "How do I go about adopting him?"

A FEW DAYS LATER, Blue's foster parents met me in the parking lot of the farm store near their home. Blue wasn't sure about getting into my truck. He looked warily over his shoulder at the people who had become his family.

"It's OK, Blue," Mark said gently. "Go ahead and get in." He pointed at the open door of my truck.

With a final look over his shoulder at his foster family, Blue (whom I renamed Boedy, after the alpine skier, Bode Miller) jumped into the backseat of my truck. I scratched him on the head before closing the door and sliding onto the driver's seat. Thanking Mark and his wife, I started the engine and began the thirty-minute trip back to Kalamazoo. Boedy leaned across the gap between the front and back seats and placed his head on my right shoulder. Aside from the moment our eyes met briefly at the adoption event, this was the first time Boedy had done anything to acknowledge me. I smiled and reached my hand up to scratch his velvety soft head.

I didn't know what to expect when I brought Boedy into the house for the first time. Dief was my first and only dog, and therefore my only experience came from owning him. I figured Boedy would run around the house, checking out all the rooms and sniffing all the unfamiliar smells, as that was what Dief would have done.

Boedy didn't seem interested in the rest of the house. He briefly sniffed around one end of the family room and then lay down in the middle of the floor and stared at me. As I watched Boedy watching me, a strong sense of gratitude washed over me. A strange sensation. Although I could feel the emotion within me, it was not coming *from* me. It came from the dog. An amazing and emotional experience I will never forget.

CHAPTER TWENTY-NINE

The first course of my master's degree program was the most intriguing I had taken thus far in my studies at WMU. This was also my first course with Dr. Jim Henry, who, in addition to teaching at the university, had cofounded the Children's Trauma Assessment Center (CTAC), an organization serving abused and neglected children, and children with exposure to prenatal drug and alcohol abuse. Dr. Henry introduced me to the concept of the social map, a way of describing how each individual makes sense of the world (personal reality). Information (inputs) received during developmental years shape our reactions and interactions from the point of input, forward, whether we are able to recall that moment of input (a specific memory) or not.

The book *Mindsight*, by Daniel Siegel, MD, was required reading for Dr. Henry's SWRK 6500 (Families) course. The book explored how memories are made and stored during a child's developmental years and how even as an adult, new neural pathways can develop as various events (inputs) create memories. I found myself intrigued by what Siegel wrote about how certain situations can trigger a seemingly nonsensical body response. One example Siegel wrote about involved a female client who had an extreme phobia of water. She felt panic and impending doom whenever she came near a pool or open water. Since she had never had a bad experience with water, the response didn't make any sense to her. Her fear of water seemed illogical, but she could not deny its debilitating effect on her life.

Something seemed familiar about that. I thought back to all those nights I spent tortured with guilt and anxiety, seemingly irrational fears I could not name. Plagued by a sense of impending doom and fear I would get in trouble for something I couldn't identify, I stayed in a constant state of anxiety. Therapist Lady had told me my fear was illogical and basically I should just knock it off. Could there be something more to it? I didn't think so.

I turned back to my reading. The woman continued to work with Siegel, talking about her strong fear around water. He encouraged her to do what he called a "body scan." During this body scan, she would think about being close to water. When the inevitable happened and she felt panicked thinking about the water, Siegel encouraged her to not retreat from her feelings of fear but instead to stay with it, to "follow the fear" and see where it led.

With Siegel's guidance, the woman thought about being close to water, then felt panic coming over her. Instead of pushing the feeling down, she followed it to find the source. Eventually she recovered a repressed memory of nearly drowning as a small child. Her parents had never talked about it with her because they believed she didn't remember the experience and did not see the point in bringing it up. This was only partly true—the woman did not *consciously* remember the near drowning, but her body remembered. The event created a neural pathway in her brain where certain stimuli (in this case, proximity to water) triggered the body memories—panic, extreme fear, sense of impending doom—of her near-drowning experience.

Siegel believed there was an original life event—in this case, near drowning—that is the source of the learned reaction (panic when near water). He further posited the significant life event had actually changed the brain and "taught" it to always respond a certain way to certain triggers (or, created a new neural pathway in the brain). The only way to "untrain" the brain is to teach it a new response by discovering the original source of the reaction (frequently an unresolved trauma) and dealing with it.

I found Siegel's explanation of how trauma changes the brain fascinating but did not see how it could possibly apply to me. I'd had an easy childhood. I'd felt loved by family. Nothing bad had ever happened to me. *Had it?* My problem involved a deviant part of my mind named Mean Cheryl and the fact I was crazy. The reason I felt afraid was because of the paranoia that someone would find this out. But maybe Siegel's book could help me another way?

What could I address using Siegel's techniques? I thought for a moment. *My weight.* It seemed no matter what, I couldn't maintain a healthy weight. I'd either engage in extreme exercise and starvation, which resulted in weight loss, or I'd binge and gain weight rapidly. There seemed to be no middle ground. The problem had gotten worse since the fall from Farletta. For the first time in my life, I wasn't able to flip that switch on, the one that, albeit through unhealthy means, allowed me to lose weight. I'd tried several times since the accident. Each instance quickly aborted the moment the scale showed a loss of a few pounds.

I closed my eyes and cradled my face in my hands, resting my elbows on the table. Taking a couple deep breaths, I thought about losing weight. My thoughts went the way they usually do when I think about weight loss—fitting into fun clothes, being able to move, riding Farletta easily and comfortably without being self-conscious about the way I looked. Not worrying about fitting into whatever chair someone offered me. I knew Siegel would want me to look deeper. This was just surface stuff.

I tried a different approach.

"*Well, Cheryl,*" the animated voice of an imaginary game show announcer spoke in my mind, "*you've just lost one hundred pounds. How do you feel?*"

I let my mind go blank and listened to the question again.

"You've just lost one hundred pounds," the announcer said giddily. *"How do you feel?"*

"Scared," I said aloud.

Scared? my mind questioned. *Scared of what?*

Bam! A switch flipped. I couldn't breathe. My chest tightened, and I gasped for air. I instantly felt just like I had that day sitting in the car with Sarah. Exactly like I had that evening sitting on the ground after falling off my horse. Panic gripped me, but I stayed with it. *Follow the feeling*, Siegel had said.

What was I afraid of? What would it mean to lose a hundred pounds? Why wouldn't I want to do that?

My eyes shot open as the answer came to me surfing on a wave of terror. From deep behind the black curtain, the little girl with the imaginary black horse spoke in a barely audible whisper: *It's not safe*

I did not allow myself to dwell on the words of that little girl behind the black curtain. Instead, I buried myself in my graduate work and had little time to think of anything else—totally fine with me.

I tried a few more times that summer to ride Farletta. The outcome was always the same—nothing but tears, anxiety, and the cruel rage of Mean Cheryl.

By autumn I stopped trying to ride Farletta. Work, school, and weight gain combined to make the perfect excuse. I visited her regularly, but something had changed between us. Farletta seemed so tense in my presence, almost like she could hardly stand to be around me. She simply could not stand still, constantly moving backward and forward within the confines of the length of rope tying her to the wall. Each time I tried to brush her, she'd tolerate a few strokes, then move away. I came to hate the sound of her hooves on the cement of the barn aisle—it felt like the sound of my own inadequacy. When we reached the arena to do some ground work, Farletta had no interest at all. She seemed dull and listless, going through the motions with her eyes glazed over and empty. At times she moved like she could barely lift her hooves, making long lines in the sand as she dragged her toes across the arena surface. It made no sense to me. How could nothing remain of the relationship we once shared? Farletta did still seem happy to see me when I arrived at the barn, but she certainly didn't want me to handle her. What had happened to us? *"That horse hates you."* Mean Cheryl spat the words at me. They landed like daggers, tearing at my heart.

CHAPTER THIRTY

In grad school, many of my electives were in holistic health. I found myself drawn to the idea of holism, which looks at the whole picture rather than focusing on only the presenting problem (or symptom). The idea of holism made sense to me. I'd long looked at horse behavior problems in this manner. Unlike people, horses do not act out of spite. Almost always you will discover an underlying health issue or inadequate foundational training when working with a so-called problem horse. I wondered if there might be something more going on between Farletta and me, something beyond what appeared to everyone else to be simply a behavior problem. I knew there had to be something I could address, some way I could fix this.

My holistic health class was held over three weekends in Traverse City, located in the northwest portion of Michigan's Lower Peninsula. On the final day of that first weekend, the small class met at a lovely yoga studio nestled in a quiet community not far from Traverse City. We were to spend the day engaging in self-care (a foreign concept to me).

After everyone arrived and settled in, we began our day with relaxation and meditation. The first relaxation position involved lying flat on my back with my lower legs resting on the seat of a chair, my knees and hips bent at right angles, as if I were still seated in a chair that had toppled over. The instructor spoke softly, encouraging us to relax our bodies into the floor, feeling the sensation of the surface below us. She wanted us hear the sounds of nature outside the windows, to feel the gentle breezes, to listen intently as we focused our energy inward.

To my surprise and dismay, one by one tears slid down my face, silently rolling off my cheeks and down my neck. I took a deep breath and held it, angrily wiping my cheeks.

"Breathe in deeply, letting the air out of your lungs slowly through your mouth," the instructor reminded us.

I released my breath, and a soft whimper escaped my throat. Embarrassed, I lifted my head and looked around, hoping no one had heard me. Deciding my whimper had gone unnoticed, I laid my head back on the mat and tried to focus on my breathing, as instructed. Once again I concentrated on the sensation of the floor beneath me, feeling how it supported my body.

"Relax into the floor. Let it support you fully," the instructor continued.

I tried to do as she said, but the tears came again. They were not soft or gentle this time, and soon a shroud of inexplicable sorrow engulfed me. My chest tightened, and panic settled over me.

What is happening to me? I lifted up the neck of my T-shirt to dry my eyes. I felt blasted by emotion, as if a tiny plane were dropping emotional bombs all around me. I held my breath, trying to suppress the tears. This served only to increase my panic. I was losing control.

As quietly as I could, I rose and crept out of the room. I dashed into the small bathroom, grabbing a handful of tissues as I passed through the open door. I looked at my face in the mirror, red and tear stained, my eyes puffy and wet. I held my breath, attempting to force the tears away while I pushed down the strong emotions.

Why now? Why couldn't I control this?

My shoulders ached with the tension of physically pushing down my emotions. I had been doing it for so long, it was a familiar feeling, along with the tight, hollow sensation in my chest when I held my breath. The class instructor appeared in the doorway. I didn't want to talk to her. *Please no! Not now. Go away!* I had been hiding this side of myself for so many years. *Please, God, don't let her find out!* Terror gripped me. I couldn't hold my secret much longer.

"Is everything okay?" the instructor, Michelle, asked.

I could lie as I usually did and say I was fine, but I didn't think she would believe me, given my red, tear-streaked face.

Maybe you could try to talk to her? The little girl spoke from behind the black curtain. Could I do that—could I tell her? My mouth quivered as I formed my response. "Um, ah …" I took a deep breath. "I …"

I put one hand up to my face, covering my mouth and nose, as if trying to keep something from forcing its way out. *No,* the little girl behind the black curtain thought, *not out. In.* I pulled my hand away slowly, closing my fingers around my lips and tugging at them as I stared blankly at the ground.

With my hand still covering most of my face, I glanced up. "No." The tears flowed freely once again.

Later, after that mini meltdown, I shared a lot with Michelle. My accident and my relationship with Farletta. How our relationship felt broken, my terror at mounting her, the way I couldn't breathe when I thought about the day I fell off her. How I had been seeing yet another therapist but didn't think we were making any progress.

I needed to talk to someone who could not only address my anxiety and depression but could respect and appreciate the importance of restoring my relationship with Farletta. Someone who could understand she wasn't just a horse or a pet to me. There was something special in our connection, something that had been lost and needed to be found again.

Much to my relief and gratitude, Michelle said she understood the role Farletta played in my life. She knew of a therapist in my hometown who she thought would be just the person I needed to talk to. Michelle connected me with Ruth.

I LIKED Ruth's office immediately. A wall of windows looked out onto a small wooded area dense with underbrush. Bird feeders attached to the windows attracted a variety of birds, which flitted about, taking turns eating the seed. Squirrels emerged from the thick brush and planted themselves beneath the feeders, waiting greedily for seeds to fall on the ground at their feet. Inside the office, a dozen or so rocks of varying size and type were joined by other items from nature. Plants and flowers sat on a low table near the windows, and a small tree stood in one corner.

I sat on the corner of the couch nearest the windows and farthest from Ruth. I positioned several small throw pillows on my lap and on either side of me, like a nest.

It didn't take long for Ruth to see something in me that no other therapist or counselor had ever noticed, a subtle coping mechanism I had been using for years to protect that dark secret, the one the little girl kept behind the black curtain in my mind. That first day, Ruth asked me to make a timeline of my life, specifically focusing on stressful events. Each time I came to a stressful event I was to record whether I felt supported at the time.

I drew a timeline and dotted it with various life events, focusing on the bad things that had happened. If I felt supported, I drew a stick person on top of the line. If not, I drew a stick person hanging from the line. In a couple instances I felt compelled to draw a stick person falling from the line into nothingness.

I brought my timeline to my next appointment. Ruth asked me about the various events, and we talked about some things that had happened: the death of a few good friends, selling Corky, losing Splatters, and falling off Farletta. Ruth asked me to tell her more about the accident with Farletta. I told her about how I had to stay home alone and was fairly immobile for a while.

"Were you in the hospital?" Ruth asked.

"Yes, but only for one night. Then I went home." I glossed it over and moved on.

"Did you have anyone at home to help you?"

I wasn't expecting more questions about the details of the accident or the aftermath. I wanted to talk about Farletta and what was going on with her.

"Dief was there," I said cheerfully.

Ruth smiled. "Did you have any family to help you?"

"Well, no. My family lives here in Michigan, and at the time I was living in Kentucky."

"Didn't anyone come to help you?" Ruth prodded.

"My stepdad was sick with cancer and Mom had to care for him. Everyone had their own stuff going on, and I lived so far away."

I paused, waiting for Ruth to give some validation or agreement so we could move on. She said nothing. She simply watched with interest, waiting.

"But I had a few friends in Kentucky. They helped me out and brought me food and stuff," I added quickly.

"Yes, but did anyone stay with you?" Ruth asked again. "It sounds like it was pretty hard for you to get around and do basic things. Was anyone with you at night if you needed help?"

I stared at her. Why was she prying like this? What did my living situation following the accident have to do with anything? That was ancient history. It was over. I had already lived it. It didn't matter anymore.

"Dief was there," I offered again. "He was a great help."

"Yes," Ruth said, "but he couldn't really help you in an emergency. What if you fell and couldn't get up or needed help in the night?"

"I could call a friend," I said, knowing full well no one could get on the farm at night without someone opening the gate. I'd never really thought about those complications, which now sounded scary.

"How did you feel when your mom said she couldn't come?" Ruth asked.

How did I feel? How could I feel? Rick needed Mom at home. He was dying. I was not. Such was life. I shrugged. "Disappointed, of course, but I understood. What could she do? Rick was dying from cancer. He needed her there. Everything turned out fine. It wasn't a big deal or anything."

"It sounds like a big deal," Ruth replied.

Her words took me by surprise and left me speechless. No one had ever responded like that to my "no big deal" statement. When I described a subject as "no big deal," it had always been dropped—by friends, by family, by therapists, by strangers—everyone. Once I dismissed the issue, nobody brought it up again. Over. *Finito*. Moving on. Not so with Ruth though. She saw what I was doing, something I was unaware of. Minimizing and dismissing a situation are coping mechanisms that for years effectively prevented me from having to discuss how I really felt about anything. If I said it wasn't a big deal or it could've been worse, I could dismiss and avoid the subject.

Once I understood this, I could see many places in my life where it had become a habit. Particularly when I didn't feel supported anyway. Whether because I felt people didn't understand the impact of a certain event in my life, or, as with the suicide attempt, I simply didn't tell anyone, there were several significant life-altering events that I had dismissed as "no big deal." *I* didn't matter, so why should anything in my life matter? It wasn't an oh, woe-is-me, boo-hoo, waaaaa pity party. I hated myself so much I could see no value in anything I had to offer the world. The thought that anyone could genuinely care about me seemed like a big joke that everyone was in on except me. I believed people were nice to me out of pity or some misplaced sense of duty because we'd been friends for a long time or perhaps were related. Or worse, at times I felt convinced people pretended to like me or be my friend until I trusted them, at which point they would publicly humiliate me and ridicule me for allowing myself to believe they would ever really be my friend. Of course, most of these ideas came from Mean Cheryl, but it had happened enough times in grade school and high school that some reality existed for Mean Cheryl to base her theories on, even as I moved on into adulthood.

By recognizing how I minimized my traumas and, in turn, helping me to understand this behavior as a coping mechanism that no longer served me, Ruth enabled me to talk about things I had never discussed. A real turning point in my healing process. Stuff I had held down for years came out. I talked about losses, bad things I'd suffered through in silence, how I'd felt growing up, and how I felt about myself now.

Ruth taught me to honor the painful memories and respect the person who had survived them—*me*. Slowly we peeled away the barrier I had built around myself. To do this I had to stop living life only from the neck up, which not only allowed me to deal with past trauma but also made me vulnerable to discovering the one event I had hidden so well, even I did not remember it. Mean Cheryl at one time had served an important purpose, but that was before she was Mean Cheryl, back when she was just a scared and confused little girl.

Ruth placed a thin, black thread in my hand. The other end of that thread was firmly attached to the bottom edge of that black curtain in my mind. Out of curiosity I tugged at it, and the curtain unraveled. Crumbling around me, my carefully constructed reality threatened to come crashing down at my feet. As I stood in the demolition zone, I realized too late I might be crushed in the process.

CHAPTER THIRTY-ONE

I suspect few memories actually reside in our consciousness. We imagine memories as something we file away in our brains, but I've discovered many are held in the body, invisibly linked to the subconscious with tiny communication wires that allow the memories to influence our behavior without our being aware of it.

Years ago I heard about an Arabian mare, a retired circus horse. In the circus, the mare would perform a specific routine to a certain song. She did this performance alone, without a rider or handler cueing her. The idea was that the horse would appear to be dancing to the music.

As the story goes, the mare performed this same pattern of movements to the same song night after night for thirteen years. After she retired, she became a lesson horse, teaching kids to ride, but she never forgot her previous job. Occasionally during a lesson, the mare would suddenly launch into her old circus routine, trotting and cantering around the arena at will. Those who observed the behavior said it was as if she had somehow gotten the song into her head and was dancing to music only she could hear.

I think it is more likely some of the movements the mare performed during the lesson were in the same sequence she had performed over and over in her dance routine. By performing that sequence in the lesson, she triggered her memory and went on autopilot, mentally returning to the circus and her days of performing—physically she was in the present, but the reality she was experiencing was in the past. When this type of physical reaction combined with mental disconnection (dissociation) is linked to trauma, it is called post-traumatic stress disorder (PTSD). I drew the connection between this and what Siegel had written about, how trauma affects the brain, programming a response to occur over and over, even if the logical mind didn't understand why.

As I reflected on the story of the old circus horse, my mind skipped into the past, and I recalled unusual behaviors I hadn't thought on in years—hiding under my bed or closing myself in a small closet as a child. The tighter the fit and darker the space, the better I felt. It was good to feel invisible.

I recalled an incident in second grade. Larry, an older kid on the bus, put his hand up my skirt and fondled me while he whispered dirty words in my ear. I screamed and squirmed away from him.

"Sit down!" the bus driver yelled, looking at me in the mirror.

"But I ..."

"Sit now!" he yelled again.

Had he seen what happened? Was he angry with me? There was no one else on the bus, no one to look to, to determine if I had done something wrong. I reluctantly sank back into the seat next to Larry. Watching the driver's face in the mirror, I slipped into a different seat. The driver glanced at me in the mirror but said nothing. I moved to another seat farther back.

"That's enough—stay there!" the driver yelled.

With tears stinging my eyes, I pressed myself against the cold, hard steel of the bus wall.

I later told my mom what had happened with Larry on the bus. Together we went to see the principal, Mrs. Norman, and told her what had happened.

"This is a very serious accusation," Mrs. Norman said, looking at me sternly. "Are you sure that's what happened?"

I felt instantly confused and scared. Was I sure? What did she mean was I sure? I didn't know what I had done, but I had the feeling I was in trouble. I had done something bad, something Mrs. Norman didn't approve of.

"You're sure?" Mrs. Norman asked again.

My lower lip trembled, and the corners of my mouth twitched downward in a frown. Tears welled up.

"Yes," I squeaked.

It had certainly happened, but now I wasn't sure which one of us had done something wrong. I had a funny feeling gnawing and twisting in my belly. I wanted to get out of Mrs. Norman's office right away. I had made a mistake coming to her, and I felt guilty.

Days later I saw Larry in the hallway at school.

"You didn't have to do that." He scowled at me. "You didn't have to tell on me."

A distinct, gnawing, twisting feeling of guilt again sank into my belly.

"I got in trouble," Larry continued. "I can't ride the bus."

I didn't say anything, but my lower lip trembled. Stinging tears welled from my eyes and escaped down my cheeks.

"I just did it because I like you," he said. "I just thought you were pretty."

Did he just say that? Did he say he touched me there *because he liked me? Because I was pretty?*

After my mom and I talked with Mrs. Norman in her office, we never discussed the incident with Larry again. I never forgot it though.

Things were beginning to make sense, the isolation, the fears around being liked by a boy, being pretty … these words had always felt dangerous.

Another memory, years later, I had unknowingly parked in a poorly marked fire zone. Someone had left a nasty note on my truck, calling me selfish and inconsiderate, accusing me of believing the rules didn't apply to me. Somehow this stranger had discovered the horrible person I was. I screamed at myself and hit myself repeatedly. Then replied to the note, writing that I knew I was a horrible person and I should kill myself. I hung the note on a tree near where I had parked. As I drove home, I became convinced someone was chasing me. I pulled into an empty parking lot and hid under the tonneau cover in the bed of my truck, my body shaking uncontrollably.

Just like the fall from Farletta and the suicide attempt, I labeled these memories as no big deal, minimizing and dismissing them in my usual style. By helping me discover this minimizing and dismissal was actually a coping mechanism, Ruth effectively enabled me to remove my last line of defense against that terrible secret lurking in the darkest recesses of my mind. Minimizing, dismissing, and ultimately forgetting worked as a defense when I was a child, but in adulthood it only served to perpetuate the lies Mean Cheryl had been telling me for decades. Now, nothing stood between me and that awful secret I'd been hiding from for most of my life.

The first memories that surfaced were feelings of being trapped, unable to escape, unable to help myself or protect myself. There were no images to go with the feelings, no way to identify the source of the fear, only a deeply held understanding that I was in danger and had no control over what would happen next. *Get away! Get away!*

But I couldn't get away from whatever I felt inside me. I didn't ruminate on these feelings of fear that teetered on the edge of panic, and tried to dismiss them as quickly as I could. But then my chest constricted, I gasped for air, tears welled, and my body shook. I felt out of control, panic and anxiety choking the breath out of me. I buried my face in my hands like a small child unable to process intense emotions. *What the hell is happening to me?* Days later the sensations washed over me again. Feelings of fear, being trapped, and unable to escape some unseen danger flooded my senses. Then images accompanied the sensations. I felt cold tile touching my skin, white with gray flecks, like you'd see in a school or some other public building. Someone knelt over me, holding my body against the tile. I tried to see him but saw only a vague shadow. Next I saw the leg of an old desk next to my head. I alternated between being the body on the floor and floating just above it. I shifted between seeing what happened and feeling it. I pinched my mouth shut, pressing my lips tightly together, turning my head from side to side trying to avoid ... *Someone is trying to put something in my mouth.* I could see an old metal-sided desk and ... then I was hiding under the desk, covering my face.

Panic rose, and I couldn't breathe. Only that part was real, happening not in my memory but right in that moment. I lay in my bed, gasping for breath. My chest tight, I felt trapped. I struggled for air, feeling like the wind had been knocked out of me. The feeling was familiar—it was the same as the night I'd fallen off Farletta, the same as that day in Sarah's car, the same as when I'd told Michelle about the accident, the same as when I thought about losing weight, the same as when I tried to get on my horse. It all felt the *same.*

I woke up the next morning with the (*memories?*) images burned into my mind. They replayed over and over—the desk, the floor, my arms pinned, my mouth pressed shut. I shook my head, trying to rid myself of the scene and the awful feelings that accompanied them. Whatever this was, I didn't want it. But it happened again and again, as if a carefully protected portion of my memory had sprung a slow, irreparable leak. Bit by bit the memories seeped out. Sometimes they came in tiny, disconnected drops, other times in messy bursts like water sloshing out of a violently jostled cup. I couldn't make sense of the images or the sensations. There was no coherence. Like a deck of cards tossed into the wind, I never knew which ones would appear first, or when.

I shared what I'd seen and felt with Ruth at our next appointment. As I relayed the images and sensations, I lost my breath once again, my chest constricting. I covered my face, pinched my lips together, and cried.

"Cheryl? Cheryl, what is happening right now?" Ruth asked, her voice soft and gentle.

"Something bad," I whispered behind my hands. "Bad. Bad. Something bad." I pressed my body into the couch cushions, wishing I could disappear into them. Ruth spoke again, but I could no longer hear her. I had disappeared. Ruth later told me that when I spoke to her in that moment, my voice was that of a small child. Not only in sound, but even my vocabulary had regressed many years.

I, too, had heard the childish voice come out of me. Before I "disappeared" completely, I experienced two distinct realities at the same time. I was both an adult, sitting on a couch in Ruth's office, and a little girl experiencing a terrifying event. Just like when Mean Cheryl took over my thoughts, the feelings and words of this little girl overpowered me, and in that moment her vision was my reality.

Ruth explained that I'd experienced what appeared to be an episode of dissociation, a phenomenon common with victims of trauma.

Trauma? Victim? I didn't like those words. They did not apply to me.

In the days and weeks that followed, the images and accompanying physical sensations continued and expanded. The body pinned on the tile floor. The little girl, she had my face. I could feel the floor beneath her. I could feel the pressure of his weight pinning her arms. I could feel …

"NO!" I screamed, shocked at the sound of my voice blasting against the bathroom walls. I clamped my thighs shut at the feeling of a hand between my legs. I could feel his fingers, his hot breath on my neck, his scratchy beard on my cheek.

"Stop it!" I screamed. "Stop it! Get away from me!"

I ran from the bathroom and jumped into my bed. I curled up on the mattress and clenched my eyes shut. Hysterical sobs shook me, and once again my chest tightened and I gasped for air.

"Leave me alone … leave me alone … leave me alone," I repeated over and over, my voice like that of a small child. What was happening to me?

"Oh God, make it stop! Make him stop!" I cried, my eyes clenched shut. Just then I felt a slight movement of the bed. Cautiously I opened my eyes. Boedy sat on the floor beside me, resting his head on the mattress, watching me closely with his amber-colored eyes. I willed myself to unclench my fist and reached a shaky hand toward my dog. I stroked his velvety soft ears and rubbed his head. As I interacted with Boedy, the awful sensations dissipated, and I regained my composure.

"What the hell was that?" I asked Boedy, absently wiping half-dried tears from my eyes. Boedy lifted his body up, resting his front half on the bed. He stretched his long neck and put his head on the pillow right next to mine. Boedy stared into my eyes, and I stroked his soft ears. He moved his head and rested it on my shoulder, pressing hard against me. I scratched his neck. "Thank you, Boedy." Boedy's stump tail moved from side to side. We stayed like that for a while, Boedy half on the bed and half off, resting his head on my shoulder.

I took a deep breath in and let it out, smiled, and thanked God for bringing Boedy into my life after I lost Dief.

I can't say things quieted down after that night, but they did stay the same for a while. I continued to experience the awful physical sensations, sometimes at the most inopportune times (as if there is ever a good time to have such a sensation). I would sit in class or at church and squirm while my body replayed the memory. Often I wasn't immediately aware of what was going on, but soon I would become cognizant and have to leave the room to regain my composure.

One day while sitting in a crowded room listening to a speaker, a young man I knew sat directly behind me. This man had a mental disability and would sometimes act strangely or make odd noises. On this day he made sounds of heavy breathing and grunting. The sounds were quiet, and I was sure most people in the room could not hear him. Although aware of the source of the sounds and knowing they had nothing to do with me, his vocalizations still triggered my body memories. Soon I once again relived all those now regretfully familiar sensations. Panic closed my throat and tightened my chest, cutting my breath into short gasps. I tried to maintain my composure but could not. Like a car going down a mountain road with no brakes, I had lost control of my reaction and didn't know where or when it would stop. I excused myself and ran to the bathroom, not wanting anyone to see the tears or the terror in my eyes.

These sensations continued for months. At first I only told Ruth about my experiences, but eventually I also shared some with Sarah. Deeply ashamed, I didn't share too much though. I didn't want to tell anyone else anything until I had more concrete memories, and more importantly, until I could identify the faceless man in the memories. Still just a shadow in my mind's eye, I couldn't identify any features, a name, or even a time period. The thought that perhaps this had been someone I knew, or worse, a friend or family member I still had contact with, terrified me most of all. What would I do then?

There were not many men in my life now or in the past. My uncle, dad, and stepdad were my three main male figures. Of course there had been teachers, the pastor of my church, guidance counselors, and other authority figures. The few male friends I had were either married or gay. Both types felt safe, as I assumed neither would show any romantic interest in me.

I didn't even go on my first date until I was twenty-five, an event I enjoyed at first but quickly shut down when, toward the end, I could tell he wanted to kiss me. We were alone in the barn and I was showing him Danny's horses. Every time I looked up at him, he'd close his eyes and lean in … *oh God! What is he doing?* I kept praying Danny would come into the barn. How could I be so stupid to get myself in this position? Alone in a secluded place with a man I didn't know. I squirmed inwardly every time he looked at me. Eventually he caught the hint and took me back to my truck in the parking lot where we'd met. Always hyper-vigilant, I had asked to meet there, not wanting him to know where I lived.

Men did attract me, but at the same time, they made me uncomfortable in any situation that could be viewed as anything other than just friends. I never really thought much on this, not even connecting the incident on the bus with Larry as a possible cause. Because all my friends had been involved in multiple relationships through the years, and some were now married, I recognized my situation as unusual. After all, with my excessive weight and the constant reminders from Mean Cheryl about my complete worthlessness and foul appearance, I simply figured that men found me undesirable and unworthy of a serious relationship. Knowing there had been few men in my life perhaps added to the anxiety of discovering the identity of the man in those memories. This lack of male contacts increased the likelihood it was someone I still cared about. At the same time, I really wanted to know. I needed closure. If I discovered who the individual was, then I could wash my hands of the whole mess and be done with it.

    If only it were so simple.

CHAPTER THIRTY-TWO

I spent a lot of time actively denying what I remembered. Truly, how could something so horrible, so vulgar happen to a little girl? How could no one know? How could I have forgotten it? I didn't want to be a part of this group I'd never identified with before—was I a *survivor* now? A survivor of sexual abuse? I don't know how to be a *survivor*. What do I do? How do I act? Do I talk to other survivors? I didn't want to. I didn't want to be a part of that group. It shattered the image of what I thought my life had been to this point. It changed my identity. This knowledge disturbed me, and consequently I worked hard to push the voice and memories of the little girl back down where they had come from.

I don't want you here, I would tell the little girl that was me. She would linger though. She had waited many years to tell her story and would not be denied. A reoccurring image flashed in my mind, that of a little girl standing on a desk in an empty room. Her face red, her eyes clenched shut in anger or frustration, she holds her arms stiffly with her hands balled up in tiny fists. Her mouth is open, her throat raw and bleeding as she screams. She screams until her head hurts, tears streak her little face, her chest heaves as she gasps for breath and screams again. But she is there alone, her screams fall flat, there is no one to hear her. No one at all.

"LADIES AND GENTLEMEN," the captain's voice crackled out of the overhead speakers, "we are approaching Las Vegas and will begin our descent momentarily. The temperature is eighty-three degrees under sunny skies." Crackling sounds and a loud *click* replaced the captain's voice as he turned off the microphone. I squeezed my pillow closer to my body, gazing out the window at the brown desert landscape far below. I would soon be in Las Vegas for the Equine Assisted Growth and Learning Association (EAGALA) National Conference.

I first learned about EAGALA when an undergrad a couple years earlier. EAGALA has an excellent therapeutic model for equine-assisted psychotherapy (EAP) and equine-assisted learning (EAL). Unlike therapeutic riding, which generally focuses on the physical and mental benefits of learning to ride, EAGALA-model therapy is all unmounted (no riding). It is believed the lack of formal instruction in the therapy sessions enables the client to more easily tell their own story and make personal discoveries.

The EAGALA-model's focus on providing the resources to help the client find their own answers is similar to one of the main principles of good social work. In my social work program, we were taught the job of a social worker is to provide resources (support, information, advocacy, etc.) to help the client help themselves. You can't make a person change, you can't make them heal, but you can give them the tools they need to learn how to change or heal themselves. In EAGALA-model EAP or EAL, the tools (or resources) include horses. In the sessions, the horses often become metaphors that help the client tell his or her story, develop self-awareness, and make personal discoveries.

Near the end of my master's degree program, I planned a future where I could combine my knowledge of and passion for horses with my social work degrees, allowing me to find work in the field of equine-assisted therapies. I had already been certified in the EAGALA model and had an internship at an EAGALA-model facility near my home in Michigan. I came to the three-day conference hoping to learn, network, and, with graduation fast approaching, hopefully get a good lead on a job.

The conference presentations could be an information overload, particularly when dealing with topics such as mental health diagnoses and treatments, victims of abuse, and other sensitive subjects. The presentations could wear on a person both physically and mentally. By the final presentation of the first full day of the conference, I already felt wiped out. I also found myself distracted. By what I was not yet sure.

When I arrived late to the final presentation of the day, the speakers had already begun and the seats were mostly full. I found a spot on the floor near the front of the room and sat with my back leaning against the wall. I don't remember the subject of the presentation—not because it was a poor presentation, but because I wasn't really there. Drawn back into my mind, I was distracted by an image of a desk. Sheet metal, painted bland beige, made up the bottom portion, and the drawers, while cheap pressed wood with fake wood-grain veneer, made up the desktop. I couldn't concentrate on anything but this desk. The image wasn't fully formed. I could only see the one side, and ... *What is there?* I knew without seeing, something hid underneath the desk. Just what I could not yet tell.

I picked up my pen and notebook and started sketching.

First I drew the parts of the desk I could see, vaguely aware that I viewed the desk from the perspective of a small child. In my visual field, the top of the desk was about chest high. I sketched the top line of the desk and worked my way down the sides to the legs. From this vantage point, I faced where the chair would slide in. Slowly drawers formed on the right side. I sketched them in roughly and then added depth to the drawing until a two-dimensional desk shape appeared.

At this point I felt myself disconnecting. No longer sitting on the floor in the conference room, I instead floated just above it, looking down at myself sketching. I remained at that safe distance and watched the image appear from the pen strokes onto the paper. My hand moved more quickly, and shapes took form. A small circle appeared under the desk, followed by more shapes and lines, shadows and ... *What is this?* I drew frantically, arms and legs forming in the shadows. The circle turned into a face covered by little hands.

I paused for a moment looking at the notepad. I had sketched a little girl sitting under a desk with her knees drawn up to her chest. She wore a dress with short ruffled sleeves. Her hands covered her face. Dark pen strokes, so firm they made deep indentations into the page, formed the image of the little girl's panties down around her ankles.

With more to see, I kept drawing. My pen moved to the drawers on the right side of the desk. I added in the pulls and the shadows. I worked my way around the right side of the desk, my pen adding specifics as the desk materialized before me. I continued down the right side ... there was something there, something on the side of the desk, something attached there. I sketched more and then paused, working the pen up and down, just above the surface of the paper, drawing in thin air. Finally I settled the pen back on the paper, making soft lines. There was a picture on the side of the desk, a small child's drawing.

Oh God, I know who it is.

An hour later I sat on the bed in my hotel room looking at the sketch in disbelief. I stared at the little girl hiding under the desk, her hands over her face and her panties down around her ankles. I could feel her back pressed so hard against the cold metal, like she was trying to will herself to disappear into the shadows.

That little girl is me, I thought with a shudder. *And that desk belongs to ...*

I drew in a breath sharply and held it until I felt I would explode. Finally, I released the breath with a whimper.

"I can't deal with this," I said aloud, my voice barely a whisper. I tossed the notebook down on the bed. It fell with a soft flutter of the pages, the recently sketched image still staring up at me.

"I can't do this, God!" I cried out. "I can't do this! I can't deal with this! Please, God, I've had enough!"

Several minutes passed before I cautiously picked up the picture again and stared at the right side of the desk in the image. The desk in the picture belonged Mr. Vandersmelden, a well-loved, well-respected man among many families in our community, including mine.

"How can I tell anyone about this?" I asked the empty room.

Will they believe me? Will anyone? Everyone loves Mr. Vandersmelden—they will be angry at me for accusing him.

"Why does it have to be him, God?" I cried aloud. "Why can't it be someone nobody cares about?"

Who was I supposed to talk to? I couldn't tell anyone who liked him. My mom? My sister? My aunt, uncle, and cousins? How can I tell them when they all thought he was so great?

One memory I have never forgotten suddenly came to the forefront of my mind. It was not an event as much as a tiny snapshot of time, a still image of me sitting on Mr. Vandersmelden's lap, his swivel chair turned to one side so his legs were next to rather than under the desk. It was where he sat when he read aloud, kids sitting on the carpet at his feet, listening to *Aesop's Fables*.

The memory had always seemed strange to me, because in it, the other kids weren't there—just me and him. I'd never allowed myself to dwell on it though. Now, as I focused on the memory, the reality became alarmingly clear. That was how it had begun. Not exactly sitting *on* his lap, but rather sitting on his *hand* in his lap. I dropped the notebook, and it landed in a tent shape at my feet. I put my hands over my face and cried.

Hours later a soft knock came at the door.

"Cheryl?" A familiar voice came from the hallway. "It's Ulla."

Ulla was my supervisor for my EAGALA-themed MSW internship. She was also here in Vegas for the conference. Unable to deal with the new information, I called her to my room. I'd been working with Ulla, a licensed psychologist with her own EAGALA facility, since the previous July and considered her a friend and a mentor. Someone I could trust. She already knew some information about the resurfaced memories.

I let Ulla in and then retreated to the bed. Ulla sat next to me on the edge of the bed. I showed her the drawing and explained I now realized who the person was in the memories. Ulla placed her hand on my shoulder near my neck. I cringed away from her and started to cry again. I remember trying to press myself into the inch or so of space between the bed and the bedside table. At some point I retreated from the bed, ran across the room, and hid under a table.

"Get away from me!" I screamed. "Don't touch me! Get away!"

My voice was that of a little girl. I pressed my back against the wall under the table as hard as I could.

I kicked my legs and screamed. "Don't touch me! Get away from me! NO! Leave me alone! LEAVE ME ALONE!"

Some small part of me was aware I was in the hotel room in 2012, but I didn't really believe it. Physically and emotionally I was living that memory all over again, unable to separate the memory from reality.

"Cheryl?" Ulla called calmly to me from the foot of the bed.

She told me I was safe. I was in a hotel room, and no one could hurt me. The terrified little girl did not believe her.

"Make him stop!" I screamed from under the desk. "Make him stop! Why won't he leave me alone?" I kicked my legs and screamed, "Get him off me! Get him away from me!"

Eventually Ulla calmed me down using the same technique Ruth had used, asking if she could talk to the adult Cheryl. She had heard the little girl, but now she needed to talk to the adult.

I had experienced another dissociated memory, one where the little girl in me, the one who had been hurt all those years ago, was finally able to tell what happened to her. As terrifying as this was, it made me feel alive, more so than I had at any other time in my life. Perhaps because I finally gave a voice to that little girl? After all these years she could finally tell someone what had happened to her.

When I returned to Michigan, I told Ruth what happened in Vegas and my fears about telling my mom or any other family member what I'd remembered. I had not told anyone in my family about any of what I remembered thus far, wanting to wait until I knew who had done it, feeling I needed the information to add validity to my story. Now that I finally put a face to my abuser, I felt like I could never tell anyone who had known Mr. Vandersmelden. Ruth encouraged me to share with my family, reminding me that they loved me very much.

I kept the secret for a while longer while I scoured the internet for current information about Mr. Vandersmelden. Perhaps someone else had come forward and accused him? I checked the database of sexual offenders and found nothing. I searched using his name and other identifying information. There were no stories at all about Mr. Vandersmelden, good or bad. He simply did not exist online, at least not within the scope of my abilities to uncover information.

I told Sarah first, and like Ruth, she reminded me that my family loved me and that no matter what, she would always have my back. When I finally told my mom, sister, aunt and uncle, one by one, they were shocked and angry. But they weren't angry at me ... they were angry at him. I felt like the worst was over. I'd remembered something terrible and now remembered who had done it. It could only get better from here, right?

CHAPTER THIRTY-THREE

During the same time I worked with Ruth dealing with the recovered memories, I also read many books that explored the therapeutic value of the horse-human relationship. While reading a portion of *Tao of Equus* by Linda Kohanov, I became intrigued by a story she told of a woman who came to her farm for therapy with the horses.

In the story, Linda asked the woman to brush a particular gelding. However, when this woman tried to go near the gelding, the horse appeared stressed, dancing around and generally difficult to approach. Linda noted this as unusual behavior, although the horse, Noche, had a history of abuse and thus was highly sensitive and hyper-aware (also common with human abuse victims). After watching the woman and horse for a while, Kohanov asked her client what she was thinking about. The client mentioned feelings she was experiencing and then indicated she was trying to hide these feelings from the horse, believing she needed to show confidence no matter how she really felt.

Through her research, Kohanov determined horses are programmed to pay close attention to visceral readings from other animals. It is part of their survival mechanism. They are naturally wary of any creature with incongruent behaviors—presenting one way on the outside when they are different on the inside—like pretending to be comfortable when you are terrified. Kohanov suggested the woman be honest with the horse and tell him what she felt. The woman agreed and shared aloud what was really on her mind (conflict over returning to an abusive relationship). When the woman told her story, Noche soon quieted and she could easily approach and handle him.

As I read this story, I thought of Farletta and how she moved constantly when I tried to groom or handle her. I decided to try being honest with her and tell her whatever I was feeling in that moment. I figured it couldn't hurt and it might help.

I went out late that evening, long after the other boarders had left. I wanted to be alone with Farletta for my little experiment. Bright moonlight lit my path when I made my way to the barn, Farletta following me. When we reached the barn, I tied Farletta loosely in the aisle, as I typically did. She immediately shifted her weight from foot to foot in her restless dance. I closed my eyes and focused on my feelings.

As soon as I turned my focus inward and listened to myself, feelings of anxiety and sadness welled up. Instead of pushing these feelings away, I allowed myself to feel them, experience them, and understand where they were coming from. Images flashed through my mind, some from the past, some more recent, and some from my recently recovered memories. Each image brought a wave of emotion crashing over me.

I opened my eyes and spoke to Farletta, telling her about each memory, each image, and explaining the emotion that came with it. Farletta stopped moving and turned her head to look at me. Letting out a deep sigh, the mare licked and chewed, working her mouth gently as horses do when releasing tension. Her body softened, and she was visibly more comfortable.

I picked up a brush and groomed her soft multicolored coat. Farletta stood quietly while I gave her a thorough grooming. For the first time in ages she seemed comfortable in my presence.

I put away the brushes. "Would you like to go for a walk?" She looked at me with light in her eyes. Three little wrinkles appeared below her left eye, a face she made when she was particularly happy. A face I hadn't seen in a while.

"OK." I pulled the end of the lead rope to release the knot holding her to the wall. "Let's go."

We turned toward the large double doors at the end of the barn. Farletta's bare hooves made a soft clip-clop sound on the cement aisle. I paused to flip off the lights, and then we walked together into the crisp night air.

THE NEW ORAL anti-inflammatory Dr. Brown prescribed the previous fall still seemed to be helping Farletta's eye. As a precaution I had her stay in the barn during the brightest part of the day, but by the afternoon her paddock was mostly shade, so I let her go out with her friend Ernie. Although pleased to have her leading a semi-normal life again, I still wondered if she could ever be outside without worrying about her eye.

Ever since I'd started being open with Farletta and telling her why I felt sad or anxious or any other emotion I would normally hide from others, our relationship had been returning to the way it was before the accident. Farletta stood quietly when I worked with her, and once again she seemed to enjoy my company.

A summer breeze wafted down the aisle, gently lifting Farletta's long mane as it billowed around us. *Thank you, God, for bringing us back together.* I picked up the blue comb and set to work detangling her tail.

Mounting still proved to be an issue. I had been working on that in my mind in recent months though. I understood my fear did not relate to riding but rather to the act of mounting. As I thought on this, I discovered how to isolate exactly what bothered me about mounting. Obviously, a big part of my problem was Farletta's refusal to stand still at the mounting block. But I felt fairly certain she was responding to my apprehension. Basically my energy and body language were telling her I was terrified, while my voice told her she should ignore that and stand still anyway.

When you mount a horse, you place your left foot in the stirrup, push off with your right foot, and swing your right leg over the saddle, landing in the seat. This should be all one fluid movement. For me, as soon as I put my foot in the stirrup and prepared to push off the mounting block with my right foot, Farletta would start moving, and I would panic. I realized it was the point after my foot left the mounting block but before my right leg swung over the horse that I felt vulnerable. It was a point where I had to fully trust my own balance and athletic ability to complete the motion safely whether my horse stood still or walked off.

The fall from Farletta a few years earlier created a painful and terrifying realization that my level of athletic or equestrian ability apparently could not be trusted. After all, if I could be thrown that severely, how could I expect to do any better now that I was both heavier and far less fit? With such thoughts and memories weighing on my mind, I put Farletta's blue comb away and picked up a kelly-green polo wrap.

Kneeling, I carefully wrapped Farletta's front legs. "Would you like to go for a ride today?"

Farletta turned her head and watched me, her lower lip stretching down, showing me her bottom teeth and gums. (I love her smile.) I scratched her neck.

"You are such a good girl." Those three small wrinkles I loved appeared below her eye, and her lips stretched and twitched.

"Good scratches, huh, girl?"

She flapped her lower lip up and down in response.

I hadn't ridden Farletta in a couple months because of my fear of mounting her. That day there was no one around the farm, and I relished the quiet. This meant no one would witness my experiment—also a good thing. I had an idea, a way I could get on Farletta without putting my foot in the stirrup or putting myself in the vulnerable moment where I'd be suspended between the safety of the mounting block and the security of being safely seated in the saddle.

I placed the western saddle on Farletta's back. She turned her head and watched me intently, her lower lip twitching. After securing the saddle I returned to the tack room and soon emerged with Farletta's bridle and my helmet.

"Are you ready?" I asked the mare.

Farletta took a couple steps to the right, giving me more room to bridle her, still twitching her lower lip. I unhooked the throat snap of her faded gray nylon halter and slipped it off her head, causing it to swing against the barn wall with a metallic thud as the halter's hardware struck the wood. I lifted the bridle, and Farletta eagerly dipped her head and opened her mouth, allowing me to slide the bit into place.

"I guess you are ready," I said with a smile, positioning the head piece and straightening the bit.

Grabbing the reins and bringing them over Farletta's neck, we then walked down the barn aisle and outside into the warm summer sun. The farm, located in a beautiful, secluded spot well off the main road, had a large parking area, which serviced a twenty-four-stall barn with an attached indoor arena. A large sand outdoor arena sat next to the parking area, while white-fenced paddocks stretched out toward the back of the farm. Deep, thick woods surrounded the entire property. The wooded areas provided miles of trails on which Farletta and I frequently hiked, but due to my fear of mounting, we seldom rode on them.

I walked Farletta across the large parking area to where my old GMC Sierra was parked. I had backed into the parking space so that the back of my truck lined up with the soft grass of the barnyard. I dropped the tailgate and sat on it with my legs dangling over the grass. I looked at Farletta and explained to her that I wanted to ride her today and we were going to try something new. She cocked one hind leg to a resting position and listened carefully while I spoke.

When my nerves had settled some, I carefully stood up on the tailgate. From this vantage point, my view looked down onto Farletta's back. I asked her to approach me, which she did obediently. I then reached over the saddle and gently tapped her flank, asking her to move her hindquarters closer, until she stood flush with the tailgate. I put the reins over her neck, took a deep breath, and prepared to mount. At this height, with no gap between Farletta's body and the truck, I simply had to lift my leg over the saddle and sit down. I could do this without ever taking my left foot off the tailgate until after I sat securely in the saddle, effectively eliminating that terrifying moment of vulnerability. My heart raced as I stood next to my horse. I spoke softly, telling her that I was nervous but we weren't in danger. Farletta let out a sigh and worked her mouth contentedly. She understood and she was ready. I whispered a quick prayer and lifted my right leg up, letting the inside of my calf touch the seat before pulling it back and replacing my right foot on the tailgate. I took a deep breath and lifted my right leg again. This time I completed the motion, swinging my leg over the saddle and sitting in the seat.

I did it! I'm on!

My demon hadn't been conquered, but it had certainly been dealt a deadly blow.

"Good girl!" I sang.

I reached down and stroked Farletta's smooth neck. Next I gently touched her sides. She obediently walked forward. I steered her carefully across the asphalt parking area, and we then traveled down the short path to the outdoor arena. Farletta seemed content, and I was elated. I'd finally found a way I could get on my horse without being terrified. I reached down and stroked Farletta's neck, running my fingers through her silky mane. I hadn't felt this connected to her since before the accident almost five years earlier.

CHAPTER THIRTY-FOUR

The gentleness of the fall-like breeze caressed me in the daytime, but with it came a sense of cold dread from somewhere deep inside me. Somehow the shift in the weather pulled at something within, tugging at … something I didn't want to discover. Already certain there was more to remember about what I'd endured at the hands of Mr. Vandersmelden, a kind of terror rumbled deep inside me. Along with an uncomfortable sense of knowing that what I had already remembered barely broke the surface of the murky pool that clung to and obscured my memories—something so much worse still lurked in the shadows.

Early August brought a welcome change from a blistering summer. High heat and humidity were replaced by pleasant temperatures in the low to mid-seventies. Each day seemed to bring crisp blue skies dotted with fluffy white clouds and a gentle breeze coming across the landscape. The rains finally came, and the ground greedily drank in the life-giving water, renewing the grass and flowers like a second spring.

We had gone from unusually hot to unusually cool. Though it was only mid-August, the essence of fall hung in the air. Fall is my favorite season. I love the crisp, clear nights and the unmistakable smells of decaying leaves and freshly turned dirt as the farmers harvest their crops and prepare the fields for the long, cold winter. I love the colors of the changing leaves and how they crunch under my feet after they float from their branches to carpet the ground in a beautiful mosaic of orange, red, and brown.

As much as I love the fall, this shift was occurring much too early. The abrupt change in weather gave me the feeling I was propelling forward much faster than I was prepared for. Toward what, I couldn't know. Yet there lingered a persistent sensation of cresting a steep hill in a car with brakes of questionable quality.

I'd felt the newest memory coming on for several weeks, but tried to ignore it. I did not feel prepared to deal with the uncontrollable crying, the deep terror, and the feelings of utter helplessness and despair that accompanied these memories as they finally broke the surface and sliced ruthlessly into my consciousness. The new image coming through was that of a small child with a full mouth. She looked at me with terrified eyes. I turned away, squeezing my eyes shut as hard as I could while shaking my head violently from side to side until her image disappeared. I wiped at my mouth, as if trying to remove something that has splattered all over my face, but there was nothing to remove, nothing I could see with my eyes or feel with my hands.

On a hot, mid-August night I no longer could squeeze my eyes shut and make that small child with the full mouth disappear back into my subconscious. Her eyes were filled with terror, her small body trembled, and salty tears streaked her face. She was trapped, but I couldn't help her. I saw darkness all around her, as if she were locked in a small, dark room, and I peeked in at her through a tiny secret window. She was not alone in the room. I knew it was him, and I knew what he was doing but ... *Please, God, I don't want to remember.*

I lay curled up in my bed praying sleep would come and take me away from this. Just as I drifted off, I'd jerk awake with a start, as if someone had screamed and startled me. This happened again and again until I was no longer close to sleep but rather lying atop my crumpled sheets, my heart pounding in my chest, faster and faster. Nausea swept over me, and I shivered. For the fifth time I got up, this time at four thirty. Sitting on the edge of my bed, I rocked back and forth, praying to God. *Please! I don't want to remember this!*

Once I'd successfully shut out the image, I crawled back under the covers.

"Please be over. Please be over …" I whispered a continuous loop into the dark night.

Closing my eyes, I saw the little girl again. She looked at me with her hazel eyes.

I am her.

I see his dark hair—not on his head. I was the girl with the full mouth. He grabbed my neck with both hands. I couldn't move … The memory came into focus.

Gripping my pillows tightly, I buried my face as uncontrollable sobs washed over me. My body trembled with the intensity of them.

"I don't want to remember!" I screamed out as I cried.

But it was too late. The memory had arrived, and I fell into it.

Mr. Vandersmelden made strange grunts and noises, and he gripped my neck tightly. I couldn't breathe. I shifted between the adult part of me, safe in my bed, and that little helpless girl being forced to do unspeakable things. What was real? It was so hard to tell. I cried louder and shook harder and squeezed the rock Ruth had given me to help me stay connected to reality. I tried to focus on the feeling of the rock in my hand, to stay present in the moment and not fully become that little girl again. But it was too late. My screams filled the room.

"No! No! No! Get away! Get away from me!"

My words were lost in a torrent of painful sobs.

My mom's alarmed voice came from the doorway. "What's wrong? What's wrong?!"

I couldn't speak, only cry harder.

She entered the room. "Please tell me what's wrong!"

"I don't want to remember," the little girl squeaked out. "Please hold me," I said to my mom.

She did while I cried and shook. Mom held me and talked to me and comforted me until the tears finally subsided, but I continued to shake for a long time. I was so relieved in that moment that I'd told her my other memories, for I could not imagine trying to endure this alone. I clutched my rock in one hand and Mom's hand in the other, and she held me until I knew I was all right.

Much later, sleep finally, mercifully, came for me, but I was changed forever. I had another piece of the puzzle.

Is this it? Surely it can't be worse than that, can it? Can it?

Journal Entry—August 24, 2012

Following the return of the memory of having Mr. Vandersmelden's penis in my mouth and hearing him grunt and moan like a disgusting pig I have once again left my body far behind it seems. The dissociated feeling is familiar but I am much more aware of the difference between being in my body vs. being dissociated and now I feel completely lost which makes it difficult to write this. I can't focus and I find that as before, I don't want to do anything or see anyone again. I think I understand now how I lived in solitude for all those years without getting lonely. You have to be in your body to feel loneliness. I think of the past few months and how I have been keenly aware of how much time I spend alone and how I literally have one friend I feel like I can reach out to. I have always been alone but I never felt truly, deeply lonely until recently. To return to my body means to allow feelings to return as well and to be aware of them and acknowledge them.

Now I am gone again and I feel nothing at all. There is an amount of comfort in this numbness but a part of me wants to rediscover that feeling of being present and really living in the moment ... that feeling of being alive. I kind of feel like I am floating above myself, drifting off to the right but I have a weak grasp on a thin string which connects me to my body. I could let go if I wanted to; or a strong wind could come along and rip the string from my hand leaving me to float around aimlessly with nowhere to land; no home-base to return to. How do I get back? Do I want to come back? If I don't feel, I can't hurt and I can't fear but, I also can't truly live. I can't feel the joy of seeing Farletta or the warmth of our reciprocal love and friendship. Why don't I want to do the things which once excited me?

I stay up until I can barely keep my eyes open so that when I finally lay down to sleep I don't have the time or energy to accidentally conjure up more memories. Can it be worse than what I've already remembered? I hope not ... please let this be the end. I still struggle with disbelief. This can't have really happened, right? This doesn't happen in real life. Did I really have this experience? I begin to doubt myself and my memory. Why would I physically and emotionally react the way I do if the memory wasn't real? The literature I've read on survivors of childhood sexual abuse indicate it is normal to have doubts as that is a way to protect yourself from the memory. I don't even know how to be that person. I never knew I had been sexually abused. I was just a girl who loved horses and could think of nothing else; a little weird and obsessive, perhaps, but nothing to get worked up about. Now I am someone else.

Hello, my name is Cheryl. Yup, I'm an adult and I love horses and still obsess about them. By the way, when I was a little girl a man used to stick his fingers in my vagina and then take me in a closet and make me suck on his penis. How are you?

I hate this. I think I'll stay out here on the end of this string a bit longer ... it seems safer out here.

IT HAD BEEN NEARLY a week since the night I spent terrorized by the newest memories. I was once again experiencing that disconnected out-of-my-body sensation that is characteristic of dissociation. I thought it would go away as time put distance between me and this newly remembered experience, but day after day I still felt disconnected, as if I were floating just above the surface of my mind. Prior to this, I'd felt I was finally living fully in the moment for the first time in a very long time. I'd been riding Farletta with some regularity, feeling like we were rediscovering each other and rebuilding our relationship.

I'd finally felt excited about going to the barn again, loving the opportunity to spend hours just being with my horse. But now, instead of feeling joy and connection in Farletta's presence, I felt nothing at all. Knowing I loved Farletta and wanted to spend time with her seemed more like something I'd learned somewhere along the way—as if I'd read it in a book and memorized as hard facts or instruction in how to enjoy my horse. I felt capable only of going through the motions, trying to reproduce a feeling from a distant memory.

My body numb, I could not feel the emotions and love that resided in the very fiber of my being, deep within my soul. The love, the joy, and the connection were all still in me, but I could not access them while I floated above my life, tenuously hanging on to my balloon string. Terribly confused by this utter lack of emotion toward Farletta, I wondered what had happened to our blossoming relationship.

Why did I suddenly no longer feel like riding her or spending time with her? I did not want to return to that dark place where Farletta and I weren't together. It felt as if Farletta were in a glass box—I could see her and I could stand close to her, but I could not feel her. I couldn't feel *us*.

CHAPTER THIRTY-FIVE

*A*n awkward ebb and flow interfered with the recovering relationship with Farletta. I'd ride her a few days in a row, reveling in the power and connection moving between us. Then my mind would fill with excuses—no time, too much homework, too tired—and I'd stop riding her. It was up and down—connection, retreat, connection, retreat. I didn't understand it.

Sometimes the recovered memories would sneak up on me, like a predator lurking in the woods, waiting for a flash of vulnerability before launching a surprise attack. The images and sensations would replay over and over, pulling me into the past, a victim once again, trapped inside the terrified mind of the little girl. This was not something I could predict. I learned to avoid certain television shows with stories of child molestation, but then there were the seemingly unrelated incidents—an innocent touch, a spoken word—that would sucker punch me and leave me gasping, grasping at flailing strings of reality in an effort to avoid slipping back into the dissociative state. I'd hear others speaking around me, but their voices sounded hollow and distant, like a forgotten television playing to an audience of empty chairs in the next room. My hands and arms tingled, but my body felt like an empty vessel, devoid of warmth and feeling—it was simply there. Nothing felt real. Nothing seemed important or relevant. I didn't feel sad or depressed, just empty.

THERE IS a truth in good horsemanship, one revealed to me through many years of riding and training: to be effective in your work with horses, you must remain present, in the moment, truly feeling the energy in and around you as life unfolds before you. As a student, retail employee, and later as a graduate assistant for the WMU social work field office, it was easy to remain in my head. I could function like this—disconnected from my body—in that academic setting without difficulty. It was such a familiar state to be in—having been there for most of my life, I didn't notice how much I did not allow myself to feel. But when I rode Farletta, I had to open myself to feeling not only her but also all those things I didn't want to feel. I'd protect myself by disconnecting, but in that act of dissociation, I'd lose my ability to connect to Farletta. Through our accident and her actions in the years that followed, Farletta had forced me to remember the abuse I'd suffered and to recognize, and deal with, the trauma it left me with. Now, my need to stay connected with my horse would be instrumental in helping me reconnect with myself. Farletta became a conduit, the cure to bring me back into my body.

Summer returned to the Midwest. The air, warm and heavy, blasted me when I slid out of the air-conditioned coolness of my truck. *No excuses. I need to try to ride her. I don't want to lose us again.* A gentle breeze touched my face. The sun slipped behind a cloud, making the air cooler and more inviting, as if God were giving me a little nudge of encouragement.

Farletta pushed her finely chiseled head over her stall door as I entered the barn. I never tired of looking at her beautiful features. She had her father's face, expressive and elegant. Every time I saw her, even on my darkest days, Farletta always greeted me with the same bright-eyed look. With her shapely ears pricked forward, she gently lifted her chin toward me, as if pointing to me and saying, "Hey, I'm glad you're here." I greeted her with soft touches and a gentle hello. Farletta nuzzled my shirt and turned her head toward the halter hanging on her stall door.

I lifted the halter from its hook. "Is this what you want?"

I held the gray-and-pink halter in front of her. Farletta dipped her head into the contraption. She backed up without my asking, allowing me to open her door, and then followed me into the barn aisle. Like always, I listened to the clip-clop of her bare hooves on the cement aisle when she stepped out of her stall. Moving fluidly and symmetrically alongside me, her steps sounded normal, healthy. I smiled.

Tying her in our usual spot, I asked, "How about it, Farletta? Are you up for a ride today?"

Farletta stood quietly while I brushed her already glistening coat. I felt myself mentally edging closer to my body, moving a few inches down my balloon string. I put on her protective leg gear and the western saddle. Farletta turned her head to look at me, the skin just below her eye developing the three wrinkles I loved so much. I removed her halter and grabbed the bridle. Farletta enthusiastically dipped her head into the bridle, automatically opening her mouth to receive the bit. She kept her head low so I could slip the headstall over her ears, then lifted her face and looked at me. The wrinkles returned under her eye when she pulled her lower lip back in that happy smile.

"Let's go." We turned and walked toward the door.

Mounting was still a process. Farletta waited patiently while I ensured all her tack was adjusted perfectly and everything was just right. I led her over to my truck, where I'd already dropped the tailgate. Nerves gripping me, I sat on the tailgate, letting out a deep breath through my parted lips, making a soft whistling sound as I exhaled. Farletta looked at me with patience, but I could see she was ready. I needed to trust her. I stood up on the tailgate and turned to find Farletta had already positioned herself. Her left side was pressed firmly against the edge of the tailgate so there was no gap between her and the truck. I gathered up the reins and lifted my right leg over the saddle, sliding onto her back. She waited until I was seated, and then we moved off.

As we entered the arena, a bay Thoroughbred in a nearby paddock took off at a wild gallop. The ground rumbled while he tore around in large circles. He screamed a high-pitched whinny. The other horses stirred, shifted nervously, and looked around, wide eyed. Soon all the horses were running in their paddocks, bucking and spinning in a giant cloud of dust produced by their thundering hooves. Farletta lifted her head to look at them. I sent her a picture in my mind to assure her there was no danger. The horses were simply excited—it would soon be dinnertime. Farletta relaxed into my hands, moving smoothly under me.

Years of horsemanship taught me that if I stayed focused on Farletta and what we were trying to accomplish, she would stay with me, rather than allowing the energy of the running horses to draw her into their excitement. The horses galloped and played around us, but I soon realized I was no longer holding the balloon string or floating above my mind. Rather, I had come back into my body. I could feel the motion of my horse, the firmness of the saddle, the stirrups on the balls of my feet. I could smell the fly spray mingled with Farletta's wonderful horse aroma.

I melted around my horse, and we became one being, moving effortlessly around the arena. I now fully realized how the act of riding had the power to end my dissociative period and bring me back into my body. I was relieved to discover a way to bring myself back. I also had a new understanding for how horses worked their magic in a therapeutic setting, the field of study I was building my new career around. Joy filled my heart. I could feel *us* again. Farletta knew how to bring me back. I suspected she had always known.

The horses settled down in their paddocks, and I took Farletta for one more loop around the large arena. I steered her toward the center of the enclosure, guiding her more with my mind than my body. Exhaling, I sank deeper into the saddle, cueing Farletta to halt. When I slid off her back, Farletta turned to me, the three wrinkles under her eye and her lower lip pulled back in her beautiful smile.

"Thank you, Farletta." In silence we turned toward the barn, dust kicking up and swirling around our feet. *I am the luckiest girl in the world.*

Journal Entry—September 16, 2012

I think now I understand why I go through these on and off periods—riding for several days and then slipping back into the non-riding mode. Riding (or at least riding well) requires me to be fully present in the moment. I need to feel my horse and respond to and direct her energy; it is the only way to be an effective rider. However, to be this present I risk letting other sensations seep in; those feelings and memories I've worked so hard to keep out over all these years. Riding becomes an activity which has the potential to be both exciting and terrifying at the same time. I don't really have a fear of falling (OK, I do but it's not a debilitating fear—it's more of a healthy respect for gravity and the fact I'm not fifteen anymore) but I do have a very real fear of the emotional impact of being present enough to ride—to do this I must also make myself vulnerable to remembering and feeling stuff I'd just as soon forget.

Even as I write that I realize that the healing which has taken place in my life is a direct result of being present in my body and feeling and remembering (Farletta has helped me with this). But that knowledge doesn't make it any less painful or scary.

I CONTINUED to be haunted by the image of that little girl screaming in an empty room. She had something to say, something important, and I was the only one in a position to hear her. In our sessions, I talked to Ruth about the little girl. We talked about arrested development, about how trauma during childhood could cause a portion of an individual's personality to stop development and remain trapped in the state at which the trauma occurred. She said this is not uncommon in abuse victims, as it is a way the mind protects itself from an event so horrifying the child is unable to deal with it at the time it occurred. I came to realize a part of me was still inside that little girl. To deny her and shut her down hurt both of us.

"You are not that little girl anymore," Ruth told me one day.

She went on to explain how I had the power now to listen to her and help her step into her future. She didn't have to stay trapped as a victim in the past.

"You have a niece around the same age, don't you?" Ruth asked. "What would you say to her in this situation? Would you listen to her or ignore her?"

I decided to listen. The healing began.

CHAPTER THIRTY-SIX

At first it wasn't easy to listen to the little girl's story. I felt vulnerable, scared, naked, and utterly alone as we relived the memories together. I struggled to remain present, to stay connected to my adult body rather than retreating into the mental state of that little girl. Something completely unexpected happened as I cautiously explored the memories and, through writing this memoir, finally gave a voice to that little girl. I not only grew to know who that little girl really was, but I also learned the true identity of Mean Cheryl and, more importantly, the purpose she once served. I listened to the little girl, and my life, my belief of my insanity and social ineptitude—it all began to make sense.

Until I finally started recovering the memories, I'd spent my life believing I was not only crazy and socially crippled, but also deeply flawed. I looked around me and saw seemingly normal people, peers with lots of friends and, as we grew older, romantic relationships. All around me were people who liked to go out in groups, hang out at parties, and have fun. Some of them wanted me to go with them. I went to a few parties in junior high and high school, which were anxiety filled and often painful experiences. For the most part I pushed people away, preferring to sit in silence, read, and think about horses. When anyone of the opposite sex showed anything resembling interest in me, I panicked and retreated.

About the third grade I'd begun to gain weight. I soon outgrew my short lavender-and-white skirt I'd begged Mom to buy me for school. What a relief when the skirt became too small. I never wore another for a long time. In junior high we had a terrible sex-ed class, where the teacher told the girls if we were ever raped, not to fight, just relax and try and enjoy it. I was horrified. I hid myself in mounds of fat, believing the weight would keep me safe from rape. Who would want to touch fat, ugly me? At the same time I constantly berated myself for being a fat, ugly, and horrible person.

In my world, sex was dirty and something to be feared or ashamed of. I hated hearing sex-themed songs on the radio—they felt both shameful and uncomfortable. Nothing has changed, even now. As I grew older and became interested in boys, and later, men, I lived in an eternal state of conflict—attracted to the opposite sex, but at the same time my mind screamed "This is not safe!" When my girlfriends entered into relationships with guys, I worried for them, constantly filled with conflict wanting my friends to be happy, but also feeling like they were putting themselves in a vulnerable and potentially dangerous situation. For me, men in general were not to be trusted. This feeling, unfortunately, extended to my dad and my stepdad. I struggled for years with my relationship with both of them.

There were other events in my past that started to make sense when viewed through the lens of the traumatized little girl. One in particular is the morning at breakfast when I took a drink of orange juice, gagged violently, and immediately spit it all over the table. Orange juice was my usual breakfast drink, but the feeling of the pulp in my mouth made me gag and nearly vomit. When I put the memory together with what I knew happened with Mr. Vandersmelden … I haven't had orange juice since that day over thirty years ago.

I had never liked anyone touching my neck, but the aversion escalated after the memories returned. One afternoon I was sitting in my chair watching TV, when my mom came up behind me and placed her hands on my shoulders, the inside curve of her thumbs and forefingers touching the sides of my neck. My shoulders shot upward, clamping her hands against my neck.

"Don't touch my neck! Don't touch my neck!" I yelled and began to cry.

Mom had to pull her hands free. I was unable to make my shoulders drop and release them.

"He grabbed my neck," I tried to explain through my tears. "He grabbed my neck and told me not to tell anyone because everyone would hate me and they'd know I was a bad, bad girl. He told me not to tell or he would kill my mommy!"

The words squeaked out of me in the voice of the little girl. I fought to stay in the present. When I finally looked up, there were tears in Mom's eyes. This was new to her too, and I could see she struggled with the sorrow of learning too late what had happened to me. I stood up, and we hugged for a long time.

Making sense of past events and behaviors delivered a huge relief for me. That I was normal became validated, as now I could see there was a legitimate reason for all of those things that for so long had me believing I was crazy—the odd social behaviors, seemingly irrational fear, self-hatred, self-harm, and feelings of worthlessness, all of it. I was *normal*. The things I went through were symptoms of PTSD stemming from the sexual abuse. Even though I hadn't remembered the abuse consciously for so many years, it still affected every part of my life—relationships, health, employment … my whole world.

Another liberating discovery was the true identity and purpose of Mean Cheryl. That hateful voice in my head actually started life as a coping mechanism. When children struggle with a difficult situation or traumatic event, they will often blame themselves as a way to make sense of what happened. This is seen over and over in divorce cases, when the children can't understand the complexities of a relationship that is broken beyond repair. Therefore, they decide it must be something they did to cause Mommy and Daddy to split up. The child will reason that the divorce is because of constant fighting with siblings, poor grades, or simply not being loveable enough. The child will build an entire story around this belief. It is the only way they can make it understandable to a mind that is still developmentally residing in the narcissistic stage.

In my case, not only was I in that self-centered stage of development when I believed everything that happened was because of something I did, Mr. Vandersmelden also told me I was at fault.

"You're such a pretty little girl," he'd said.

In my younger mind, my being pretty was the reason Mr. Vandersmelden had molested me. Clearly being pretty wasn't safe.

I had a favorite Snoopy pencil that had been used so frequently, it was just a few inches long. One day Mr. Vandersmelden took the pencil from me and threw it away. I retrieved it from the trash and continued to use it. This angered him.

I have always remembered this incident with the pencil, but I now made the connection that the molestation had occurred after I had been defiant toward that man. I had learned that making a mistake or a wrong choice, or even simply standing up for myself, all were also not safe. The realization hit me like a sonic boom—how that man's actions had influenced mine even years after he no longer had access to me. Choices I'd made in the name of protection, my inability to promote myself, defend myself, even see my own value—all of these were "protections" to keep me safe. Don't rock the boat ... don't bring attention to myself ... don't make a mistake ... don't *dare* challenge anyone in authority. Further, I could see how the deeply ingrained fear of that terrified little girl (*she is me*) turned her (*me*) into an adult who pandered to and placated male authority figures, needing them to tell me I was doing a good job because I couldn't risk the danger of telling that to myself. Or worse, and far more dangerous, I couldn't risk challenging their authority—always backtracking, always downplaying my knowledge, my ability, my skills, and not even aware that I was doing it, or why.

Way back then, Mr. Vandersmelden had also warned that everyone would hate me if they knew what I had done with him. When I thought about what Mean Cheryl had said to me over the years, much of it sounded like what Mr. Vandersmelden had told me, and the conclusions I'd come to about why he had molested me in the first place. The other purpose Mean Cheryl served was to never let me look too deeply into what I was feeling. Any time a bad thing happened in my life, Mean Cheryl made sure to insist it was my fault. She insinuated I was stupid and worthless, ugly and horrible. That everything bad was my fault—a very important part of the coping mechanism was that if something was indeed my fault, I had the power to stop it. Therefore, I still held the control.

While growing up and struggling with depression and anxiety, Mean Cheryl steered out of control. But with recognition of the abuse, she no longer served to help me cope with something I couldn't understand (however dysfunctional her "help" may have been) but instead became a destructive force, directing blame for all things onto me with no hope of ever rising above it. When I reached adulthood, Mean Cheryl was no longer recognizable as a coping mechanism. She had become like a one-trick pony that had somehow risen to a management position. The once useful member of the management team had become a Godzilla-like monster, wielding her power with reckless abandon.

The former, moderately useful middle manager had become a serious liability.

CHAPTER THIRTY-SEVEN

Farletta was already outside when I arrived at the farm on a warm summer evening. It had been the kind of day where, despite the heaviness in the air, you felt relief from the sun dipping below the horizon, where its brutal rays could no longer bake your skin. Heat rose up from the sand-covered lane while I walked out to get Farletta from the paddock she shared with her boyfriend, Ernie. When I arrived at the gate, Farletta stood by a tree, swishing her tail absently at flies, her head hanging low. I whistled and called to her. In a single lackluster movement, Farletta lifted and turned her head. She paused for a moment, as if summoning the energy to make the next move, or perhaps to decide if she even felt like making a move at all. Finally, she lifted one front leg, then a hind leg as she drifted in my direction.

She doesn't seem quite right. I quickly shut down the negative thoughts forming in my mind. Her bad eye had been doing so well for so long, I had let myself believe this flare-up–free existence was her new normal. When Farletta arrived at the gate, I slipped her halter on her head and led her out of the paddock.

I placed a hand on her sleek neck. "How are you doing, girl?"

When we entered the barn aisle, Farletta drifted to the right and clipped her shoulder on the door. *She didn't see that.* I shook my head. *Maybe she just wasn't paying attention,* my mind retorted. We arrived at her stall, and I looped her rope around the tie ring, securing it with a slipknot. I patted my mare's sleek neck, working my way up toward her head, absently pushing the black half of her mane over to the right side of her neck as I moved my hand to remove her fly mask. I pulled at the mask's Velcro closures, which released with a crackling sound, and I lifted the mask off her Farletta's face.

Like a kick in the gut, what I saw floored me. Farletta's left eye was clear but lacked the light and energy I was used to. I ducked under her head to look at her right eye. I found it almost swollen shut, the lids jerking and jumping with spasms. I attempted to push the eyelids apart with my fingers. I saw it only briefly before she jerked her head away. It was cloudy with a bluish-green tint. The pupil was almost completely constricted. She had run into the door because she couldn't see it. With her eye in severe flare-up, she was almost completely blind on her right side. Fluid leaked out of the corner of Farletta's eye as the lids continued to twitch and jerk with the constant and painful spasms. Farletta's lips were pulled tight in a grimace. Her nostrils had acquired a pinched, oval shape indicative of either pain or anger. In this case, it might have been both.

"Oh, baby, I'm so sorry." I went to the other end of the barn aisle to turn off the lights. Any light seemed painful to Farletta when her eye was in flare-up. I wondered how long she had been like this. She'd been fine the last time I saw her, less than forty-eight hours before. I knew the farm manager would have called me had she seen her eye like this, so it must have come on abruptly—terrifying, as it had never advanced this quickly before.

The next hour was spent applying cold washcloth compresses, trying to get the swelling down enough that I could get medication into her eye. Eventually the oral anti-inflammatory and compresses reduced the swelling enough I could push her eyelids open to administer the medications. Forcing her eye open caused the lids to swell even larger, and now her eye was completely swollen shut.

I stayed with Farletta late into the evening, waiting for the pain medications to kick in and give her some relief. She didn't want to be handled or brushed, so I just sat with her, talking to her and waiting. It was well after dark when she finally seemed to experience some relief. The air had cooled some, but the earth still held the heat of the day, and I could feel it radiating like hot embers as I walked Farletta back down the lane to her paddock.

"I love you, baby," I said, letting her through the paddock gate. "Be careful and feel better soon."

Farletta twitched her lower lip in a halfhearted smile. I obediently gave her a treat.

"And you be nice to her, Ernie. She doesn't feel well."

A snorted response drifted into my ears from somewhere in the darkness. I gave Farletta a final pat on the neck, latched the gate, and headed back toward the barn.

"This can't be happening again," I said aloud to the stars. They flickered an indecipherable response, like they so often did.

FARLETTA PUSHED her head over the stall gate, pressing her muzzle softly against me. Searching my hands with curious lips, she retrieved her prize, then retreated to the darkened corner of her stall. Her right eye looked a little better than it had the day I'd discovered the flare-up. It was no longer swollen shut, but I could see the eye itself was still discolored and painful. Farletta had been receiving oral and ocular medications four times each day for the past few days in addition to restricting turnout to only after the sunlight had disappeared from the sky. She'd improved briefly and then seemed to relapse—something that had never happened before while on medications.

Farletta stood in the corner of her stall, her head lowered and her right eye twitching and squinting. She was clearly still uncomfortable and seemed to be bothered even by the dim amount of daylight coming through her stall window. The gate opened with a soft squeak as I entered the stall. I placed a hand on her haunches to let her know I was there and approached her on her right side.

"Hey, girl," I called softly.

She turned her head toward me slightly, without lifting it, her lower lip twitching. I placed my hand on her neck—she felt cold and clammy despite the heat of the day.

I had been at this point before, where treatment was ineffective and Farletta was suffering greatly. The previous winter I had scheduled Farletta to have the eye removed. I'd even driven her to the clinic, leaving her there for surgery to take place the next day. I'd felt empowered by my decision, taking the initiative to make a difficult and unpopular choice for the well-being of my horse. There is no cure for uveitis in horses—eventually, she would lose it anyway, and therefore I could see no reason to prolong her suffering over something we could never save.

The morning of the surgery, Dr. Brown called me and said he would not perform the enucleation, as he felt the eye still looked too healthy to give up on it. His words had felt like a punch in my gut, forcing the breath out of me before I burst into tears. Not the trickling, quiet, hide-my-true-feelings tears, but the uncontrollable sobbing of an inconsolable child who has just watched her horse rundown by an eighteen-wheeler. The intensity of my reaction took us both by surprise.

I felt helpless, completely disempowered, like that little girl trapped in the closet with the monster. It was a horrible sensation, not feeling in control of what was happening to my horse—worse, it felt like a death sentence for Farletta. Indeed, a true overreaction on my part, unless you could understand where I was drawing from—filtering the situation through the mind of that traumatized little girl.

Now, here I was again at the same precipice. I called Dr. Brown, telling him about the flare-up and how Farletta was worse after treatment rather than better. He wanted to give her a bit longer to respond to meds before discussing eye removal. What could I do? I couldn't make him take her eye out. He had the right to refuse. I didn't feel right approaching a different vet when it was Dr. Brown who knew her history and treatments. I also fully trusted his expertise and didn't want some stranger performing surgery on my mare. However, at the same time, I worried whether he would follow through with his promise to remove her eye, "no questions asked," if she weren't able to return to a normal life on the new anti-inflammatory medication he'd prescribed after refusing to remove her eye the previous winter.

"This is definitely not normal." I slipped the faded nylon halter on her head. "C'mon, girl," I said as I led the mare from her stall.

The summer sun shone bright outside the barn. The stalls and barn aisle were open and airy, which was great for ventilation but did not afford Farletta much protection from indirect sunlight. She stood tied in the barn aisle, head lowered, eyes squinting. The light had never bothered her indoors. Farletta turned her right eye away from the doorway. My heart groaned, sinking deep within me. I felt so useless. *What am I doing wrong?* That same old narrative of self-blame resurfaced. *Why can't I fix this?*

An idea interrupted my thoughts. I went to the tack room, which housed a wooden box holding Farletta's things.

After rummaging around for several minutes, I finally emerged from the tack room with a green hood, the style that racehorses wear on the track, often referred to as "blinkers" or a "blinker hood." It was a hood with a fully enclosed opaque eye cup, which Farletta had worn following her surgery at Michigan State University, where they had placed a cyclosporine implant in her eye almost two years before as a treatment for the uveitis. A surgery that, like all the other treatments I'd tried, was ultimately unsuccessful.

"Do you want to wear this?" I asked Farletta, holding up the green hood so she could sniff it.

She pushed her head forward and leaned into the crossties, as if she were trying to get as close to the hood as possible.

"I'll take that as a yes." I unhooked the Velcro closures on the green hood.

Once the hood was secured, Farletta was visibly more relaxed. Her body seemed to deflate as she released the pent-up tension. She licked and chewed, working her mouth softly—a sign of release and contentment. Finally, a long, soft sigh escaped her, and she lowered her head into a relaxed position.

"Feel better?" I asked, relieved I was able to do something to help her.

The hood completely blinded her right side, but it also protected her bad eye from any light. Contented, she wore the hood without being bothered at all by the loss of vision. The sensitivity to light bore a clear sign that the uveitis had come back with a vengeance, so much so, that she needed light completely blocked out in order to get some relief.

After a couple of weeks, Farletta's eye returned to some version of normal. The pupil no longer responded the same to light as it had before and was frequently more constricted than the pupil in her normal left eye. The right eye also took on a bit of a haze, which never quite cleared up.

Dr. Brown wanted to wait and see if Farletta could go several months without a flare-up, as she had prior to this last one, before he was willing to again discuss eye removal. I could see his point. One or two flare-ups a year were better than the five or six she'd had before going on the new anti-inflammatory. However, I could see no point in risking her enduring another flare-up as bad as the one she had just gone through. It was cruel to do that to her, knowing eye removal could completely and permanently end her pain. I reluctantly searched for another equine eye specialist.

SEPTEMBER ROLLED INTO OCTOBER, and cool fall breezes chased away the heat of the long summer. I slid out of my old truck, admiring Farletta's new residence. I'd relocated her a month earlier because the farm we had enjoyed for the past two years would soon be closing.

The leaves burned with brilliant color as they died and eventually drifted to the earth in their beautiful dance of the changing season. A warm, soft sweatshirt now covered my summer T-shirt. I walked into the barn. Farletta was out in the pasture enjoying the remaining warmth of the October sunshine, the large red bay swatches of color on her body picking up the orange light of the waning sun.

"You're getting all fuzzy and cute," I said when I reached the pasture gate. "Actually," I continued, fingering the lengthening winter hair on her neck, "you're always cute, fuzzy or otherwise."

Farletta snorted her response before lifting her head from the grass and placing her muzzle into my hands. Finding no treat there, she tilted her head to one side and pricked her ears, like a dog cocking its head when it hears its master's voice. Farletta's lower lip twitched as she drew it back, exposing her lower gums. At the same time, the skin below her eyes pulled down slightly, forming those three small wrinkles.

"I love your beautiful smile." I reached into my pocket and produced a treat. "Even your eyes smile."

Farletta accepted the treat from my right hand. Chewing her prize, she moved her delicate muzzle across my sweatshirt to my left pocket, just in case another treat resided there too.

"You'll get another later. You know you always do."

I slipped the halter over her head, and she followed me into the barn.

Farletta's eye had not flared up since the last episode the end of August. It still did not look normal, but she seemed comfortable much of the time. I did notice she occasionally came in with nicks and bumps on the right side of her face and body, and I suspected she had lost more of her vision during the last flare-up. *Maybe she would be OK keeping her eye after all?* I thought with a tiny glimmer of hope.

But Farletta's next flare-up occurred just a week or so later. It began as any other flare-up, with swollen eyelids, the tender pink skin of her inner lids streaked with angry red lines of inflammation. Her pupil constricted, and her eye grew hazy and green. I started treatment with eye medications and Banamine, but this time progress was minimal. Farletta became dull and listless. She bumped into walls and gate posts as she navigated her surroundings with her head hung low and her right eye squinting and painful. Soon the pupil disappeared into a tiny slit, and her beautiful multifaceted brown iris discolored to blackened mud.

I hadn't yet found another eye specialist for Farletta, as I'd only been searching halfheartedly. Despite my difference of opinion about the ethics of delaying eye removal, I still respected Dr. Brown and trusted his expertise in her care. However, I suspected there would be an argument when it came time to make a final decision about eye removal. I feared Dr. Brown would not remember his promise from the year before.

I called Dr. Brown to let him know what was going on with Farletta. He wanted to see pictures of her eye before he made any sort of decision and asked if I would email current pictures. In the meantime, he wanted me to keep Farletta on her meds as usual. I took some pictures later that day and emailed them to Dr. Brown. I was discouraged with the timing—it would soon be the weekend, and I knew I likely would not hear back from him until Monday.

The weekend was cold and rainy. Most of the leaves were down for the season, and the bare trees looked naked and unprepared for the icy, cold breath of winter. The damp air seeped through my layers of clothing and nestled deep into my bones, chilling me from the inside out. Farletta stood in the corner of her stall, her hay mostly uneaten, loosely piled at her feet. I called to her as I opened her stall, the wheels of the sliding door making a metallic swooshing noise as they slid across the overhead track. Farletta stayed motionless with her head in the corner. I whistled softly to her and pressed my hand against her haunches, asking her to turn toward me. Farletta stayed where she was, unmoving except for a subtle flattening of her ears against her head. Her nostrils were pinched and oval in shape. She was in pain.

I walked slowly over to Farletta, speaking softly to her. Slipping a hand into the pocket of my hooded sweatshirt, I retrieved a treat and presented it to her. Farletta flicked an ear and tipped her head in my direction, lipping the treat briefly before extending her lips and bringing it into her mouth. She held the treat in her teeth and bit down, breaking the horse cookie before opening her mouth and letting the uneaten pieces fall to the ground.

Farletta was miserable. It was clear her medication was making her sick. Her inflamed eye in constant spasms told me the meds were also no longer working. The light had gone from her eyes, her bright and gentle spirit doused by the constant pain. Worse, there was nothing I could do, nothing I could give her to stop the pain or colic symptoms, as the medications I would use to treat her for colic were the same medications that were making her sick. She had reached a point of intolerance; her meds were toxic to her. There was no longer a question of the ethics of removing a "relatively healthy" eye. It was now about removing an eye to save Farletta's life.

I did not wait to get an email response from Dr. Brown regarding the pictures I'd sent. I went home and emailed him that night explaining how sick Farletta was and that I feared for her life. This was a big step for me, advocating for myself and my horse—a thought that had completely crippled me with terror less than a year before.

Dr. Brown called the next business day, and we scheduled an evaluation for Farletta. Dr. Brown wanted one last look at her eye before agreeing to remove it. If, following the evaluation, Dr. Brown determined it was time to remove her eye, Farletta would stay at the clinic and have the surgery the next morning.

My nerves twisted and turned in my gut as I remembered the events of a year ago and the devastation I'd felt when Dr. Brown refused to remove Farletta's eye. I had felt so powerless and unable to help my horse. Having made so much progress in understanding and dealing with the PTSD symptoms from the sexual abuse, I was now in a better place to deal with whatever Dr. Brown said. I knew he did not hold the ultimate power over my horse and my decisions.

Later that night, the uncertainty and helplessness were still with me despite the knowledge I held the power. I still wanted Dr. Brown to perform the surgery. I closed my eyes and asked God for help. After I finished my prayer, I sat in the silent room, my eyes closed as I listened for His voice. Suddenly, an amazing feeling of peace washed over me, and I knew, without a doubt, Dr. Brown would remove the eye without question. I felt as certain of this as I was of my own name.

It had been nearly three years since Farletta's initial diagnosis. Uveitis is a brutal foe, a cruel and debilitating disease that does not offer a fair fight. It affects each horse differently, causing terrible pain and suffering while offering no chance of a cure and no real hope of discovering the true cause. No matter how hard you fight, eventually you lose. I would not look at a horse's eyes the same again.

I tenuously walked the fine line between pain control and drug toxicity while waiting for Farletta's appointment. I tried to explain to Farletta what was going to happen, to tell her the vet could end her pain but she wouldn't be able to see on her right side anymore. Ever. In the days leading up to her surgery, Farletta wore her green hood with the fully enclosed eye cup. Her body was hard and tense, and her flanks were drawn up with pain and distress.

No smile greeted me when I arrived at the barn the day of the appointment. Farletta stood in the corner of her stall, her head lowered into the shadows, uneaten hay strewn about her feet. I applied protective shipping boots to her legs. Farletta hadn't been a difficult horse to load into a trailer for many years, but she was always hesitant, wanting to give the trailer a thorough inspection and frequently stepping in and out two or three times, trying to determine just how serious I was about a particular trip. As I prepared her for her trailer ride, I told Farletta she was going to the vet and her eye would never hurt her again. Once again I promised she would never suffer another flare-up. This time I knew I would be able to keep my promise.

I slid open the heavy door at the end of the barn aisle, and Farletta and I emerged into the gray light of another cloudy autumn day. Farletta flicked her ears forward when she saw the open door of the horse trailer—she pulled me toward it. Not waiting for me to ask her to load, never even a pause, she simply walked to the open door and hopped in.

The drive to the clinic took an hour. I had mixed emotions while I navigated the truck and trailer north to the small Michigan town where Dr. Brown practiced. Farletta stood quietly in the trailer behind me, not even giving her customary few kicks when we first started out the driveway. At the clinic, I unloaded Farletta and brought her into the barn. We had been here many times over the past few years. I waited for Dr. Brown, remembering the first visit when Farletta was initially diagnosed. I recalled the despair of learning her prognosis but also the relief and hope in hearing it might take several years before she lost vision in her eye. None of us had any idea it would progress so quickly and viciously.

Dr. Brown came through the door that adjoined the clinic offices and the barn. "How are you today?" he asked Farletta.

I always appreciated how kind and gentle he was with her. I restated what I'd told Dr. Brown in the email, explaining how sick she'd been and how I feared for her life and well-being. Using his optic scope, Dr. Brown examined Farletta's eye. Looking up from the scope, he clicked off the tiny light. His face was hard to read as our eyes met, but as always there was kindness and concern.

"Yes. I'll take this eye out for you."

CHAPTER THIRTY-EIGHT

A day after the surgery, I once again navigated my truck north toward the equine medical clinic to pick up Farletta. Boedy sat in the backseat, watching the southwest Michigan landscape slide by outside the window. I wasn't sure what to expect when I arrived at the clinic and saw Farletta for the first time without her eye. Would it be swollen and bulging? Would the sutures look gruesome? An image from the music video for "Man in the Box," sung by Alice in Chains, kept playing in my mind as if it were stuck in a continuous loop of tape. At the end of the video, they show a man in a black cloak with his eyes sewn shut. Rather creepy.

Boedy stretched his neck over the gap between the front and back seats and placed his head on my right shoulder. I reached up with my right hand and scratched behind his ears.

"It won't matter how it looks, will it, buddy?" I patted Boedy's head. "She'll still be the prettiest horse in the world, won't she?"

Boedy pressed his chin firmly against my shoulder, then nosed my cheek before returning to his observation post in the backseat.

A twinge of nervous excitement spiraled through me when we pulled into the clinic drive. I let Boedy run around the big open field behind the clinic while I maneuvered the truck to hook up the horse trailer. Bending over the hitch, I carefully checked and rechecked all the connections. Satisfied all was proper and safe, I whistled. Boedy came bounding across the field in leaping strides, his ears bouncing up and down with his happy gait.

"Get in the truck," I said as he approached.

With a single brilliant leap, Boedy flew through the open door of the cab and landed softly on his seat. I drove the truck and trailer around to the front of the clinic and parked it in the loading zone.

"You stay here," I said to Boedy as I exited the truck.

I entered the barn area, and looking on down the row, I could see the partially open door of the next stall after the feed room and headed that direction. There was a vet tech in the stall with Farletta.

"Hello," I called, leaning into the open doorway.

"Oh, hi," the tech said as she turned her head to look over her shoulder. "I was just in here cleaning her up for you."

Farletta's right side faced the wall. Her green hood with the fully enclosed eye cup covered her head, with the closures hanging open beneath her jaw. The tech removed the hood and turned Farletta so I could see the right side of her face.

Farletta's eyelid was indeed sewn shut, but she did not look gruesome or creepy. I had opted to have a prosthesis placed in the empty socket. The prosthesis, an eyeball-sized globe made of what looked like hard black rubber, was placed in the empty socket so it would appear there was an eye under her closed lids. It was a more aesthetically pleasing alternative to an empty socket, which in my experience gave a sunken-in look to the entire side of the head over time. At least that was what I had seen with the few one-eyed broodmares I had known. Dr. Brown had placed several of these globes over the years and never had a problem with one. There was a small amount of swelling that made her eye socket bulge, but it didn't look too bad. A thick silver "bandage" had been sprayed over the entire eye. There was a single visible suture at the front corner of the eye.

"Just one suture?" I had pictured at least half a dozen along the edges of her lid.

"Yes," the tech said, "just one on the outside. There are several sutures inside, which will dissolve within a couple weeks."

"It looks great."

Reaching into my pocket, I retrieved a special treat I had picked up at the tack shop on the way to the vet clinic. The treat was an unbaked cookie made of grains and molasses. A red-and-white-striped peppermint candy was pressed into the center. Farletta gobbled up the sugar-laden treat and eagerly searched my hand for another.

"There are more in the truck," I told her as her lower lip twitched. "Be patient. I have to pay your bill first."

Farletta's recovery went smoothly over the next two weeks. She wore the green hood with the full eye cup to prevent her from rubbing the sutures as she healed. The swelling went down gradually, and the boney structures that made up her eye socket became more prominent. Although her lids were sewn shut, Farletta still had a blink response. The muscles around her eye still worked, and much to my happy surprise, the three wrinkles still appeared under her missing eye when she smiled.

Within a couple days of returning home, Farletta's mood brightened and her spirit returned full force. Seeing the light return to her lifted my own spirits. I had made the right decision. I'd advocated for my horse and made a difficult choice. This was a big deal for me. Standing up for what I thought was best, and giving voice to my opinion, for decades had been associated with danger. Albeit subconsciously, the self-preservation of remaining unheard and unseen had long been part of my post-trauma safety net.

One warm afternoon in late October, I stood in front of Farletta as I brushed her silky black forelock. Once the hair was smooth and straight, I used the soft bristles of the brush to rub her forehead gently. Farletta leaned into the brush and moved her head slightly up and down, her left eye closed as she savored the sensation of the bristles rubbing her itchy forehead. Stepping back from the brush, Farletta shook her head and gave a satisfied snort. She then stretched her lips out toward my hands.

"I have no treats." I lifted my hands for her to inspect.

Farletta worked her lips over my hands and, discovering no treats, grabbed the brush in her teeth and snatched it from me.

"Hey!" I reached for the brush.

Farletta held the brush tightly in her teeth while nodding her head up and down. After a moment she released the brush at the top of her nodding motion. The brush flew through the air in an arc and landed near the stall door with a clank of the wooden handle hitting the cement floor.

"Cute." I grinned.

Inside I was dancing. It had been years since Farletta had been playful like that.

I stroked her neck. "You must be feeling better." I had forgotten what a happy and playful horse she was—it had been so long since she had shown me this side of herself.

At the end of two weeks, I gently snipped and removed the one suture in the corner of her eye. There was only a very thin line where the lids were joined. Dr. Brown had done a beautiful job. He had passion and love for his specialty, and I knew that would translate into excellent, aesthetically pleasing work.

Now that she had recovered, I began lightly longeing Farletta. She had been trained with both voice and visual commands for longeing. I wondered if she would struggle traveling to the right, as she would not be able to see the visual commands. Farletta adapted quickly and easily to longeing with unilateral vision. It took several trips to the right, making odd ovals and amoeba shapes, before she found a true circle. Farletta had previously been more responsive to hand signals, and it took her a few minutes to focus on what I was saying and to also develop a feel for when she reached the outside perimeter of her circle. Each time she drifted in toward the center of the circle, I gave her the command "Get out," and she moved back to the end of the longeline. Soon she was traveling at the walk, trot, and canter in both directions.

The next step was riding. While things had been going fairly well with mounting and riding prior to the surgery, I still battled with severe anxiety and a riding schedule governed at least partially by fear and apprehension. Any sort of change to equipment or environment still made my anxiety skyrocket and had the potential to paralyze me with uncertainty as I prepared to mount my horse. Now I was planning to get on a horse with just one eye, a horse that had two eyes the last time I had ridden her—a big change.

My mind filled with questions and doubts. Would she spook more easily? Would she be hard to turn to the right? Would she know it was my leg touching her right side, or would she be afraid and try to get away from it? My biggest fear was she would bolt out from under me the first time my leg touched her right side (which would occur during mounting). Could she put it together? Would she understand that what she felt was something that had happened hundreds of times before? I thought about how it had taken her a while to remember to focus on my words while I was longeing her. Was her memory of being mounted primarily visual or tactile? I didn't know, and it worried me.

I found myself spiraling into a deceptively deep pool of self-doubt. As soon as I dipped my toe into the dangerous waters of anxiety-laden uncertainty, the sandy bottom slipped away like a dangerous rip current pulling me deeper, threatening to drown me.

I couldn't let that happen.

How could I ask Farletta to trust me when I couldn't trust myself? She was the one dealing with something new and potentially scary. She needed my support. How could I be a strong and comforting presence for her when I was drowning in my own fear and insecurity?

ON A MILD NOVEMBER EVENING, my favorite time of day, when the temperature is cool and comfortable and the air is crisp with the smell of fallen leaves, I walked through the dry grass toward the barn. Today was my thirty-sixth birthday, which would also be the day I rode Farletta for the first time since she'd lost her right eye.

The barn was quiet and empty when I arrived to Farletta's run-in stall.

"You're getting all wintered up, Farletta," I said to my friend, observing her thickening coat.

Farletta turned her head toward me, her lower lip twitching. I hooked her flapping lower lip with my finger and pulled it gently. Farletta grabbed my finger between her lips and pulled it toward her open teeth, where she held it carefully for a moment before releasing it.

I stroked her neck. "You're a silly girl."

The previous day I'd practiced saddling Farletta, then led her around the arena just as I would with a horse that had never been ridden. Since her eye removal, I developed a habit of explaining everything when I stood on Farletta's blind side. "Here comes the broom," I'd say as I swept around her feet. "Here's your brush," I'd say as her stiff-bristled brush touched her right side.

I continued with this habit when I prepared for our ride. "Here comes your saddle pad," I said when I lifted the thick wool pad and positioned it on her back. Farletta stood quietly, like she'd done this hundreds of times before, which of course, she had. "Here comes your saddle." I hefted the bulky western saddle and placed it gently over the wool pad. Farletta sighed and worked her mouth, licking and chewing in contentment. She cocked one hind leg in a resting position, further displaying her comfort with the process.

Slowly I tightened the cinch and then reached up and released the right stirrup, which was lying across the seat of the saddle, letting it fall into place. Just a moment too late, I realized I hadn't warned Farletta the stirrup was falling on her blind side. I quickly grabbed her halter to steady her and stepped out of the way in case she spooked in my direction. The stirrup fell with a thud, and Farletta did not flinch at all.

I was feeling more relaxed about the upcoming ride. Farletta seemed to be comfortable with everything I did. Apparently her memory was not 100 percent visual and she took comfort in the familiarity of certain sensations she had experienced many times before.

Farletta's nonchalant attitude gave me renewed confidence. Everything was going so well, I believed this first ride would occur without incident. I bridled Farletta, grabbed my helmet, and led her out to the arena, where I walked her around in a few circles each direction. I snugged up the cinch one last time and led her to the dropped tailgate of my truck. I approached the truck, my stomach lurching as butterflies swarmed within me. Taking in a deep breath, I blew it out, making a whooshing sound when the air exited my lungs. I took another deep breath and held it, letting the pressure build up in my chest before I forced it out my nose with a soft whistling sound.

"Are you ready?" I asked Farletta.

She flicked an ear in my direction and watched me out of the corner of her one remaining eye. I lifted my hand and rubbed her soft neck. "OK, let's do this."

I walked Farletta over to the tailgate of my truck and sat on it, absently stroking her side beneath the edge of the saddle pad. She turned and touched her nose to my thigh, leaving it there for a moment before moving upward and shoving it hard into my shoulder.

I pushed her head away. "Ow!" Farletta had made her point though—if we're going to do this, let's get on with it!

I turned and pushed my body up until I got my feet under me and stood. Reaching across the saddle, I touched Farletta's right side with my first two fingers, asking her to move closer to the tailgate. Farletta moved over obediently, stopping when her body was flush and tight with the edge.

I gathered up her reins in my left hand and placed my right hand on the front of the saddle. "Whoa girl." Farletta stood quietly as I lifted my right leg up and gently placed the side of my lower leg on the seat of the saddle. There I hesitated as fear and anxiety crept into my body, clouding my mind with worry, questions, and doubt. Farletta lifted her head and laid her ears back, a sour expression crossing her face, and she sidestepped away from the tailgate.

Oh crap. I'm messing up. My hesitation and doubt was making Farletta uncomfortable. How could I ask her to trust me when I was unwilling to put my own trust in her or in myself?

"Oh, to heck with it," I said. "You'd better buck up and get on with this or forget the whole thing!"

I quickly asked Farletta to move her body back to the tailgate. She did so willingly and stood quietly, though I could tell her patience was wearing thin. I gathered up her reins once again and lifted my right leg above the saddle.

"Please, God, let us be OK," I prayed aloud.

I shifted my weight and slid onto Farletta's back. She stood unmoving as I patted her neck and praised her. My right leg settled gently against her right side. She flicked her right ear backward, but that was all.

"Big deal, huh, girl?" I said as relief enveloped me like a cozy, warm blanket on a cold night. "Big effin' deal."

I stroked Farletta's smooth neck and ran my fingers through her silky mane as I whispered a quick prayer of thanks. For me, the scariest part was over. I had a renewed sense of vigor and enthusiasm. Now it was time to see how she handled being ridden.

An idea came to me. I lifted my right leg away from her side and gently touched her with it a few times.

"Do you feel my leg touching your side?" I asked. "Do you feel my hand on your rein?" I lifted my right hand, wiggling my fingers on the rein. "My hand and leg will guide and protect you. I will not let you run into anything. I will not let you stumble. My hand and my leg will guide you. I will be your right eye."

Farletta stood silently for a moment, then sighed and worked her mouth, licking and chewing with contentment. I ran my fingers along the crest of her neck, ruffling her long black-and-white mane. Gently touching her sides with both legs, I asked Farletta to move forward. She walked off easily, and I moved my right hand slightly while touching her with my left leg, asking her to make a looping turn to the right, which she did without hesitation. I guided her through the open arena gate, and we walked around the perimeter of the enclosure, first traveling clockwise around the arena so Farletta could see what was going on outside the fence line. She did well, so I turned her to the right, guiding her back to the fence, now traveling counterclockwise.

Farletta was less comfortable going with her blind eye facing the outside of the arena. She could hear the horses in the field nearby but could not see them. She traveled with her head high, trying to twist her neck around to look outside the arena with her left eye. I gently straightened her head with the reins, asking her to travel straight along the fence. She obeyed but soon lifted her head again, twisting her neck, trying to see everything outside the arena. I remembered my promise to be her right eye and told her what I could see outside the arena, similar to the way I told her what I was doing when working on her right side.

"We're going past the gate now," I began. "Your pasture buddies are out there grazing."

Farletta's head remained high, but she stopped trying to twist her neck around.

"We're walking past the driveway and my truck."

Farletta's head and neck dropped as she relaxed.

"Do you hear that hissing noise? That is the hose near the gate."

Farletta let out a short, sharp snort, another sign of relaxation.

"Here comes a cat, Farletta," I said when a cat ran in our direction. "She is going to run right in front of you, and then you will see her with your other eye."

The cat darted in front of Farletta and continued across the arena. Farletta did not flinch when the feline suddenly appeared in her field of vision.

Soon Farletta was traveling in a relaxed frame, content and no longer trying to lift and turn her head to see outside the arena. I became more relaxed as I sat and enjoyed the ride, the creak of her saddle, and the feel of the soft fall breeze on my face.

The sound of thundering hooves galloping in the nearby field, heading in our direction, interrupted the stillness of the evening. Farletta's body tensed. The horses were on her right side, and she could hear them but could not see them. I thought of the galloping horses a few years earlier on a fall evening in Kentucky, the evening I'd fallen off Farletta and everything had changed. I shook the negative images from my mind.

I touched her neck. "It's OK, Farletta, It's just your buddies running in the field. Aren't they loud and silly?"

Farletta sighed deeply as the tension left her body. She lowered her head and neck into a tranquil position and worked the bit softly in her mouth.

"That's right, sweetheart." I closed my fingers on the reins, signaling her to halt. "I'll watch out for you. I'll be your right eye, and we'll be just fine together."

Farletta turned her head and neck to the right, bumping her nose along her shoulder, as if searching for something. I kicked my right foot out of the stirrup and gently touched her nose with the toe of my boot. She held her muzzle there against my boot for a moment.

"That's right, girl. I'm right here, always."

Farletta straightened her head and neck and breathed out with a long sigh, like the sound of air being released from a large inner tube. She worked her mouth on the bit.

I reached forward and scratched her neck just behind her ears. "Thank you, Farletta, for such a great ride. And thank You, God, for such an amazing horse."

CHAPTER THIRTY-NINE

"Hey, girl," I called to Farletta.

The mare stood gazing longingly out at her pasture mates, grazing in the large field at the back of the farm. During her recovery from the eye removal surgery, Farletta had to stay confined to a small space, because anything that got her blood pumping too strongly (such as running), increased the risk of rupturing the sutures. Her sutures had already been removed, but I decided to confine her a bit longer to acclimate her to her missing eye before reintroducing her to the herd.

Fall leaves of brown and gold swirled around the barnyard, collecting in wind-blown piles along the fence of the small paddock connected to Farletta's stall. I breathed in their earthy scent.

I had ridden Farletta a couple more times in the days following our first post-enucleation ride. She continued to do well, just as she had that first day. In fact, she was riding as if nothing had changed. In everything she did, it was clear she was far more comfortable than she had been in a long time.

Farletta turned her graceful head to look at me. I whistled softly to her. She walked to where I stood with her halter in my right hand. Farletta lifted her nose and touched me with her muzzle. I reached in my pocket and gave her one of the special treats I had picked up on the way to the clinic following her surgery. Farletta eagerly pulled the treat into her mouth with her outstretched, ever-searching lips. I slipped the halter over her head, careful not to rub against her still-tender right eye. (I didn't know what else to call her non-eye.) Farletta followed me into the barn, where I tied her and brushed her long winter coat.

"Sorry, girl," I said to my friend after I finished her grooming. "No time to ride today. I just came to say hi and give you some lovin'."

We walked through Farletta's open stall and back into the paddock, where I slipped her halter off over her black-tipped ears. Farletta searched my hands and pockets, her lower lip pulled back in an expectant smile. I scratched her withers, and she stretched her neck outward, twisting her head back and forth, her lips outstretched in pure ecstasy as I worked on her favorite itchy spot.

"Tomorrow's a big day," I said as I moved my way up toward her ears, flipping the black half of her mane back over to the right side of her neck along the way. "Tomorrow you get to go in the field with one of your friends."

My heart vibrated with anticipation over having Farletta out with her buddies again. She hadn't had regular, twenty-four-hour turnout with a group of horses since before she was diagnosed with uveitis. She had been out with the horses at this particular farm before her surgery, but when she still had her eye, she was restricted to cloudy days and wearing a fly mask day and night year round.

Horses are herd animals—their feeling of safety and sense of well-being are strongly tied to being in contact with other horses. When they are alone, their instincts tell them they are vulnerable. Yes, tomorrow would be the beginning of a truly normal life for Farletta, something she never could have while afflicted with uveitis.

The following afternoon, Farletta and I stood near the gate of the pasture. All but one of the horses had been moved to the back field, where they stood watching the events unfold across the fence. The farm owner was down at the near corner of the large field, holding one of her mares, a bay that would be the first horse Farletta would be turned out with since having her eye removed. I led Farletta through the pasture gate and secured the latch.

"Are you ready?" I shouted down to the farm owner, Sam.

She indicated she was.

I should tell her to let that mare loose, I thought, knowing it would be safer if her horse did not feel confined when Farletta approached her. I shrugged my shoulders and removed Farletta's halter, letting the thought slip away, assuming Sam could take care of herself. Farletta stood next to me and searched my hands for her treat.

"You have me so well trained." I opened my hand and revealed another of the special treats with the candy pressed into the center.

Farletta gobbled up her prize, then set off trotting across the short end of the field to where Sam stood with the bay mare. *Tell her to let that mare go,* my inner voice spoke again. I said nothing and trotted after Farletta.

Farletta slowed to a walk as she approached the other mare. The two mares sniffed noses and squealed, typical behavior when saying hello to a fellow equine. Farletta then took a few steps away from the other mare.

"Well, that was uneventful," I mumbled to myself.

I'd spoken too soon.

Farletta stood at an angle to the right of, and facing away from, the other mare, but positioned in such a way she could see her with her left eye. The bay mare shifted her hindquarters a half a step to the right. Farletta turned her butt and backed a couple steps toward the other mare, her body language saying "Stay back!" The bay mare then spun around and backed the remaining distance between the two horses, and a kicking match ensued. Farletta let off a couple kicks before running away down the field. She did not travel far before she stopped to graze.

I looked over at Sam, settling her mare down and checking her over. Having seen many horses get reacquainted, I felt things had gone pretty well. I walked over to Farletta and could see she had a fresh kick mark to the left of her tail but otherwise was fine. The kick was not severe. I told her she was a good girl.

I went to talk with Sam. The bay mare looked a bit lame on one hind leg, but I saw no mark or injury on the leg. I knew the mare had a history of hoof and leg pain, and I figured she had made it sore kicking my horse, but I didn't say as much, not wanting to start trouble or put Sam on the defensive. Overall, it seemed this first reintroduction had gone fairly well, and Farletta had successfully taken the first step of her new, normal life.

The next day I went out to find Farletta in the same field, but now with a different horse. This other horse, an overo mare, stood with her head over the gate. Farletta was eating grass a short distance away.

"Hmm, that is strange," I said to the overo mare as I unlatched the gate. "What are you doing in here?"

Sam and I had agreed it would be best to give Farletta a few days with just one horse before introducing another.

Sam walked over while I brought Farletta through the gate. She explained she was worried about her other mare with the sore legs and thought the overo mare would be a better choice. That made sense to me, and Farletta seemed fine with this mare, so I figured it was a good plan.

The next day I arrived at the farm to find the overo mare and a two-year-old filly in the field with Farletta. Again, Farletta seemed OK. However, I was curious and concerned, wondering what had happened to the plan to give Farletta a few days before introducing a new horse. The farm owner was still at work, so I let it go since the three seemed to be fine together.

A few days later on a beautiful, warm, and sunny fall day, I pulled into the driveway of the farm. Excitement filled me. I had several hours available, and I planned to spend them all with Farletta, riding, grooming, and enjoying being in her good company.

I headed across the yard toward the barn. My eyes scanned the field for Farletta. Surprise changed into confusion when I found Farletta in her small private paddock.

"I wonder what's going on," I said to the empty barnyard.

I'd taken about five steps into the barn, when Sam emerged from the shadowy interior. "We need to talk. There are going to be some changes around here."

No greeting, smile, hi, or hello from the woman who, up to this point, had always been friendly and warm. My insides clenched. I felt like a little child about to get a severe scolding. My mind frantically searched through memories of my actions over the past few days, trying to identify what I could have done wrong to deserve a greeting like this. I came up empty.

"Um, OK," I stammered. "What's going on?"

"Farletta will not be going out in the field with the other horses anymore," she said tersely.

"Why? What happened?"

Sam explained how she had been unable to catch Farletta the evening before and how my mare had chased the two-year-old filly around and tried to kick her. Then after they removed the other two horses, Farletta proceeded to run around the field screaming frantically. Apparently Sam was unable to catch her for over a half hour. She said she would not have a dangerous horse like Farletta around her horses, and she would not be handling her anymore. Farletta would be confined to her stall and paddock unless I was at the farm to provide supervised turnout in an empty field.

I searched for a response. Why on earth was I hearing this now, twenty-four hours after it happened? She should have called me. I could've caught Farletta. I would've checked her over for injuries. Why would Farletta behave this way, and why was this woman reacting like this? Prior to yesterday she'd loved Farletta and had spoken of how sweet and kind she was. Today she was speaking of Farletta like she was a dangerous, half-wild animal bent on destroying any horse or human in her path.

Sam left me shell shocked and numb. I stood unmoving in the barn aisle, where she'd stopped me. Overrun with guilt and shame, I felt like I had done something horrible. I wanted to run away and never come back. I wanted to hide. These feelings were agonizingly familiar, much how I felt when I relived the memories of trying to escape from Mr. Vandersmelden.

I ran out to the paddock and threw my arms around Farletta's neck, crying into her wavy mane. "I am so sorry I wasn't here for you. I am so sorry you were scared. You are a good horse, a good, good horse, and I love you so much!"

My body shook and my chest heaved as I gasped for breath.

I stayed in the paddock with Farletta for almost an hour. I no longer wanted to ride or even be at the barn, but at the same time I didn't want to leave my horse. That somehow didn't feel safe. A part of me knew my reaction was too strong. Mean Cheryl tried hard to make it my fault, as she had done so many times before, but for the first time, the cruel words she spoke did not make sense. I couldn't agree with her. I knew Sam was wrong about Farletta. She was not dangerous, and she was not a bad horse. Something had caused her to behave that way, and I needed to find out exactly what was going on with her.

I went home that night and battled mentally with Mean Cheryl. She told me I was a horrible person and a horrible horse owner. I couldn't accept her words. Unbelievable—not too long ago I would never have been able to fight off Mean Cheryl's negativity with logic. For once I didn't see myself as the problem. Something important had just happened to me.

I never knew what really happened with Farletta and Sam that day, but based on what I'd learned later, I suspect the two-year-old approached Farletta from her blind side, an action my mare was no longer comfortable with. Farletta chased the young mare off as a warning to never do that again. Since they removed the other two mares from the field first, Farletta was left alone, and panicked—thus the running and screaming. Obviously Farletta's actions had scared Sam badly, because she apparently was unfamiliar with common horse behaviors in this type of situation. She was now acting as if Farletta was some sort of demon spawn, and no amount of apologizing or reasoning would sway her newly formed opinion. Farletta noticed the change right away and reacted negatively to the bad energy, which only reinforced Sam's notion that Farletta was a dangerous animal.

I now hated going out to the barn. My stomach flipped and

churned every time I pulled into the driveway. I couldn't wait to get out of there, afraid of another confrontation. Had I misread Sam? Had I somehow been mistaken thinking she was a kind and gentle woman? For sure I didn't trust her not to flip out on me again.

This particular farm was no longer an emotionally safe place for me —an important realization. For the first time able to consciously recognize an emotionally unsafe environment, I could now take the appropriate actions to protect both me and my horse. I had to move Farletta, and quickly. With this new insight, I informed Sam and her husband of my intention to relocate immediately upon finding a suitable farm.

At last I'd learned to listen to my gut, recognize danger, and act on it appropriately without owning shame that didn't belong to me. A new and incredibly liberating sensation: I had control of my emotions and my situation.

CHAPTER FORTY

For the first couple years, on the anniversary of my suicide attempt, I recorded in my journal the things I had accomplished that year, things that would not have happened had my life ended on May 11, 2006. It was a way of trying to show myself my life had value. It didn't work though. Perhaps that was why I stopped. Despite recent progress advocating for myself, the idea that there could be actual value to my life was still a foreign concept. It isn't easy to explain, but it was like an idea that is so advanced, I didn't have the intellectual capacity to comprehend it. I didn't understand how it worked, and I simply couldn't wrap my head around it. I didn't know how to love myself or even why I would want to.

Others tried to instill that concept of self-value in me: my mom, best friend, sister, and various therapists. They seemed to value me, but I truly couldn't understand why. Mean Cheryl decided they all had some misplaced sense of duty. Like the popular kids at school who decide to do a good deed by inviting the hopelessly awkward outcast into their group to "help" her. They are doing it because they are supposed to, or perhaps to feel good about themselves, not because they really want to be the lonely girl's friends. After a few hours or a day of doing their good deed, the popular kids abandon the lonely girl, not realizing they have done more harm than good. If they were only going to abandon her later, she'd have been better off without the manufactured kindness in the first place.

I filled my journals with entries asking God why He kept me around. What was the point? Why did I have to stay here? The worst times were when someone died. Filled with guilt and questions, I'd demand God tell my why He would take a good person, someone who would be missed by many people, and leave a worthless loser like me here. My heart felt like a blackened, burned-out, empty cavernous shell. There were days and weeks where the only emotions I could feel were self-hatred and deep, hopeless sorrow. Only in my mid-thirties, the thought of living another forty, fifty, or God forbid, sixty years taunted me like a cruel joke.

Journal entry—July 5, 2011

Black dead heart,
Sad and alone
Hope is gone.
No one is there,
No one to care.
Black, dead heart.
Alone
All done.

I COULDN'T SEE A FUTURE. I couldn't feel hope. I couldn't understand why some days I felt like I was making progress, and others I felt like I was stepping backward out of newly discovered sunlight and into cold darkness. I tried harder to hear the little girl's story, a story she'd held on her tiny shoulders for nearly thirty years. Eventually, I began to write the story. As I wrote, that image of the little girl standing on the desk, emitting her silent scream to an empty room, finally disappeared. As I listened and released her story through writing, hope became real, and for the first time in a long time, the future felt like something I was interested in living to see.

The improvement on my outlook on life was not consistent. Mean Cheryl was still a part of me, and she did much to destroy my fledgling hope and dissuade me from looking toward the future. A large part of my struggle centered on my post-graduation job search. As the months of unemployment stretched into and beyond a year, I grew increasingly discouraged. The self-hatred grew in strength, snuffing out the tiny glimmer of hope and desire to follow my dreams and live to see my future.

I sent out dozens and dozens of résumés as I worked my way through the listing of EAGALA-model facilities found on the organization's website. I answered ads for which I had any qualifications. These ranged from purely horse-related employment, to jobs specifically within the field of social work. A few of the jobs I was a strong candidate for—combining my social work degrees and horse expertise. Ninety-five percent of my résumés went unanswered. A handful received a "Thanks but no thanks" letter, and a few more actually resulted in a phone interview but went no further.

In addition to my discouraging job search, I also struggled with self-worth as a viable, contributing member of society. I originally moved in with Mom upon my return to Michigan in 2008 to keep her company after my stepdad passed, and also for the ease of going back to school. Now my temporary move was stretching well into the fifth year, and I was feeling like one of those failure-to-launch cases—adult children who won't leave home.

In school I felt mostly OK being thirty-something and living with Mom. After all, she assured me my company made her happy, and I knew it was the only way I would be able to get through school quickly. As the months stretched on and on following graduation, I felt like a parasite, a pathetic, unemployable loser mooching off my mom and devouring her retirement fund. I found some contract work at the university, but I made little money and had no hope of moving out and supporting myself financially.

What money I made went to paying Farletta's expenses, and I quickly burned through the remainder of my student loans, reallocating the portion reserved for my living expenses to cover her board and care. I'd been desperate to relocate Farletta after the fallout with Sam and, as a result, had found a suitable farm, but it was much fancier than I needed and therefore considerably more expensive. However, it is difficult moving a horse on short notice in an area where good boarding is hard to find, therefore, I was glad to have found a safe place with trustworthy people. But the cost was devastating to my pitiful budget. As the months of unemployment and rejection letters piled up, I slipped out of adulthood and into feeling like a child without the confidence or experience to make it on my own.

The pre-accident version of me, the one who had fearlessly moved from state to state in search of new adventures and new opportunities, had been replaced by a fearful adult-child who lacked the confidence to step out without an ample safety net. Even with all the emotional turmoil and self-hatred before the accident, I could at least hold a bit of dignity in my ability to remain self-sufficient. Now that version of me was a distant memory.

Post-accident Cheryl had her confidence severely shaken. I didn't feel like I knew what I was capable of or what was too dangerous. How did I keep myself safe? The day of that accident was a wake-up call. Before that awful day, I'd felt physically strong, confident in my riding ability and in my ability to read my horse. Afterward, I felt like everything I knew was wrong. I didn't trust my judgment with regard to my own abilities, and I no longer felt capable of keeping myself safe in any situation.

These were not conscious decisions. It was more like a subconscious knowledge that affected my confidence and decision-making without my being aware of it. They were well-worn paths in my brain, the CD set on repeat since the days of Mr. Vandersmelden, playing over and over—affecting every part of my life, every decision, every relationship, every job interview, *everything*.

I continued my job search, particularly interested in a few ads posted by colleges looking for an equine program director or instructor. My social work programs had given me many of the skills needed for such positions, plus I had a couple decades of horse experience in a variety of areas.

In the cab of my pickup, preparing to leave the farm after visiting Farletta, I took the call from a small out-of-state college looking for an equine program director. The woman on the other end of the phone asked if I would come for an interview on May 14. That was just a couple weeks away. Didn't she know where I lived? Just then pre-accident Cheryl poked me in the heart and said, "Go for it."

"Yes, I can be there on May fourteen," I said. "What time is the interview?"

After the woman explained when and where, we said our goodbyes, and I clicked the End button. The number and the state she'd called from flashed on the screen.

Montana.

My head did somersaults. *How will I get there? Will Mom come with me?* The insecure child in me wanted to know. The pre-accident Cheryl rose up within me once again, challenging me to reclaim my independence and adulthood. If Mom joined me on the trip, it would be easy to fall into the role of a child, asking Mom to make the decisions and keep me safe. Pre-accident Cheryl would see this trip as an adventure and would not want to be tied to someone else's timetable or decision-making process. I decided I would drive rather than fly, and I would make the trip alone. Well, not really alone—Boedy would be my traveling companion.

I figured up the mileage and the best route. It turned out I-94, the interstate that runs through Kalamazoo, went all the way to my destination of Miles City, Montana. I divided the trip up into driving days of eight hours and found a destination city for each night. My plan was to arrive in Miles City the afternoon before my interview. The route I'd planned would travel through a portion of nine different states.

Journal entry—May 10, 2013

Doubt keeps creeping in, and it is hard to keep it at bay. I hold on to the peaceful feeling that encompasses me when I remember God is with me and I have nothing to fear.

I know what I can do, what I know, and what I am capable of. I know I can do anything through the strength of Jesus Christ. So what do I have to fear? Doubts, fears and negative words are the tools of the devil. Will I empower him by letting fear and doubt overtake me? No!

I talked to Danny today ... hard to believe it has been ten and a half years since I left Kewanee. So much has happened since then. So much has changed. I have changed so much—in what I know and understand about myself and where my place is in the world. I'm learning to honor my gifts and see my own value. I am stronger. I am wiser. I am better at caring for myself. I still have far to go but I am ready for the journey.

I can do this. Jesus has my back. Let the adventure begin. I'm heading west tomorrow. I don't know what the future will bring but I'm going to run head first into it with the exuberance of a child and the wisdom of an adult who has lived through unimaginable horror and came out stronger on the other side.

ON SATURDAY MORNING, May 11, four days before my interview, I packed up my truck, and with Boedy in the backseat, we set off on our adventure.

The first destination was Eau Claire, Wisconsin. I intended to make a few stops so that anytime I saw something interesting, I could pull off and have a look. On a brisk and windy day, while traveling through Wisconsin, a giant orange fiberglass moose caught my eye. I took the next exit and went to check out the unusual statue. Boedy posed for pictures with the moose and his larger-than-life companion, a buck leaping over a log. When we stopped for lunch, we discovered an enormous fiberglass cow, her udders larger than Boedy! It seemed there were an inordinate number of oversized fiberglass animals in Wisconsin, and soon the novelty wore off once we drove past the twelfth oversized mouse with a ten-foot hunk of cheese. I wondered where they built these. Was there a fiberglass menagerie somewhere?

That evening we reached our hotel in Eau Claire, near the Wisconsin-Minnesota border. After unpacking, Boedy and I went in search of a path to hike. We found a small park with a paved trail—not quite a hiking route, but it did travel through a wooded area. Because it was nearly dark, this would have to do. Boedy and I ascended the hill leading up to the trailhead, and a cool breeze caressed my cheeks, lifting my hair before dropping it back onto my shoulders. I breathed in pine-scented air. Peace refreshed my tired soul.

"Check out that sunset," I said to Boedy, pointing at the pink-and-blue-streaked sky above the line of pine trees to the west.

Boedy panted in reply, his long, pink tongue hanging comically out the side of his mouth.

"Beautiful night, eh," I continued. "Are you having a good time?"

Boedy withdrew his tongue and closed his mouth thoughtfully. His amber eyes searched mine as he cocked his head to one side.

"You're a good boy!" I said cheerfully.

Boedy leapt into the air, and for a flash his eyes were nearly level with mine. What an amazingly athletic vertical jump. He twisted away from me, landing, and immediately leapt through the long grass in his bouncing, puppylike stride, where he moved more up and down than forward.

"Goofy dog. C'mon, buddy. It's getting dark, and we have a big day tomorrow."

Boedy spun around and raced back to the truck, leaping into his seat like a deer jumping a fence.

The next day we departed early for the longest driving day—destination of Bismarck, North Dakota. That cool morning we crossed from Wisconsin into Minnesota. A gray sky filled with rain clouds sometimes broke to allow beams of sunshine to bathe the earth below in a warm yellow glow. One of these beams illuminated a rocky hill jutting out from the tree-covered landscape.

A mountain! Of course, it wasn't really a mountain, but a large hill. However, when you are from a hilly but decidedly non-mountainous state, a huge, rocky hill dotted with hundreds of large pines qualified as a mountain. Fascinated, I pulled off at the next exit to see what else I could discover.

My detour took me through a beautiful rural part of Minnesota. The countryside rose and fell with large hills of rock and trees, the two-lane road winding around and sometimes right through them. Empty, decaying houses and rotted, partially collapsed barns stood as lonely reminders of a time long gone. After an hour of turning every time an interesting road beckoned me, it was time to find my way back to the interstate. I turned on the GPS and punched in my destination. The computer ran through its maps and produced a route, which I promptly ignored when I saw yet another interesting road and turned off to investigate.

About a mile down this road, I found a small parking area and a trailhead.

"Time to go for a hike," I said to Boedy. "Are you ready?" Silly question.

Boedy sprung to his feet and wagged his stump of a tail. I opened his door, and he flew off the seat, then bounced across the parking lot.

"Nope," I called to my dog, and I whistled.

Boedy bounded back to the truck and leapt in the air in front of me, landing at my feet.

"This is a protected area, buddy. You have to wear your leash." I pointed at the trailhead sign. Boedy eyed the leash and sat down on the gravel, his stump tail wagging wildly, producing a tiny cloud of dust as it moved across the surface.

"Good boy." I leaned over and clipped the leash to his collar.

The hiking trail took almost two hours to complete. By the time we returned to the truck, the early-spring sun was fading to the west. It wouldn't be long before it disappeared beyond the tall trees and slid beneath the horizon. Because of our detour, we had at least six hours before we reached our evening destination in North Dakota.

"Better get going." As I settled back into the driver's seat, a smile of satisfaction spread across my face. I hadn't gone for a real hike since before the accident. The reclamation of Cheryl had begun.

Boedy and I headed out early the next morning. Pink streaks lit the predawn sky behind us. The drive from Bismarck to Miles City would take four and a half hours, which would put me at my destination shortly after noon. The sun brightened and warmed the gently rolling North Dakota grasslands. Not long after we started out, I passed a sign promoting something called the Enchanted Highway.

"Wonder what that is," I mumbled as another mile of asphalt rolled away under my tires.

This particular stretch of I-94 lacked anything resembling civilization. Miles of long, brown grasses spread out on either side of the roadway, the rolling landscape occasionally interrupted by a round-topped hill or a dilapidated shell of an ancient farmhouse or barn, which I longed to explore and photograph. I scanned the horizon searching for some indication of an exit ahead but found none for miles. The decrepit buildings seemed trapped in another time, the roads of progress passing them by like a rich Wall Street tycoon far too busy to notice the old beggar dying in the gutter.

After many miles, a sign notified me of an upcoming exit. I had passed another old, falling-down farmhouse a couple miles back, so I took the exit, hoping I could to find my way back to the abandoned home. But as I left the interstate, something else caught my eye. To the right of the road, perched high atop a hill, was an unusual-looking structure. I spied a one-lane gravel roadway stretching upward from the highway, reaching toward the sky before disappearing around a bend. Along the roadway were dozens of blackened steel rods stuck into the ground. Atop each rod posed a steel cutout of a goose in flight.

"Well, that's just too curious to pass up." We turned onto the primitive road and navigated up the steep incline, the gravel surface crunching noisily under the pickup's tires.

Black steel goose sculptures lined the road on each side, the geese frozen in various stages of flight, each heading the same direction we traveled. A huge gust of wind rocked the truck when we crested the hill, revealing the largest sculpture I had ever seen.

The center of the sculpture was an oval that resembled the shape of the human eye. Dozens of rods shot out from around the eye shape, like rays of sunshine. It reminded me of the all-seeing eye found on the back of a US dollar bill. Attached to the outstretched rays were large cutouts of geese in flight, constructed of black steel. According to information I found later, the entire sculpture was 110 feet high, 154 feet wide, and weighed over seventy-eight tons.

The sculpture creaked and moaned as the wind tore along the plains and whipped around it. Grains of sand stung my bare legs, the wind gusting so hard that my truck rocked with the force of it. Dozens of guy wires held the sculpture to the hilltop high above I-94. Standing alone in the middle of the gravel parking space was an informative sign.

According to the sign, I had stumbled upon the Enchanted Highway. The sculptures had been created from scrap metal by Gary Grett, a native of Regent, North Dakota, the town the Enchanted Highway (actually CR 4531) led to. The first sculpture, *Tin Family*, was erected in 1991, with the most recent being *Fisherman's Paradise* in 2007. *Geese in Flight*, erected in 2001 and overlooking I-94, was the first stop along the highway. The next was just a few miles away, so I drove up to take a look. I felt like a kid, when I'd go on an adventure and bravely explore the wooded trails behind our house. Excitement awakened my senses. What would I find next?

The detour down the Enchanted Highway was well worth it. The scrap metal sculptures included Teddy Roosevelt on a horse, a stage coach, a sixty-foot-long grasshopper, and a forty-foot-tall pheasant. When I reached the end of the thirty-mile Enchanted Highway, the GPS directed me to Highway 12, which would take me directly into Miles City.

I'd been on the road for two and a half days and traveled over a thousand miles. The landscape was surreal to me now, as if it were somehow plucked from a film set in the Old West. I grew up in Michigan, where every open space is lined with trees, thickly wooded areas are plentiful, and you are never far from a massive body of water. As I watched the landscape drift by through the windshield of my truck, I found the land both fascinating and unsettling. There was no sense of familiarity, no comfort in identifying anything that resembled the Midwest, where I'd spent my entire life.

Highway 12 yawned long and gray before me. Hours had passed since I'd seen an occupied home or a person. Rusted twists of barbed-wire gripping ancient, weather-beaten wood posts stretched on for miles. The presence of fences told me the land had an owner—there were people somewhere—but there was no evidence of homes or humans to occupy them. I photographed several abandoned dwellings. Tiny one- or two-room structures leaned heavily, the wind whipping relentlessly around and through them. The ancient wood looked gray and brittle, bleached by the hot sun and beaten by decades of brutal weather. Others were nothing more than a pile of splintered wood, the brown grasses of the plains growing over the forgotten assembly as the earth slowly reached up to reclaim it.

Shortly before Highway 12 took me into Montana, I spied a narrow, steep gravel road branching off to the right. I almost dismissed it, assuming it was a private road or some sort of a farm road, but when I neared it, I saw a marker saying OLD HIGHWAY 16. LOW MAINTENANCE ROAD. IMPASSIBLE WHEN WET. Apparently it was a public road. There was no other car on the road in front of or behind me, so I stomped on the brakes, backed up a few feet, and turned. The gravel road rose sharply from the highway, and my rear tires spun, unable to grip the loose stones, with no forward momentum. If I were driving a car, I likely would have given up, but I had been a truck girl for a long time. I kicked the truck into four-wheel drive and made my way up the steep incline.

The road did not improve as we climbed. I stayed to the center of the old roadway, avoiding the deep ruts running down the slope where the lane had washed away. A sharp curve approached as we climbed, and I wondered what I'd do if we encountered a car from the other direction. Boedy stood on his seat, leaned over the gap, and placed his head on my shoulder.

"I wonder if we're going to be able to get back down this," I asked as I scratched Boedy's silky ears.

The road was cut into the steep hill. On either side of the crumbling road bed were deep ditches. Willful trees poked out of steep walls of grass and rock rising up on either side, offering no visibility aside from what was directly in front of me. I navigated around the sharp curve and came upon a strange sight. On either side of the road were rusted-out automobiles lying lazily in the ditch. They appeared to be from the 1930s, complete with bullet holes scattered along the doors and fenders.

The cars were little more than rusted hulks. The paint had succumbed to the elements in a time long forgotten. The aging rubber tires had cracked and fallen away, leaving the rusted rims exposed to the wind and sun. The headlights and windows had long ago been smashed and buried in the dust and weeds. Rusted springs poked through the tattered remnants of the seats. The eerie scene looked as if the cars had slid off the road and into the ditch some icy day eight decades before and been abandoned there. The era of the cars and the bullet holes pulled at my imagination, which quickly concocted a scene of prohibition-era gangsters with Tommy guns in a shootout where no man was left standing.

"Hmm," I said to Boedy, "maybe we should get going."

We continued up the steep grade until the truck finally poked its nose over the summit and onto a relatively flat steppe. The area offered a stunning 360-degree view, the highest point for miles around. The road continued on a bit farther before turning from gravel to a deeply rutted path, which disappeared into the grasslands. Although there was no indication that this was not a public road, I felt as if I were trespassing, those old fears of doing wrong and being punished creating an uncomfortable squirming sensation in my belly.

I turned back. The trip down the hill was easier than I'd thought it would be. Soon we were back on Highway 12 heading west toward Montana.

FOLLOW ME, FRIEND

You don't belong here. The quiet voice within my mind took me by surprise. *This is not your home.*

"This is not my home." I spoke the words aloud as I drove and realized it was true. This area did not feel like home to me. I could not picture myself living in such a desolate area. I also could not picture subjecting Farletta to a cross-country road trip. The land was beautiful, but I felt incredibly alone.

I had lived in many places since leaving home for the first time at the age of nineteen. However, I longed to return to only one. It had been nearly five years since I'd left Kentucky, and my heart ached to return to the land I felt such a profound connection to. I couldn't explain the feeling, the strong need to return to the Bluegrass Region. I just knew that was the one place that truly felt like home. Confusing. I had grown up in Michigan and spent most of my life there, but Michigan felt like the home of the little girl I used to be, not the home of the woman I had become.

In fifth grade, a friend had given me a book. I'd spent hours gazing at the cover picture of a young boy with a leather chain shank in his hand, standing next to a magnificent chestnut horse, preparing to snap the chain end to the stallion's leather halter. The stallion did not seem to see the boy but instead gazed off in the distance, his head held high, nostrils flared, eyes shining with intensity. I imagined myself in that painting, feeling the dew-covered grass beneath my feet and seeing myself walking over the slight hill behind the horse and the boy to find the magnificent farm where the chestnut stallion lived, spread out like paradise before me. The book was Walter Farley's *Man O' War*.

Farley is famous for his Black Stallion series of books for young readers, but *Man O' War* is by far my favorite. As a young girl, I'd lived inside Farley's story of the great racehorse, Man O' War. I stood outside Mahubah's stall when she gave birth to the mighty red colt on March 29, 1917. I traveled to Saratoga and saw the yearling Man O' War being walked through the sales ring. I sat on the fence and watched him breeze around the training track. I stood along the rail while the magnificent horse devastated his competition, trouncing over all comers, smashing track and world records, all while carrying an impossibly high amount of weight. I rode with him in the train car when he returned to his native Kentucky to stand stud. I watched him graze in the Lexington sunshine, roll in the green grass of his paddock, and sleep in the shade of a grand sycamore tree under the watchful eye of his devoted groom, Wil Harbut.

The haunting strains of Stephen Foster's *My Old Kentucky Home* have always evoked deep emotion and brought tears to my eyes. Perhaps it is only the happiness the book brought to me as a child, or maybe there was something deeper and not so easy to explain that connected me to the land where the great Man O' War lived. One thing for sure—my heart longed to be in Kentucky. Each time I crossed the state line into Kentucky, my heart sang and I felt like I'd come home.

I drove along the empty stretch of Montana highway, reflecting on my job search over the past year, and noticed a pattern. I told myself I would move anywhere for the right job, but each time I applied for one in a distant state, I found myself calculating how long it would take me to get from there to Kentucky. It took nearly half of a three-thousand-mile trip to figure it out, but I now realized Kentucky was where my heart longed to be. I was finally ready to listen.

CHAPTER FORTY-ONE

On the return trip from Montana, I stopped on the way through Iowa and visited Corky, now twenty-four years old. I hadn't seen him in ten years, and the emotion was overpowering. I cried and hugged him tightly. He had turned almost completely white with age but was still a beautiful and graceful creature. I brushed him and gave him treats, and we posed for many pictures. It was a wonderful reunion.

The interview in Montana had gone fairly well, but nothing felt right about the town or the job. By the time I made it home, I had decided I would not accept the position if it were offered to me. It just didn't feel right. *Intuition.*

Sometimes I think intuition is God's way of speaking to us and keeping us safe. Horses in the wild rely heavily on intuition, as their survival depends on their ability to feel the energy of a predator and take action before it is too late. I believe humans have this same ability, though society tells us to quickly dismiss these sensations as nonsensical New Age bull. How often had I felt a place or a person had bad vibes or bad energy but disregarded the warning signs, only to discover too late that my first impression was dead on? The subtle gnawing in my stomach, a general feeling of uneasiness when I come into a room, and the most often ignored sensation—that someone had lied to or manipulated me. I spent much of my life so far above myself that I missed many such warning signs and suffered the consequences in the form of poor choices in friendship, placing trust in untrustworthy people, and more than one bad boarding situation with both Corky and Farletta. In these situations, Mean Cheryl jumped in to place all the blame squarely on my shoulders, and I'd allowed myself to own shame and guilt that did not belong to me.

But now, after years of dissociation, I was finally spending time in my own body, and I discovered my intuition to be both strong and accurate.

A couple months after I returned from Montana, an unusually cool July morning found me kneeling on the cement of the barn aisle, carefully wrapping Farletta's legs for the seven-hour trip to Kentucky. I had searched online for a job, but after a few lukewarm phone interviews and several unanswered résumés, I decided I'd have better luck moving first and finding a job when I got there. A risk, yes, but it was what pre-accident Cheryl would have done. This was one way I could feel like I'd taken control of my life again—a sensation I craved.

Fluffy white clouds danced across the wild blue sky. A cool breeze swirled around my feet, lifting and twirling a few dried leaves as it raced along the gravel driveway. Farletta walked quietly into the waiting horse trailer. I followed her in and secured her lead to the tie ring.

"Are you ready for this, girl?"

Farletta pulled her lower lip down and flapped it up and down in her beautiful smile. I gave her a treat and a final pat on the neck before stepping out of the trailer and securing the large swinging rear door.

I sat in the driver's seat, thinking of all that had happened in the years Farletta and I had been together. I thought of how she had seen and touched my pain, how she taught me to listen to myself, and how she helped me tell my story. I finally understood the vision, the role Farletta played in not only my healing, but in saving my life. It was her actions that unearthed the memories in the first place.

Had I not had that devastating fall back in 2007, I doubted I would have consciously remembered the abuse I'd suffered. It took the trauma from that fall, and the parallels of the aftermath—being unable to move, unable to breathe, feeling helpless, feeling trapped—to shake loose the memories hidden so well by my subconscious mind. But Farletta's role was actually twofold. While I tried to ignore the resurfacing trauma, it was Farletta's response to my unchecked PTSD symptoms that caused me to seek the help I needed to fully recover the memories and finally move past them.

I thought of the little girl that was me, and for a moment I could see her sitting on the passenger seat by my side. Her hazel-green eyes and freckled face looked into mine. She was wearing a ruffled white sundress, the kind she liked to wear before she'd ever met a man called Mr. Vandersmelden. Her tiny face beamed, her eyes showing deep gratitude as she looked into mine and smiled.

I will honor that little girl. I will tell her story and release her. After all, she is me, and she deserves to be free, to no longer carry this story all on her own. The image of the smiling little girl faded away. I took a deep breath and a final look around before turning the key in the ignition. The engine of my old GMC truck roared to life. I glanced in the rearview mirror at the trailer carrying my friend. Boedy stood up in the backseat, leaned forward, and placed his head on my shoulder.

"How about you, buddy—are you ready for this?"

Boedy pressed his head harder against me. I reached up and scratched his ears before throwing the truck into gear, stepping on the accelerator, and pointing my truck toward *home*.

I SAT in the shade at Farletta's boarding stable in Kentucky. *Today is the most gloriously beautiful day!* Not too hot, not too cold. Perfect, especially with a cool breeze. The air, fresh and clean, caressed the earth, both renewed by yesterday's gentle all-day rain. Still, evidence of the drought conditions we'd experienced earlier in the summer lingered. Brown patches of grass, stomped flat and burned by the relentless heat of the sun, were now bordered by new tufts of lush green sward.

Thick and soft—the kind of grass I imagined must taste delicious to a horse. On days like this I felt so lucky to be alive, to have survived the abuse and the suicide attempt and to have escaped the icy-cold grip of my personal hell.

I'd never thought of myself as a survivor. That term seemed reserved for people who'd suffered through so much more than I did. A woman brutally beaten on a daily basis by the hands of a man who swore to love, honor, and protect her … she is a survivor, not me. The little girl inside me tugged at my shirtsleeve, her beautiful green-and-brown flecked eyes looking into mine, a slight frown tugging at the corners of her soft pink lips. I had dismissed her again, and the pain was evident on her little face. I took her into my emotional space and honored what she has been through. *She is a survivor. I honor her now. I honor her pain, her suffering, and her bravery.* She smiled a hopeful smile, and I tenderly embraced her. She is me. I am her. Together, we survived.

I sat outside, my laptop computer open in front of me, and reflected on the day. I was honored to have spent a portion of it with Farletta. Our once damaged relationship was showing signs of new life. I almost felt normal. I looked at the computer screen and typed about the day …

A small amount of anxiety greeted me when I prepared to mount Farletta. However, before I even asked, she stepped sideways until her belly pressed against the edge of the tailgate. Farletta had closed the gap, so there was nothing to fear. She did not move away from me. Rather, she moved closer, as close as she possibly could, and patiently waited for me to step over her back and sit in the saddle. I thanked God for her kindness. She knew just what I needed, and she was willing and able to give it to me. I spoke a soft "whoa" to her out of habit, placed my left hand on the horn and my right on the pommel, lifted my leg over the saddle, and settled on Farletta's strong back. *She is such a blessing.*

I gained my stirrups and pressed my heels down, relaxing my legs around her. Farletta's back was soft and relaxed. She never struggled with my weight, didn't sigh or groan. She simply seemed to be happy to go for a ride. I guided Farletta to the large outdoor arena, marveling again at the perfectness of the day.

I soon realized the arena could not contain the joy I felt on this day, and with a slight shift of my seat and leg, I guided Farletta out the arena gate and down the lane. She lifted her head and pricked her red-brown ears forward as she looked down the rutted path before us, excited to escape the confines of the arena. Farletta picked her way down the muddy lane, taking an interested look at each horse when we passed their respective corral. We approached the back field, and I put my legs around her, conveying confidence to her and to me. We were heading for the trail that meandered through the woods. I felt my apprehension mount. Perhaps I was not ready for a solo trail ride. I accepted this and steered Farletta in a large loop around the field and back toward the lane. It was a reminder that healing was a process, and it would take as much time as it needed to recover.

"We'll save the trail ride for another day," I told Farletta.

Her long, flowing mane lifted in the breeze before falling lightly onto her neck. Her red bay coat shone like stunning copper in the bright sun. Farletta lifted her head toward the lane. A horse in one of the paddocks had caught her attention. I took a deep breath and let it out slowly, savoring this moment of peace and tranquility with my horse.

A secret joy passed between us, the kind that comes after you have endured the worst and could finally see the light on the other side of the tunnel.

"I am the luckiest girl," I said aloud to my wonderful mare.

Farletta returned my sentiment—she felt lucky too. She had missed me as I had missed her, and I could see how pleased she was to have "us" back. I thought briefly on all we had been through together and how I'd hung on to that thin and nearly broken string of hope that someday we would again be as we once were. Smiling up at the blue summer sky, I thanked God for the beautiful day and my most wonderful friend, Farletta.

EPILOGUE

Billions of stars danced in the blue-black midnight sky. I gazed upward, taking it all in, never tiring of the beauty of a crisp Kentucky night. A cold breeze brushed across my face, reddening my cheeks and nose. My breath turned into foggy curls as it escaped my lips. In the barn behind me, mares rustled in the straw at their feet, a few sharp snorts puncturing the still night air. One mare in particular occupied my mind tonight. Leaving the starry display unattended, I returned to the barn to check on the bay. She was heavy with foal, her belly stretched large and round. She shifted her weight from foot to foot, unable to get comfortable.

The bay mare circled, pawed at her straw, circled again. Her nostrils flared, and her respiration grew heavy. Tiny wisps of steam rose from her body like fog hanging above a warm stream on a cold night. She was getting close. I walked down the aisle to the tack room to recheck the foaling supplies—they were all accounted for. Moving quickly through the barn row, I checked the other twenty foaling mares. *Wouldn't do to have one sneak up on me.* Satisfied all was quiet, I returned to the bay mare's stall and peered through the bars. Her neck and shoulders were now wet with sweat, her veins rising slightly above her sleek coat, her eyes soft and distant. It was nearly time …

The scene above could describe most any late-winter or early-spring night I've experienced in the years since I returned to Kentucky in 2013, where the part of my story contained within the pages you've just read ended—and a new story began. I didn't realize it until a few years ago, but I'd managed to insert myself into the life I read about all those years ago as a small child living within the pages of my Black Stallion books, and of course the story of Man o' War. I was now the "foaling man." Although that's not what they call us these days, since so many of us are women—something unheard of in the "olden days" of the Thoroughbred industry.

I did not pursue a career in social work or as a therapist. The truth is, I realized I'm not ready—I may never be ready, and I'm OK with that. What I gained in personal growth and self-discovery, as well as knowledge of how early childhood interactions and trauma affects the brain, plus skills in program planning and development, is more than worth the money spent. I'm proud of my accomplishments and wouldn't change a thing about my years at WMU. My education empowered me to understand my trauma, begin my healing process, write this book, and help others through my blog posts and other writings, including two training manuals for EAGALA-model practitioners, and also through giving presentations at the EAGALA National Conference in 2013 and 2016.

Sarah and I celebrated thirty years as best friends in 2017. She has encouraged and supported me in ways I can never hope to repay. In 2009 I coordinated the adoption of a two-year-old filly named Dolly Delux, a full sister to Farley, for Sarah. Dolly looks a lot like Farley, but her personality is very much like Farletta's. Fun for everyone involved. God blessed me with an amazing friendship that summer I met Sarah. I am forever grateful.

Danny and I have stayed in touch as well—we will be celebrating twenty-five years of friendship right around the time this book is released (2021). He is enjoying a well-deserved retirement from both his hair salon and the farm. Tagit Delux, Farley's sire, passed away early in 2015, with Danny by his side. Farley and the rest of the many horses Danny bred and owned have moved on to new lives and new owners. I hear the barn at Conner Equine now stands empty, which is hard to imagine. It feels like the end of an era.

The last time I saw Splatters was in 2001. I stood outside the pasture, and the horses walked over to greet us. In the golden light of the setting sun, I saw my old friend, then fifteen years of age. His back had dipped slightly, but his deep-brown eyes were soft and his baby face still held an intelligent, curious expression. Splatters died in 2006 at the age of twenty. Not long ago, while I sat remembering him, I felt a distinct presence of a horse standing behind me with his muzzle near my right ear. I could almost feel his soft, warm breath as Splatters breathed hello and nudged my cheek, like he had done so frequently all those years ago when we both were kids, playing, learning, and growing together in the warm summer sun.

As difficult as it was to let him go, I could not have found a better owner for Corky, and I'm so grateful for that. I periodically received updates from Danny, who had known the owners for many years. "They still have your horse," Danny would tell me (he never stopped referring to Corky as *my* horse). "They just love him." The last time I saw Corky in person was 2018, one last hug, one last nuzzle, one last I love you. For his thirtieth birthday, I had a FaceTime call with him (God bless technology)—many tears shed, and truly our last *I love you* and final goodbye. Corky passed away that fall. I miss him terribly still, even all these years later. He was one special horse.

Healing is a process. I've heard and spoken these four words so often that they risk losing their meaning. I don't want you to think that after a few years of therapy and work with Farletta, I am magically healed. I still live with PTSD, but now I know it, I understand it, and it doesn't have the power to destroy me any time I am triggered and the memories rush back in. I continue to work on myself and my healing. I've made progress with EMDR (tapping) therapy, art therapy, and lots of writing. In 2019 Farletta led me down another path of self-discovery, a spiritual voyage that has changed my life yet again, starting me on another journey to new and deeper healing. Visit my website (www.peacehorse.net) to find the *Peace Horse Journey* blog if you'd like to catch up on that part of our story. There is also a second book in the works.

I am a survivor. Perhaps you are as well. There is help and there is hope. I believe the path to healing begins in releasing the secret. Farletta taught me that. Each time I tell someone what happened to me, the memories lose a bit more of their power. Holding them inside keeps them strong. Let them go. This was never your secret to keep.

There are people and programs that can help you understand and deal with the pain tearing at your insides. Find the ones that work best for you, and take an active role in your healing. Be kind to yourself. Honor the abused child you once were. Embrace the powerful survivor you are now. You can do this. God bless you.

As far as I know, Mr. Vandersmelden has never been brought to justice. After I remembered his identity, I searched the sex-offender database but found nothing on him. I have not tried to seek justice, and it is doubtful I will. The burden of proof is on the victim, and I don't have memory of the details required to prosecute him. Also, there is a twelve-year statute of limitations on childhood sexual abuse, so even if I had the information, it is too late in the eyes of the law. Which is BS, but there it is.

Many people have questioned why I protect Mr. Vandersmelden's identity in this memoir. I did this to protect myself. The same exacting detail I don't have to prosecute is also what I would need to protect myself from a slander lawsuit. Therefore, details regarding Mr. Vandersmelden have been changed or omitted.

For the purposes of moving this story along, I oversimplified the explanation of Siegel's neuroscience in chapter 29. If you are interested in learning more, I encourage you to pick up a copy of *Mindsight* for yourself.

Farletta and Boedy are doing well—they are eighteen and eleven respectively (2021). Farletta never stops teaching me and helping me grow. Her job is a long one, she is good at it, and I am so lucky to have her. Boedy is still a bundle of leaping, flying, happy energy. He reminds me every day that age is irrelevant so long as you can continue to find joy in everything. Pause, breathe, sniff, run, jump, play, dance—Boedy's message to the world.

Cheryl L. Eriksen
Kentucky, July 2021
Peace

ACKNOWLEDGMENTS

Where would I be without my best friend?

First and foremost, I must thank Sarah. For truly, without her, there would be no book. Sarah has been encouraging me for years to write this memoir and tell my story. She is certain it is my main calling in life. Always my biggest cheerleader, Sarah has gently and thoughtfully helped bring this book to fruition through her encouraging words, carrying me through my self-doubt, reading version after version while offering excellent feedback. There is no greater gift than a true friend. I am so grateful for the gift of Sarah's friendship, yesterday, today, and every day going forward. Thank you, BFF (best friend forever).

I also would like to thank my mom, who has also been a great supporter and encourager in getting this book published. It was a shock to her and the rest of my family to learn what happened to me all those years ago and of the demons I'd been carrying with me ever since. I told no one what happened and effectively hid what I was going through from everyone around me. I can't imagine what that feels like, to learn so long after the fact what was happening to someone you love, after it's too late to fix it like a mother so badly wants to do. I'm grateful for her love and support and for the encouragement she has given me throughout my life to follow my dreams and do the things that make me happy. Thank you, Mom. I love you.

To Danny and Jo Conner—thank you for giving me my first job with horses and watching out for me, feeding me those glorious home-cooked Sunday dinners, taking me in when I needed it, encouraging me to publish this book, and being my friends for twenty-five years (and counting!). Danny, I'm grateful for all the horse knowledge you shared with me and the opportunities you gave me to work with such amazing horses, showing at the big shows, and having confidence in me even when I didn't have it in myself.

To Linda—what can I say? Thank you for believing in me, trusting me to train your horses, encouraging me while writing this book, and giving me the opportunity to own a life-changing horse like my sweet Farletta! I will never forget the gift you've given me, the gift of Farletta. From the bottom of my heart, thank you.

To Ulla—you helped me during a difficult time, encouraged me, and helped me grow. I'm glad to count you among my friends. Thank you.

To my original beta readers Brenda Burns; Ulla Frederiksen, MA; Lindsey R. Hatch; my "other mother" Pamela Keesler; Alanna Marie Lewis, MA; Linda Richards; Shane Speaker; Rebecca Stuurwold; and those who wished to remain anonymous—some of you were the first strangers to learn my story, a significant hurdle in this process. Thank you all for your kind and encouraging words and your constructive criticism and helpful comments. Your first reading of the original manuscript six years ago and the resulting feedback encouraged me greatly that I had something worth sharing, and also helped me understand where I needed to go next on this long and meandering path as a first-time author.

To Emily Donoho and Linda Strader—your comments and suggestions after reading my reworked manuscript (following the first round of beta readers) were invaluable to developing a publishable story. Thank you for giving so freely of your time and talents. I am forever grateful.

Finally, I'd like to thank my editor, Dori Harrell. You believed in this project, saw my vision, and put your magical editing touches on it, allowing my message and meaning to shine through. Together we made my story into something I could put out into the world in such a way it will have the greatest chance of reaching those who need it. I celebrate our accomplishment, and I'm grateful I don't have to carry this story solely within me anymore. Thank you.

A final acknowledgment must go out to the extremely patient and talented Kai Wilson-Viola, who formatted the print and ebook files, and Mallory Rock, who designed the cover. Your expertise and willingness to work with a first-time author has enabled me to present a visually stunning book with which to share my story. With my deepest gratitude and appreciation, thank you.

A NOTE ABOUT THE COVER ART

Near the beginning of this book, I mention how I lived within the paintings on the covers of my beloved Black Stallion books. Those books and their covers carried me through a lot of difficult times by giving me a safe place to hide when the weight of my trauma became too much to bear. When it came time to hire a cover artist for *Follow Me, Friend*, the memory of the little girl tracing her finger along the lines of Walter Farley's mystical horses brought to life gave me an idea, which I quickly dismissed as improbable if not impossible. However, Sarah encouraged me to seek out the artist, whose name I'd learned long ago when I fell in love with her work. Thank you to Ruth Sanderson for brining my sweet Farletta to life for the cover of this book. Another painting for me to get lost in, except with this one, I really can step inside the painting and touch the horse.

ADDITIONAL RESOURCES FOR SURVIVORS AND THEIR FAMILIES/FRIENDS

RAINN 800-656-HOPE (4673) www.rainn.org
Stop it Now - https://www.stopitnow.org
Resource Sharing Project www.resourcesharingproject.org
Equine Assisted Therapy
The two largest organizations overseeing a specific equine assisted therapy modality are www.pathintl.org and www.eagala.org. Either organization should be able to connect you with a program in your area.
US National Suicide Prevention Lifeline (Open 24 hours: 800-273-8255)

UK resources
Stop it now - https://www.stopitnow.org.uk/
Samaritans - https://www.samaritans.org/

Please always seek help wherever you are. Your local resources may not match the ones listed, but there is always help, and always hope.

*Please note that I am not currently affiliated with any of the above listed resources. I found the websites through a Google search and, while not currently

working in the field of equine assisted therapy, I have worked with both PATH and EAGALA in the past.

ABOUT THE AUTHOR

Blogger and author Cheryl L. Eriksen has a master's degree in social work (MSW) and is a former equine assisted therapy facilitator. She also authored two training manuals for Eagala model equine assisted therapy facilitators.

While earning her MSW from Western Michigan University, Cheryl took a special interest in the effects of trauma on the developing brain, and she applied that learning, along with her personal experiences as a survivor of childhood sexual abuse, in her memoir, *Follow Me, Friend*.

Additionally, Cheryl has spent decades as an equine professional and extensively studied equine behavior and how it is influenced by what the human brings to the relationship. Through her work in the field of equine assisted psychotherapy and learning, Cheryl has seen and experienced firsthand the healing power of the horse-human relationship. Her books (current and upcoming) and her blog, Peace Horse Journey, explore this powerful relationship.

When not writing, Cheryl works in multiple areas of the horse industry. She also volunteers at the Kentucky Horse Park and enjoys hiking, reading, and spending time with her dog, Boedy and her horse, Farletta.

http://www.peacehorse.net and www.followmefriendbook.com

facebook.com/PathOfThePeaceHorse

ALSO BY CHERYL L. ERIKSEN

A Clean Approach to Language and Questioning in Equine Assisted Psychotherapy and Learning - www.peacehorse.net

The Clean Facilitator's Workbook (Currently out of Print)

Made in the USA
Columbia, SC
14 November 2021